The HARD Times

The HARD Times

THE
FIRST
40
YEARS

BY
THE HARD TIMES STAFF

EDITED BY MATT SAINCOME, BILL CONWAY,
AND KRISSY HOWARD

MARINER BOOKS
Houghton Mifflin Harcourt
BOSTON NEW YORK

To Mom, who finally gave me
a fucking Pepsi

The HARD Times

INTRODUCTION

There have been many retrospective books that engage in the tired debate of who started punk. The truth is that many bands, cities, and genres played a role in its formation, but ultimately, punk is an orphan with 10,000 different parents.

And each one of those parents was reading *The Hard Times*.

When it premiered in 1976, *The Hard Times* was the first publication that punks could call their own. Run by a trio of high school dropouts living in a Lower East Side squat, it covered underground bands that other publications didn't even know existed. With its in-depth reporting and unprecedented access to the pioneers building the scene, *The Hard Times* captured the new, rapidly evolving movement so accurately that its name and logo would be forever intertwined with punk itself. As famed music critic and *Creem* editor Lester Bangs said, "Punks didn't believe in the Bible, they believed in *The Hard Times*."

But whereas the Bible had disciples, *The Hard Times* had editors. At the top was Matt Saincome, a cowardly publishing neophyte with a penchant

for drugs and gambling. His right-hand man was Bill Conway, a short-tempered, barely literate bruiser too moronic to work anywhere else. And later, the glue holding it all together was managing editor Krissy Howard, a nomadic street kid ironically known for huffing glue. Somehow--just barely--it worked. Together, these underdogs, along with contributors throughout the country, managed to create a voice that the punk scene could recognize and trust.

Oh, there was another founder, Ed Saincome, but he was beheaded (more on that later).

This book tells the tale of those kids. The ones who no one believed in, and who found themselves at the top of the publishing world only to have everything come crashing down, then later be reborn on the internet. Starting from the beginning and broken down by decade, you'll read *Hard Times* articles, memories, and other recovered clippings from the most accurate, up-close-and-personal historical account of punk and hardcore that exists.

This is The First Forty Years.

The 1970s: The Hard Times Is Born

Great ideas often come from unexpected places. After being unceremoniously rejected from a job at *Rolling Stone,* punk pioneer Matt Saincome dreamed up the idea for *The Hard Times* while attending an early band practice with the Ramones. He tried convincing the guys to join the editorial staff, but they had bigger plans. The band instead put Matt in touch with Bill Conway, a classmate of theirs known for writing offensive things on bathroom walls. Matt roped in Conway and his brother Ed, and just a few years later, the zine published its first issue.

The Hard Times was first distributed outside of CBGB but quickly expanded to a solid list of mail-order subscribers all over the United States. Reading *The Hard Times* became a rite of

passage for those within the punk community. It was a sign--much like dyeing your hair, studding a leather jacket, or shaving your head into a mohawk--that you were living by your own rules, not being taken seriously by prospective employers, and disappointing your parents on a daily basis.

Compared to its contemporaries in the field of music journalism, *The Hard Times* may as well have been written in a different language. Words like "fuck," "shit," and "limp-dicked try-hard poser who can't mosh for shit" were splashed across its headlines. Copies often arrived damaged, late, or dirty. They almost always reeked of glue or marijuana. But the editorial content was a thing of brilliance--if you looked past

the numerous typos and gratuitous vulgarities. The articles were years ahead of the competition, critiquing genres and subcultures that hadn't even popped up on the radars of *Rolling Stone* and other periodicals. Notable figures such as Joey Ramone, Debbie Harry, and Darby Crash could often be found in the Letters to the Editor section. Famed frontwoman Poly Styrene even took out an ad after seeing the Sex Pistols live, the responses to which ultimately resulted in the formation of X-Ray Spex.

Dedication to the zine was so strong that NYHC legends the Cro-Mags would go on to name a song after the publication and the tagline used to advertise its mail-order services. "Hard Times!" the lyrics read. "Coming your way!"

In the '70s, as radio and mainstream record labels dismissed punk as merely a trend, *Hard Times* dove feetfirst into the action, documenting every detail and idiosyncrasy of a scene that would soon be known as one of the most important in music history. And those labels and radio stations who ignored the whole thing? Once it became clear punk was here to stay, they were forced to use the zine's articles as source material for their think pieces.

On the following pages, you'll read choice excerpts from the magazine's first decade of coverage. It shows the publication establishing itself as the number-one voice for the kids who were tired of the world's bullshit, kids who may have argued just as much about the birth of punk as they did about its death.

But we know punk never died--if it had, *The Hard Times* would have given the eulogy.

ON THIS DAY IN PUNK HISTORY

JUNE 8, 1977--

THE SCENE DIES FOR THE FIRST TIME

Less than one year after its inception, at 9:17 p.m. EST, the New York City punk scene was pronounced dead by aspiring artist Donnie Mitchell. An outspoken critic of his creative community since becoming involved with it, Mitchell declared the scene dead during a local show after a woman who wouldn't fuck him caused him to spill a beer he didn't pay for.

AUGUST 30, 1977--

"BLONDIE" LEAST OFFENSIVE NAME YELLED AT DEBBIE HARRY BEFORE 8:30 A.M.

Included as one of a record-setting seven offensive names yelled at Debbie Harry on a morning walk to her neighborhood bodega, "Hey, blondie!" was officially deemed the kindest, and the only one fit to print.

APRIL 17, 1978--

THE FIRST POSER IS BORN

Brandon Finn, the first known poser to date, was born in Lincoln, Nebraska, to parents Chuck and Deb Finn. Brandon would go on to own multiple MC5 T-shirts despite only crediting his fandom to "their early stuff" before quickly changing the subject.

SEPTEMBER 21, 1979--

PUNK-HOUSE DOG EATS RECORD NINE CIGARETTE BUTTS IN ONE NIGHT

Riverside, California, punk-house dog Peachy ingested a record-breaking nine cigarette butts following a party that ran well into the early hours of the morning. Surpassing the former record of three and a half cigarettes consumed by San Antonio, Texas, poodle mix Hank, Peachy impressed onlookers who reportedly "didn't tell her to do it, but weren't about to stop chanting 'Peachy' till she was done."

SEPTEMBER 22, 1979--

WORLD RECORD-HOLDER IN CIGARETTE BUTT CONSUMPTION MYSTERIOUSLY DIES

A mere 22 hours after setting a new world record for canine cigarette consumption, Riverside, California, miniature pinscher Peachy died mysteriously. Unable to determine the exact cause, her owners attributed the two-year-old dog's ultimate demise to be "probably just old age."

By Patrick Coyne

The Queen Fires Back at Johnny Rotten With Brutal Diss Track

LONDON--Queen Elizabeth II has broken with royal family tradition of disregarding unfounded slander by vowing to "destroy" Johnny Rotten and the Sex Pistols via her own brutal dis track, a town crier announced Thursday from the steps of the Royal Exchange.

"Her Majesty the Queen has taken to heart the lyrics of the S. Pistols' derogatory tune 'God Save the Queen,'" said Royal Crier Jonathan Fitzwater. "In response, she has purchased a Rickenbacker 330 and is teaching herself guitar. In my humble opinion, she is already much more proficient at the instrument than those street urchins could ever wish to be."

Despite a total ban from BBC radio, "God Save the Queen" has topped the UK music charts for weeks. It is suspected that the song's popularity prompted the queen to take action.

"Her Majesty has never been one to shy away from a task simply because she is woefully unqualified. Writing this song was no exception," said Royalist Alfie Taylor. "And if I am being honest, the early demos of the song that I have been privy to are quite impressive. It is raw, fast, and as gritty as an East London Bakewell tart."

Despite being waited on hand and foot her entire life, the queen has insisted on a DIY approach to songwriting, as she believes this "punk as fuck" method will stick in the

craw of "those cheeky Pistol blokes." According to reports, the Head of the Commonwealth, Defender of the Faith has been bouncing various lyric ideas off of her most trusted servants.

"I spent four flippin' hours with the ol' bird trying to come up with a proper rhyme for 'Rotten,'" said a royal servant who spoke on the condition of anonymity. "We eventually landed on 'sodden,' which is a half rhyme at best."

While many admire Her Majesty's insistence on fighting fire with fire, some, including members of the royal family, have reservations.

"Mum's suite is directly above mine in the royal palace, and day and night I hear her noodling about on that dreadful gitbox," said Prince Charles of Wales. "I banged the ceiling with a broom, but it only made her play louder. When she gets mad, she gets very aggressive--just ask those pesky Icelandic fishermen."

As of press time, white smoke has been seen billowing out from the top of Buckingham Palace, indicating that the final mix of Her Majesty's epic dis track, tentatively titled "Suck My Twat You Punk Swine," is finally complete.

Janitor at Recording Studio Not Sure Why He Also Has to Change Name to Ramone

BY BRENDAN KRICK

NEW YORK--Media Sound Studios janitor Gary O'Doyle is reportedly upset after learning that his last name has been forcibly changed to Ramone by members of the band the Ramones, an exasperated source confirmed.

"My last name is not Ramone," O'Doyle said. "Please, I don't understand why everybody keeps calling me that. I just want to do my job and go home. I am a simple man."

O'Doyle had worked as the studio's custodian for several years without incident, until late last year when the Ramones booked time to record their sophomore album, "Leave Home."

"Most of the bands who record here have been nice, but these guys are always breaking bottles and making a mess. I started having to clean up in between songs, and they'd joke around as if I was a member of the band," O'Doyle explained. "One day I saw they switched the work pants I keep in my locker for tight black jeans. Next thing I know, they're making me wear a leather jacket and calling me 'Gary Ramone.' They even made me fill in on drums for one song. It was pretty easy, but still, why are they doing this?"

Frontman Joey Ramone was excited to praise the group's unofficial member, who he now views as an essential part of the band.

"We definitely couldn't have made this record without him," he explained. "He's been here every day of this weeklong recording session. We wanted to do something nice for him to say thanks, so we shrank a bunch of his T-shirts and gave him some bangs while he was asleep on his break the other night. I could tell he appreciated it--he was totally speechless."

Despite the praise, sources close to O'Doyle say he is completely uninterested in his status as a figure in the emerging New York punk scene.

"I don't understand these Ramone brothers, and I don't know what a punk is," he said. "I just want this to stop. The bank won't even honor my paychecks anymore because the name on them isn't my name. This is not funny; I have bills."

At press time, all five Ramones were seen celebrating the official name change of their newest member on the steps of the Manhattan Civil Court.

Police Scour Woods for Sandwich Implicated in Death of Elvis

By Kyle Erf

MEMPHIS, Tenn.--A dragnet was set up around Elvis Presley's Graceland estate this after-noon in an effort to apprehend the dangerously decadent sand-wich believed to be responsi-ble for The King of Rock 'n' Roll's untimely death, accord-ing to sources.

"It's not a matter of IF we find the sandwich that caused this tragedy, but WHEN," said Chief Rhett White of the Mem-phis Police Department. "Our officers are combing the woods for any sign of crumbs, pick-les, or those little frilly toothpicks. Nobody is getting in or out of Memphis without a full-cavity sandwich search."

"We've even flown in a Ger-man shepherd named Officer Gertrude from Atlanta PD to assist," added White. "She's the world's only peanut-butter-tracking police dog."

Police arrived at the so-called "sandwich theory" shortly after searching the larger-than-life musician's home on Tuesday.

"No 42-year-old could have died from health issues this severe without an external cause. After days of exhaus-tive searching, officers have confirmed removing several dozen empty prescription bot-tles and what appeared to be a fresh pile of sticky, oily crumbs. Those crumbs were the break we needed," a press release read.

Several eyewitnesses have come forward with stories of seeing Elvis--known for his high-fat, high-cholesterol dining habits--with the snack in question. However, descrip-tions of the sandwich vary considerably.

"Sure, I've seen it," said Oakville resident Dwayne Dobbs, Jr. "It was the size of your head--naw, two heads--and filled with peanut butter, jelly, and bacon."

But not all eyewitnesses agree.

"I saw The King with the killer. It was full of bananas and was all fried up, cross my heart!" insisted another, who wished to remain anonymous. "It sent a chill down my spine; I know it was up to no good."

Sources report that the search turned up a meatloaf and a few half-eaten candy bars, but nothing so far that fits any description given to police.

"Our biggest lead so far?" said Chief White. "Well, we found a duck eating some suspicious bread over by Rainbow Lake. We have taken the duck in for questioning. I cannot comment further."

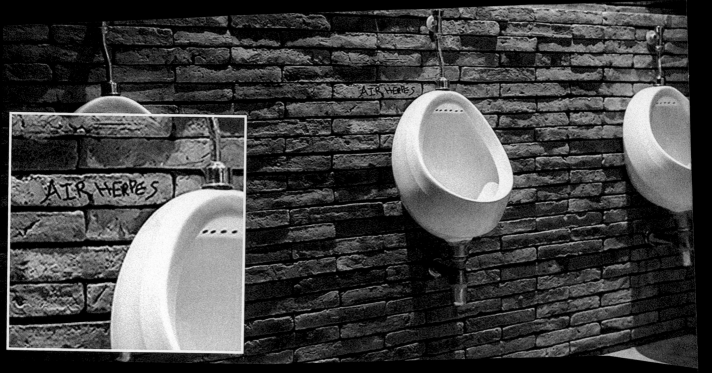

Spotless CBGB Bathroom Ruined by Scribbling of Band Name

By Cory Cousins

NEW YORK--The bathroom at local venue CBGB has reportedly been defaced by what appears to be a band name scribbled in Sharpie right above the toilet, several eyewitnesses confirmed.

"I'm appalled and disappointed," noted bartender Boots DeLuca. "Every afternoon before opening, I clean the bathroom thoroughly, making sure it's in mint condition for our customers. I take pride in that. Now some jerkoff rolls in and treats it like it's the subway? Not in my house, friend!"

Patrons who were in attendance on the night of the vandalism identified the rogue bathroom defiler as Jimmy Corrigan, an aspiring musician and local drunk.

"Oh yeah, I forgot about that," chuckled Corrigan as he lit a cigarette. "I had to pee really bad, so I went in there and started taking care of business. While I was draining the snake, I was staring at the wall thinking how it would be boss as hell if I could see my band's name, Air Herpes, there."

"Plus, other people will think of us when they pee, so win-win. Air Herpes forever!" he added.

CBGB owner Hilly Kristal had choice words about the defacing.

"It's a slippery slope," said Kristal. "Today they write their band name on the wall, tomorrow they put stickers all over the door or even the toilet itself! When people think of the name CBGB, I want them to think 'spotless.' So this is not something I'm about to take lightly."

At press time, bar staff have reportedly surrendered to the recent wave of doodlings, including three more band names, five stickers, one phone number, and what appears to be a drawing of one stick figure vomiting while another high-fives him. Management expects patrons will curb their behavior once they see how messy the bathroom has become.

The Hard Times Gets a Typewriter

As remembered by founding editor Bill Conway

When we first came up with the idea for the zine, we wanted all of the text to be handwritten. Photos we'd just steal from library books or magazines boosted from the corner store, and that part worked out. But when it came time to write the articles, we quickly discovered that none of us had legible penmanship. Even during our fleeting moments of sobriety, the best sample we could generate looked like it had been written by a horse recovering from oral surgery with a pen taped to its tail.

Then Matt, in a stroke of genius, decided we would cut out individual letters from magazines and paste them to the page. Although we've had our struggles over the years, I will give him this: That lying rat bastard was the one who invented the style that would eventually take over the punk scene's aesthetic. Unfortunately, this brief experiment in layout somehow landed in the hands of the San Francisco Police Department and put us on an FBI watchlist as potential suspects in the Zodiac Killer case. After repeated visits from federal investigators, we agreed we needed a better way--the hunt for a typewriter was on.

We had no money, and we'd been banned from every department store in New York City so stealing a top-name model was out of the question. The only typewriter we had access to was a cracked 1954 Royal HH that had belonged to Matt and Ed's father, which he had used to write beat poetry before he had children and adulthood swallowed his dreams. Ed snuck it out of his childhood home under the cover of darkness, and *The Hard Times* finally had its machine. It was not without its problems: The shift key had been damaged during the heist and was very sensitive; it typed in all caps whenever the temperature rose above seventy-five degrees or someone smoked a cigarette within thirty feet of it; the ribbon had to be refreshed with spit every fifteen words; and if the F key was used too many times during a session, the casing would heat up to a point where it would burn your skin. But we took that typewriter everywhere. Its portability made it so that we could cover breaking news on the spot, and its oversized carrying case allowed us to sneak alcohol into all-ages shows without suspicion. Without that typewriter, *The Hard Times* wouldn't exist.

Poetry Open Mic Struck by Category 5 Patti Smith Freak-Out

BY ASHLEY NAFTULE

NEW YORK--An open mic was struck by a Category 5 Patti Smith freak-out, raining down chaos and a devastating sense of ennui upon audience members gathered at St. Mark's Bookshop, multiple witnesses confirmed.

"She had this dude play electric guitar while she set my table on fire and read a poem about an injured pigeon struggling to fly," said open mic attendee Lori Karlotta. "She kept saying she was trying to summon the ghost of Baudelaire through the fire and smoke. It was definitely the coolest thing that's ever happened at this mic."

Initially predicted to be a Category 2 freak-out by poetry scenesters, experts upgraded Hurricane Patti to a 5 after eyewitnesses spotted the rocker poet fighting with Blue Öyster Cult guitarist Allen Lanier outside the Strand.

"She walked out into the middle of the road, screaming 'Allen's got a pearl in his Blue Öyster Cunt!' over and over again," said longtime friend Robert Mapplethorpe. "By the time we walked the five blocks down to St. Mark's, Patti was so steamed she was speaking in

tongues. Instead of evacuating the store, we invited more people in because we knew she would be at her best."

Prior to last night's storm at St. Mark's Bookshop, the most powerful freak-out on record was Patti's Category 4 in the back room at Max's Kansas City last September.

"She backed Johnny Thunders into a corner and kept shouting at him to do the Mashed Potato until he broke down sobbing," said survivor Sable Starr. "Johnny was never the same after that."

Witnesses said Smith spent a half hour spinning in circles, singing Monkees covers, and laying waste to the store's fixtures. By the time her freak-out dissipated, half of the venue's chairs were destroyed, and sixteen audience members had to be dug out from under an avalanche of chapbooks.

Smith expressed no remorse for her apocalyptic scene-stealing.

"Do you ask the tornado if it's sorry it stole your cow?" she demanded. "Do you wag your finger at a volcano for drowning your house in fire? Don't ask for me an apology, Jack. As a poet, it's my God-given right to fuck shit up."

Billy Carter Tapes Over Watergate Recording With Sweet Demo

By Louie Aronowitz

WASHINGTON--Billy Carter recorded his band's demo over leftover Watergate tapes, deleting evidence critical to a federal investigation and plunging himself and his brother, President Jimmy Carter, into a heated scandal, sources confirmed today.

"We thought we had finally recovered the contents of the infamous erased 18.5 minutes of tape," commented Bob Woodward, the journalist investigating the Watergate scandal. "But when we listened to it, all we had was a lo-fi recording of a band that totally ripped. While we may have lost an important piece of American history, it's undeniable that this demo is like a chainsaw to the throat."

Despite initially denying responsibility, after the positive response to the recording, Carter eventually admitted that it was indeed his band's demo.

"I've been the frontman of Billy and the Peanut Fuckers for almost two years. We have a pretty loyal following, but I never expected such a strong reaction to our most recent tape," said Carter while tapping a keg of Billy Beer. "My buddy Sal helped us record it. We were in the White House basement and I was getting really into it. I ended up kicking a hole in the wall and found a bunch of reel-to-reel tapes that I figured nobody was using. But I felt bad afterward so I put everything back where I found it. Then, a month later, some journalists wanted to talk about the band."

Kerry Willis, the Peanut Fuckers' bassist, was uncomfortable with inadvertently tampering with evidence, though he insists the band did not know.

"Goddamn it--this can't be considered treason, right? I don't want to go back to jail," said Willis after being told his band's demo may have been recorded over the most sought-after 18 minutes of audio in U.S. history. "Why would a sitting president let his brother's band play down there anyway? If this goes south, I hope he pardons us so we can tour."

Billy and the Peanut Fuckers have since been banned from practicing in the White House after it was discovered that Carter had scribbled lyrics such as "Gonna punch the president, because he's my dumbass brother. Gonna punch every Russian, then fuck their mothers" on the back of official government documents.

Following a full FBI investigation, prosecutors recommended charges be brought against Carter for his involvement in the tapes' destruction, but also noted the "demo is harder than West German concrete."

Makes Appearance for Nancy's Parents

By Tom K

PHILADELPHIA--Sid Vicious debuted his highly anticipated alter ego Sid Presentable during a Shabbat dinner at the suburban household belonging to the parents of girlfriend Nancy Spungen, relieved sources reported.

"It's time for me to evolve as an artist," said Presentable as he fixed his tie. "The 'Vicious' shtick accomplished what it needed to, but things are getting pretty serious with Nancy now. My art needs to reflect our relationship in a way that smashing a bloke in the back of the head with a pint no longer does."

The most positive reviews of Vicious' transformation came from Frank Spungen, the father of Nancy and outspoken critic of his daughter's choices in men.

"What impressed me right from the start was his commitment to the crew cut-sweater vest combination," effused Spungen from the family's rumpus room. "His dinner debut was spectacular. He had excellent manners and charmed my mother

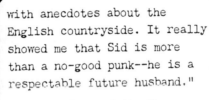

with anecdotes about the English countryside. It really showed me that Sid is more than a no-good punk--he is a respectable future husband."

Longtime fans of the Sex Pistols bass player were also surprisingly supportive of the musician's sudden change in look and temperament.

"Punk is about defying expectations, man. I've seen the Pistols at least 50 times and I have been spit on, pissed on, and had teeth knocked out at their shows," said London local Billy "The Skid" Branton. "But Sid is actually doing something shocking with this move. I have to respect him for it."

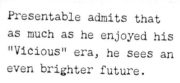

Presentable admits that as much as he enjoyed his "Vicious" era, he sees an even brighter future.

"I believe it was Donny Osmond who said, 'I never smile unless I mean it.' Thi isn't a stunt. I am here today to prove to the world and Nancy's parents that thi is who I am, this is what I wear, and, yes, that I can g antiquing on Saturday."

Sid will be heading out on tour with his new side project, Waiting-Until-Marriage Pistols, later this fall, to coincide with his enrollment in community college.

Poorly Stocked Bodega Mistaken for Warhol Installation

BY DAN RICE

FLUSHING, N.Y.--Members of the Manhattan cultural elite flocked to Queens over the weekend to visit Mano's Grocery and Lotto, a small and poorly stocked corner store that has somehow been mistaken for an Andy Warhol installation, experts confirmed.

"The man is a genius," proclaimed art critic Gus Verte while gesturing excitedly toward a single loaf of Wonder bread on a dusty shelf. "I could not be more thrilled that Warhol has taken his pop art aesthetic to the field of multimedia sculpture. The bread even has an expiration date! Such authentic Americana."

Despite continued assertions from management that the loaf of bread was not placed there by the famed artist and is, in fact, for sale, art enthusiasts from all over the city continue to visit the store in droves.

"Everybody keeps looking at that bread, but nobody buys it!" exclaimed Manolito Padilla, the confused proprietor of Mano's. "I tell them that more bread is coming Thursday and they just ignore me! Normally I'd kick a pack of weirdos like them out for loitering, but one of them paid $11,000 for a pack of Tic Tacs, so I guess I will just let them be?"

Critics are already hailing the store as a "love letter to New York" and a "natural evolution of the Warhol Factory concept."

"His latest Campbell's piece is particularly intriguing," noted Warhol warehouse regular Brigid Berlin, standing before a poster-sized advertisement for the soup. "Never before has Warhol incorporated ad copy and a price into one of his paintings. Groundbreaking."

While even the slightest investigation completely disproved the artist's assumed involvement in Mano's Grocery and Lotto, there is evidence that the bodega has caught his attention.

"Yesterday a very skinny, odd-looking man came in," recalled Padilla. "He walked up to me, asked if I was the owner, then pointed to a woman and said, 'That's Nico, she's going to be your new cashier.' She is a great worker but takes far too many cigarette breaks."

Undercover FBI Agent Struggling to Explain No Wave Scene to Supervisor

By Steve Kowalski

NEW YORK--FBI Agent Mark Denuno is reportedly struggling to describe the subgenre of no wave to his immediate superior following a grueling eighteen-month undercover operation in the city's burgeoning punk scene, according to sources.

"He thinks it's just punk. Like, one dimensional," Agent Denuno explained. "I keep trying to tell him that this is nothing like the punk music of yesterday, but he's still not getting it. This is a symptom of the merging of punk and capital. The whole scene is a deconstruction. I don't know how much clearer I can be."

Unable to properly define the subgenre known for having no consistent sound or style, Denuno's standing within the case remains in question.

"We may have left him in the oven too long, if you catch my drift," said his superior, Assistant FBI Director Bill Fritz. "He won't stop playing shit like Teenage Jesus. He thinks I don't get it. Oh, I get it. Fifteen years ago, I was undercover with the MC5. Now THAT was a counterculture. This avant-garde nonsense is kids' stuff."

Despite tensions running high, Denuno is reportedly feeling slightly more optimistic after a recent debriefing with his supervisor.

"I thought we'd really hit a wall. AD Fritz wanted to know about drug connections throughout the Lower East Side and how they relate to larger narcotics operations up and down the Eastern Seaboard," said Denuno. "So I put on some Contortions for him hoping he'd see his answer for himself. He said it kind of sounded like jazz. He's almost getting it."

Given that the operation's success relies almost entirely on Agent Denuno's intel, AD Fritz relied on a tried-and-true strategy to further the undercover investigation.

"After a while, I tell all the young agents that whatever crap scene they've been undercover with sounds like jazz," he said. "It usually shuts them up." He continued by expressing hope for what's to come.

"We've got a crop of new recruits in the academy right now that I'm personally excited about; they don't drink, smoke, or do drugs. Some of them are even abstinent. It will be fascinating to see how the underground culture reacts to that."

By David Tyler

Lazy Promoter Pioneers World's First "Secret Show"

LOS ANGELES--A new format for punk shows was pioneered last week after local punk and self-professed lazy guy Rick Gonsalves "totally spaced" on promoting a show he had recently booked, sources confirmed.

"Shit," Gonsalves stated. "That was a real boner move on my part."

The show, which is still scheduled to take place in Gonsalves' garage this Saturday night, has since been dubbed a "secret show" on account of the fact that no one knows where it is taking place or what time it starts, and that it may feature a lineup of bands from "all over."

"We've got a ton of great acts already committed, and you never know who might just show up. I'm kind of counting on some people swinging through," Gonsalves said while reading from a list that bore the title "Desperate Losers Who Owe Me One."

So far, Gonsalves has only told those performing where the show will be held.

"The last show I booked, I spent a month getting the word out and only, like, eight people showed up, and only three of them had money to get in," he explained. "What's the point?"

"If people want to come, they should just ask a punk," he added. "I mean, not this one,

cuz my phone's been disconnected since I got fired a few months back, but, like, probably anyone else would know what to tell you."

In addition to the "secret" status of the show, an unmet effort to purchase alcohol beforehand led Gonsalves to dub the show as BYOB. Despite the total oversight in planning, Gonsalves is so far content with the outcome.

"I get some bands to come by and play in my garage, and I can charge people to hang out at my house. I don't need to pick up the phone or photocopy shit," he stated. "It's actu-

ally pretty genius. I don't know why I didn't think of this sooner."

Inspired by the recent revelation, Gonsalves says he plans to start a "bringer" show early next year, where the bands themselves will be responsible for bringing a crowd or else have to pay to perform, thus removing not only all work, but also any risk to him whatsoever.

Scene Veteran Trapped in Jonestown Completely Unaffected by Poisoned Kool-Aid

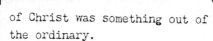

By Jeremy Kaplowitz

JONESTOWN, Guyana--New York punk scene veteran Steve Nelson told reporters he felt "buzzed" after drinking several Solo cups of poison at the scene of the mass suicide led by the Peoples Temple cult leader Jim Jones.

"Yeah, I guess I have a pretty high tolerance. We've been mixing Kool-Aid and poison to make cheap drinks at The Star Bar for years," Nelson explained to befuddled Guyanese doctors after the suicide ritual, which took over 900 lives. "The speech the main guy [Jones] gave was pretty sick, and everyone let me finish their drinks. It was a cool party."

As one of the few survivors of Jones' cult and the only member seemingly unfazed by the horrors of Jonestown, reporters flocked to Nelson to ask how he became entangled with the notorious group. Nelson, however, was confused by the notion that the Peoples Temple of the Disciples of Christ was something out of the ordinary.

"I've been around the punk scene for a while, so I'm used to all that cult shit," Nelson told reporters while sewing a Peoples Temple patch onto his jacket. "Everyone in weird, matching outfits, chanting gibberish alongside a bunch of crazy people and having sex with the narcissistic leader even though he's ugly and insane . . . I felt very much at home."

"Honestly, when I first got here, I just figured it was a super-DIY village. I had no idea it was a cult," Nelson added.

After running a battery of tests on Nelson, Dr. Emilia Chakraborty, a veteran physician, admitted she was shocked by the results.

"That he was able to survive a dosage of poison strong enough to kill 20 acres of rainforest was alarming, but when I went to take a blood sample, it was so thick and viscous it wouldn't flow through the tubing," said Dr. Chakraborty. "This man is more poisonous chemical than human at this point. It is our belief that further studies need to be done to fully understand the consequences of the ingestion."

At press time, Nelson admitted that though he thought the Jonestown massacre was a "shitty" situation, he believed it was far worse that it had been broken up by "a bunch of fucking cop bastards."

Selling Our First Zine

As remembered by founding editor Matt Saincome

Our first issue took months to complete. We had no idea what the fuck we were doing--we were just folding them up by hand and learning as we went. By the time we were ready to start production, we had wasted all of our money on high-end bathtub hooch and couldn't afford to make copies. Luckily, Bill happened to have some dirt on a security guard at The New York Public Library who granted us access to the coin-operated photocopier after hours and showed us how to override the coin slot by constantly unplugging the machine. It took us all night to make the first twenty copies, thanks to noticing a ton of factual and spelling errors, but we were finally ready to bring *The Hard Times* to the world.

We set up a table at a Dead Boys show and listed a price point of 25 cents. That first day, we sold zero copies, and half of our inventory was destroyed when someone spilled beer on our table. The fight that ensued was over quick, but we got bounced out by security.

Undeterred, we returned the next day for a CBGB show and sold our first copy. The buyer's name was Gerry Piss, the highly influential creator of the punk/water sports-themed zine *The Piss Machine*. He paid for it with the latest edition of his zine, so even though we didn't make any money on the transaction, we knew we'd finally created something people wanted to read. Also, because of the trade, we learned a lot about the underground world of piss drinking and its supposed health benefits. And with that, *The Hard Times* was ready to take off.

CBGB Owner Beginning to Think Some of These Bands Aren't Really Country, Bluegrass, or Blues

By Patrick Coyne

NEW YORK--CBGB & OMFUG proprietor Hilly Kristal is reportedly beginning to question whether bands such as the Ramones, Talking Heads, and others who regularly perform at his club are truly "country, bluegrass, or blues," as they claim.

"CBGB stands for 'Country, Bluegrass, Blues' because that's the only music bands are allowed to play here," said Kristal. "Historically, I've done a great job enforcing that rule. But lately these musicians sound unlike any country or blues group I've ever heard. Lots of our shows have younger folk playing a little louder and faster than I like, but I just chalk that up to them learning how to wrangle their instruments."

Sources confirm CBGB is one of the few New York City venues that books unsigned bands. Many musicians, including Talking Heads frontman David Byrne, have privately admitted to lying to Kristal in order to secure stage time.

"When I first went to CBGB, I put on a cowboy hat and incessantly yelled 'yeehaw!'" said the slight and soft-spoken Byrne. "I told [Hilly] I was a shit-kickin' buckaroo who used to raise steer in Rhode Island. Next thing I know, we're opening for the Ramones."

Kristal reportedly let Talking Heads play despite Byrne wearing what was purported to be an "oversized foam novelty cowboy hat." Kristal has since requested that they start writing songs featuring trucks, drinking, and other common country motifs instead of more songs about buildings and food.

Television guitarist Tom Verlaine had a similar experience to that of Byrne's.

"I tried to sweet-talk Hilly by claiming to be an uplifting gormandizer, but no luck. So then I said Television was bluegrass," said Verlaine.

"Hilly initially bought it, until he saw [Television bassist] Richard Hell, who he thought looked too 'punk.' I suppose we'll have to kick Hell out of the group or get him a pair of overalls if we want to play there again."

Kristal later explained how he conceptualized CBGB's strict music policy.

"I remember thinking, you know what these Bowery junkies and lowlifes need? Bluegrass and country-western," said Kristal. "Sure, maybe these bands don't sound exactly like I imagined, but clearly everyone downtown loves Americana music."

As of press time, Kristal is considering bending his rules slightly and allowing British folk band The Damned to play his club.

Teary-Eyed Paul Simonon Hopes 12th Bass Guitar Will Be Good Enough for Album Cover

By Kyle Erf

LONDON--The Clash bassist Paul Simonon has expressed disappointment at the prospect of smashing yet another beloved bass guitar in search of the perfect album photo, confirmed sources close to the matter.

"This is my last one," said a frustrated Simonon. "It's good that we've already recorded the album because after today I won't have any more basses left. We have a gig tomorrow and the band's just having me hum the riff from 'London Calling' into a mic. I don't want to sound like I'm not a team player, but this is getting pretty unmanageable."

Members of the up-and-coming punk outfit have reportedly pushed Simonon to destroy bass after bass in recent weeks.

"It started out like a fun idea, smashing my instruments after big shows," explained the leather-clad bassist. "But then we just kept on with it. Next thing you know, the guys are having me crush watermelons with my favorite Fender Jazz and pointing and laughing. We even did a take where I threw a bass off the roof, and it turned out we didn't even have a camera with us."

"I'm starting to worry that it's all a game to them," Simonon added while repeatedly wiping his face and insisting there "must be some dirt in my eye."

When asked to comment, frontman Joe Strummer confirmed Simonon's theory.

"All right, honestly, we were taking the piss out of Paul a bit," Strummer said. "We actually got some really good shots of the Fender he smashed in New York last week. Now we're just seeing how long he'll keep doing it."

Other members of The Clash defended the ruse, pointing out ways the so-called hazing hasn't been all bad.

"The whole smashing thing has been right useful," said guitarist and vocalist Mick Jones. "I couldn't get the lid off a jar of gherkins yesterday, so I told Paul it'd be really great for the album if he could please hit the jar with his bass. Lid popped right off, but it was hard to enjoy them with Paul crying like a little Sally the whole time."

At press time, sources report seeing Simonon utter a short prayer of indeterminate religious affiliation before lifting his last remaining bass above his head.

As REMEMBERED BY MATT SAINCOME; ILLUSTRATIONS BY ANDREW DUBONGCO

There was a good chunk of time in the '70s when a horrible cockroach infesta-tion made our squat uninhabitable, so pumping out content became very chal-lenging. We had a graff friend who offered to illustrate some of our stories for us during these dark times, and we took him up on the offer even though couldn't pay him with anything other than angel dust. I gotta say, shit came out pretty well considering how wrecked he was.

HOW TO SHOPLIFT WITH WENDY O. WILLIAMS

STEP 1: FIND A PLACE TO SHOPLIFT FROM

Before you start, pick some materi-alist bullshit store to steal from, which shouldn't be too hard. When entering the store, do your best to resist any urges to chainsaw through the front door or smash the light fixtures with a sledgehammer--there's a time and a place for that, and this definitely ain't it. For a practical way to use those tactics in your day-to-day life, check out my earlier how-to guide, How to Make a Dinner Reservation, with Wendy O. Williams.

STEP 2: BLEND IN

If you're gonna get away with stealing, you gotta make sure you don't stand out too much. You basically want to look like you're dressed for Easter dinner or a court appearance or something. To do this, try trading in your leather-bikini-with-only-clothespins-to-cover-the-nipples ensemble for a more modest leather one-piece-bathing-suit-with-only-clothespins-to-cover-the-nipples ensemble. Before you leave the house, put a pair of khaki slacks on under your ass-less chaps, and keep your mohawk to a maximum height of five inches.

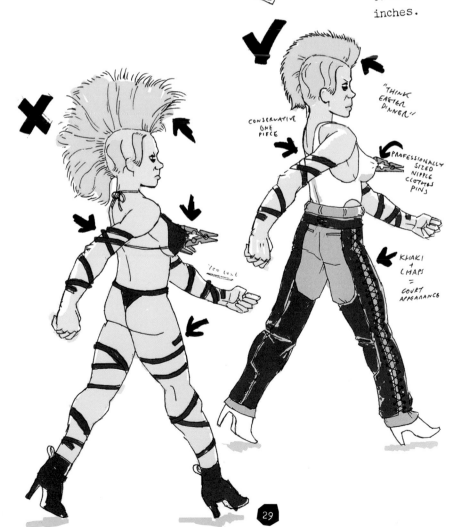

CONSERVATIVE ONE PIECE

"THINK EASTER DINNER"

PROFESSIONALLY SIZED NIPPLE CLOTHES PINS

KHAKI + CHAPS = COURT APPEARANCE

TOO COOL

THE HARD TIMES

Now that you've slipped inside the store and no one suspects a thing, look for something you want to take. This could be something you need, like a can of spray paint, or just something you want, like six cans of spray paint.

STEP 4: DISCREETLY HIDE THE ITEM

Once you have the item in your hand, tuck it somewhere it can't be seen, like in your pocket or under your nicest shredded T-shirt. If you're not about to stifle your right to express yourself by wearing a shirt, try adding extra strips of electrical tape to your pasties, which have been known to hold up to eight ChapSticks or two candy bars. Or, if you just pop in on your way home from work and are just covered in shaving cream, bring a cute tote bag to conceal the item.

STEP 5:
EXIT THE STORE

Once you've got your item stashed, leave the store with a confident stride, and do your best not to look nervous. Remember, millions of people in spike-covered Medieval arm braces walk out of Sears every day, so there's nothing to see here!

STEP 6:
DON'T TAKE NO SHIT

Got caught? Happens to the best of us--just try again later. If the cop gets rough or gropes you while placing you under arrest, don't hesitate to punch that pig in his fucking face, and fight the charges all the way to the end.

THE 1980S: GROWING PAINS

The 1980s marked the first time *The Hard Times* began to understand the monetary value of their media enterprise. MTV had changed the way corporations thought about music content, so bigger media conglomerates were now seeking out other properties for potential acquisition. *The Hard Times* may have been rough around the edges, but it had amassed a serious audience by this point, and many outside the company thought it could be prime time to cash in.

In the mid-eighties, *Hard Times'* management, like many others in the scene, traded in their mohawks and safety pins for shaved heads and X'ed-up fists. Still, the wayward punk kids running the company weren't at all prepared for the polite nature of business meetings with potential investors. And, in many ways, big business wasn't ready to sit down with *Hard Times*. There were some introductory meetings between them and a few larger corporations, but it ultimately wasn't quite time for such an innovative product to hit the mainstream. Regardless of this,

others in the punk scene saw there was serious interest, and many began to crudely imitate the *Hard Times* model.

On the West Coast, Tim Yohannan started *Maximum Rocknroll* as a direct response to *Hard Times'* overtly political nature. "It's time for punks to laugh again," Tim famously said inside a 924 Gilman Street meeting (a space known for light-hearted jokes). Always looking for a way to boost attention and magazine-stands sale, *The Hard Times* willingly jumped into a feud with *MRR*. It would spark a legendary standoff that exists to this day.

MRR's infamous thirty-six-page takedown of the zine, where Yohannan himself argued that *The Hard Times* editors were "punks without humor, independent thought, or the bravery to challenge groupthink," was supported by wide swaths of *MRR*'s carefree, easygoing readership. *The Hard Times* responded with a fierce campaign to get *MRR* "wiped from the annals of punk his-

The HARD Times

tory" by publicly accusing *Maximum Rocknroll* of punching down, being tone-deaf, and making jokes in bad taste. But then, in a crucial misstep, *Hard Times* attempted to side with Agnostic Front in their brutal war of words with their rival. Unfortunately, the alliance between Hard Times and AF never came to pass because the NYHC heavyweights misread a statement released by management and smashed up their office with baseball bats. Matt managed to escape, but Bill was seriously injured.

Razorcake and *Punk Planet,* two other *Hard Times* rip-offs, were also launched during this era but never produced any content worth mentioning.

While tied to their independent values, it was difficult for the *Hard Times* to sit on the sidelines as others in the underground punk and hardcore culture received their mainstream due. Punk-turned-rap act The Beastie Boys, who got their start as interns for the magazine, became international superstars with hits like "Fight for Your Right" and "Sabotage," but they refused to grant *The Hard Times* an interview, claiming their old employers had mistreated them, and

that they were still owed money for being forced to try various drugs as "research." The founders denied the accusations and banned the Beasties' music from ever being played in the office.

The 1980s saw *The Hard Times* evolve in scope and tone. They were a major player in punk media, but with Wall Street and other major corporations too scared to take the plunge, *Hard Times* had to look elsewhere to finance the company's growth. In this chapter, you'll get the inside scoop on the zine's expansion into new markets, and the full story of what happened when interest payments to the Death Crush Boys came due. You'll read about the increasing level of violence directed at the magazine's staff for their articles, the lengths they took to avoid beatdowns, and how Bill usually got the worst of it. It was a time of growing pains, physical pains, and the tragic but ultimately avoidable death of one of the founders. But, in the eighties, nothing could stop *The Hard Times'* renegade publishers from pushing punk to a whole new level--not even a body count.

ON THIS DAY IN PUNK HISTORY

FEBRUARY 18, 1980—
POORLY DRAWN STICK-AND-POKE TATTOO OFFICIALLY TRANSFORMS INTO DIFFERENT IMAGE

After having spent two infected weeks and eight additional months on the forearm of local punk Meghan Crespi, a stick-and-poke "giraffe giving the middle finger" tattoo officially transformed into an equally hard-to-explain "sideways trident with circles on the side" tattoo thanks to a complete lack of aftercare products and overall concern for her health.

DECEMBER 22, 1983—
FIRST UTTERANCE OF STRAIGHT EDGE AS EXCUSE NOT TO DRINK AT COMPANY PARTY

Desperate to keep her sobriety intact without giving a lengthy backstory about her decision, local woman Jenny Choi delivered the first known use of "I'm straight edge" to get out of drinking at a company holiday party, a statement that likely left her judged more greatly than had she simply admitted to her years of alcoholism.

APRIL 7, 1984—
FIRST KNOWN APPEARANCE OF POINTY S DOODLE

The ubiquitous pointy S first seen featured as the "S" in "Spinal Tap" was spotted on the locker of Petaluma, California, seventh grader Carlos de la Huerta. Insisting that he has no recollection of how the mark could have made its way onto the metal surface, de la Huerta returned to school the next morning to find that the esoteric symbol had disappeared as mysteriously as it arrived.

JUNE 12, 1988—
TOWNIE KID ACCIDENTALLY BECOMES PUNK UPON RIPPING SLEEVES OFF DAD'S HAND-ME-DOWN JEAN JACKET FROM 1972

Local teen Jake Campbell inadvertently began what would be referred to in his family as his "punk phase" after removing the sleeves from his father's old denim jacket on a particularly hot summer afternoon. Campbell would go on to adorn the item with a tag reading "MTV" in Sharpie, which was amended with the word "Sux" a few months later.

AUGUST 1, 1988—
TAPE STUCK IN WALKMAN FOR SIX WEEKS FINALLY UNSTUCK

A 60-minute Maxell cassette tape featuring Reagan Youth on one side and the Descendents on the other was finally freed after spending six consecutive weeks stuck inside a Dayton, Ohio, Walkman. Sources report that while the tape was removed unharmed, the Walkman was retired to a box in the garage.

DEBATE CLASS INSTRUCTOR HOPING IAN MACKAYE DROPS COURSE AS SOON AS POSSIBLE

By Bill Conway

WASHINGTON--Woodrow Wilson High School debate instructor Peter Schuster vocalized his wishes that long-winded senior Ian MacKaye drop the class immediately, according to exhausted teachers and administrators.

"I'm at my breaking point," said Schuster, visibly shaking in the teachers' lounge. "He just never stops. I try to give him softball topics like 'Is candy delicious?' and he goes on and on about the human rights violations in countries that export sugar, and how if he was a supplier of candy bars, he would stay up all night packaging each one by hand."

Schuster has tried a variety of tactics in order to make the class less pleasant for the controversial student.

"I am not proud of this, but last week I sat him by the window and paid some other students to stand outside and smoke. Ultimately, it had no effect," said the veteran high school instructor while pouring a small bottle of whiskey into his coffee. "For the past two weeks, we've been debating which disco artists are best, and he still finds a way to turn it into a rant against conformity or capitalism."

Students also expressed frustrations with MacKaye's presence.

"Debate is during last period, so if he starts talking toward the end of class, I know I'll be late to catch the bus," said fellow student Amy Parker. "Last week we were debating about whether cats or dogs made better pets, and he ended up talking for two hours straight about how owning a pet is false imprisonment. I ended up missing my shift at the diner and almost got fired."

MacKaye was unfazed when confronted with the criticism of his debate style.

"Listen, it's not like I'm trying to give anyone a set of rules; I'm just debating things that are important in a world that I don't find importance in," he said while nursing a can of Coca-Cola. "If the other students can't keep up, then that's their fault."

Bullis School in nearby Potomac, Maryland, claimed to have a similar issue with senior Henry Rollins, who, in addition to initiating long-winded debates, has also injured multiple students during dodgeball.

FEAR FOLLOWS SNL GIG WITH EVEN MORE DISASTROUS APPEARANCE ON "THE LOVE BOAT"

BY TED PILLOW

LOS ANGELES--Notorious hardcore band Fear, whose recent "Saturday Night Live" performance caused thousands of dollars in damages, performed a cameo on "The Love Boat" that ended in a small riot this past Tuesday, sources close to the production confirmed.

"Everybody on the set seemed really uptight," said Fear lead singer Lee Ving shortly after filming wrapped. "The producers were mad that we brought all our buddies, especially when they were slam dancing and knocked Bea Arthur and Sonny Bono overboard. Oops."

Executives at ABC were hesitant when cast member and hardcore enthusiast Gavin MacLeod campaigned to have his favorite band appear on the show.

"We wrote this great story for them where they'd be the ship's newest onboard entertainers, The Deck Swabbers," explained the actor.

"They promised the network they would only do Rick Springfield covers, but instead they played a 44-second song called 'Fuck Christmas' nonstop throughout the entire shoot."

Flanked by a crowd of LA punks smuggled by the band onto the cruise liner used for filming, witnesses reported that Fear's performance quickly degenerated into chaos. Large parts of the ship were damaged as the band provoked their friends and even some of the program's guest stars into violence and destruction.

"I couldn't believe my eyes," remarked assistant director Carol Gregory. "At one point I looked across the deck and saw Don Knotts grab the mic and scream 'New York sucks!' before booting [cast member] Fred Grandy right in the jaw. And that pretty boy Ted McGinley was trying to tear the damn chandelier off the dining hall ceiling."

Filming halted as the scene grew increasingly dangerous, and a team of security officials swarmed the deck. According to several production members, Fear managed to escape the situation via a lifeboat that they commandeered.

"We got the hell out of there," said bassist Derf Scratch. "Things were a little dicey for a minute, but then we washed ashore for a special crossover episode of 'Fantasy Island.' God, what a fucking catastrophe that turned out to be."

BAD BRAINS' PMA PUSHED TO LIMITS AFTER LETTER ADDRESSED TO JOHN JOSEPH ARRIVES IN STUDIO MAILBOX

United States Navy
5720 Integrity Drive
Millington, TN 38055-0000

John Joseph McGowan
P.O. Box 244892
New York, NY 10001

BY JEFF CARDELLO

WASHINGTON—D.C. punks Bad Brains had their positive mental attitude pushed to the limits after a piece of mail reportedly addressed to Cro-Mags frontman and longtime fan John Joseph made its way to their studio PO box, frustrated sources confirmed.

"It was from the Navy, which was weird to find in our mail, but it looked like it might be important," said vocalist HR, holding the letter addressed to their studio in care of Joseph. "And it just kept going from there."

None of the members of the band recall asking Joseph to move in, and all agreed that the relationship was moving too fast.

"When he showed up to a gig and started loading in our gear for the first time without asking, we were cool with it," said bassist Darryl Jenifer. "But here we are months later, and John's greeting us in the morning wearing only a bathrobe, serving us tofu scrambles for breakfast. His garlic-to-turmeric ratio is on point, but sometimes we just wanna record and get outta there."

Band members have raised suspicions that Joseph has turned their practice space into his living space.

"One night, I came in to grab a guitar and found him curled up on a pile of cables. I asked what was up, and he said he was 'making sure they still worked,'" said guitarist Dr. Know. "But then why did he have a blanket and an alarm clock? And I don't even wanna know how that ficus got in here."

"One time we were an hour late for practice, and when we finally showed up, he said that he'd been calling all the hospitals in the city to make sure we were all right," added drummer Earl Hudson. "It's like we have to tell him what we're doing all the time."

Joseph confirmed that he was now residing at the rehearsal space.

"Of course I moved in, motherfucker," Joseph said. "Who else is going to make sure their motherfucking guitars are in tune, laugh at their motherfucking jokes, and make them motherfucking soup when they're feeling motherfucking sick?"

As of press time, Joseph was seen at a local home improvement store procuring multiple paint swatches in hopes of "making the studio feel a bit more welcoming."

REPORT: SHEENA IS AN INVESTMENT BANKER NOW

By Chuck Kowalski

NEW YORK--The American punk community was blind-sided today as punk icon Sheena announced that she had accepted a position at Goldman Sachs, sparking widespread accusations of betrayal from scene members.

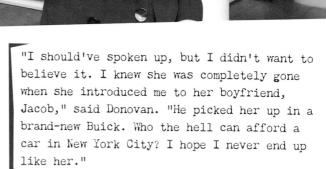

"This is the woman who got me into working dead-end jobs and huffing glue in the first place," said longtime fan Johnny Hart. "It really hits me hard to see her stoop this low and give in to the crushing world of capitalism. I bet that poser even wants kids and a family too."

Tina Rawlings and Luci Donovan, former room-mates of Sheena's, claimed to have noticed troubling signs of counter-counterculture over the final year of their living together.

"I started getting suspicious after she stopped wearing leather jackets in favor of those pastel blazers with shoulder pads," Rawlings said. "And when I found a copy of 'Sports' by Huey Lewis and the News hidden inside the cover of her copy of 'Rocket to Russia,' I knew she had turned."

Donovan stated that seeing the punk icon succumb to the demons of full-time employment and fulfilling relationships was too painful to accept, so she forced herself to ignore it.

"I should've spoken up, but I didn't want to believe it. I knew she was completely gone when she introduced me to her boyfriend, Jacob," said Donovan. "He picked her up in a brand-new Buick. Who the hell can afford a car in New York City? I hope I never end up like her."

Despite mounting criticism, Sheena insisted that her move to finance will prove to be the most punk phase of her life yet.

"Punk's a boys' club; there's limited capacity for women to fight the system," she said. "So now I deal my damage from within. Nothing screams 'punk rock' like ensuring multinational corporations have all of their documentation properly filed with the SEC."

The punk community still awaits the response of Judy and Jackie, who recently moved to Berlin to perform in the Ice Capades. However, rumors abound that both have reportedly died after experimenting with a lethal combination of night school and conformity.

DIVE BAR JUKEBOXES WORLDWIDE RECEIVE FINAL INSTALLMENT OF NEW RECORDS

BY ANDY HOLT

CHICAGO--The annual shipment of new 45s to dive bars around the globe will be the final such operation to ever take place, as jukebox selections have reached an ideal state that cannot be improved, numerous local bartenders confirm.

"Yep, that should do it," said Bob Wilkes, owner and bartender at Bob's Polish Tavern in the Ukrainian Village. "We got the new Springsteen, Aerosmith, Michael Jackson. I mean, what else do we need at this point? This ain't the Library of Congress."

In addition to cutting costs, bartenders expect that the move will please their core clientele while discouraging any disruptive newcomers from their establishments.

"I added 'Take On Me' last year, and a bunch of skinny, greasy dudes with dangly earrings would come in and play it over and over again. They would hit on every girl in the place until I kicked them out," said Trish Hanna of longtime neighborhood staple Wabash Alehouse. "Thankfully, every jukebox is equipped with 'Rock You Like a Hurricane,' and we can play that any time we need to get the energy in the room back up."

Powerful record industry groups lobbied heavily against the decision, warning that jukebox libraries would eventually become outdated, putting dive bar attendance at risk.

"Patrons are going to come to these bars looking for cutting-edge records, not outdated junk," said Patricia Flemming, a representative for the Recording Industry Association of America. "What are people going to do, get drunk and sing along to old favorites again and again, friends and strangers alike basking in a shared passion for music that transcends time and place?"

Service industry professionals disagreed with the RIAA's assessment, saying they know best what patrons want.

"I don't know why we add new stuff to the jukebox in the first place," said waitress Jennifer Turk of Roosevelt Beef & Sports while popping the lid off a five-gallon bucket of ranch dressing. "You could take every song but 'The Boys Are Back in Town' and 'We Are the Champions' out of that thing, and nobody here would even notice."

The Death of Ed

As remembered by Matt Saincome

Losing a brother, a friend, and a business partner all at once was the hardest thing I've ever experienced. In 1985, *The Hard Times* was riding high as one of the most popular zines in the nation, and we editors were taking advantage of our low-level celebrity status by partying every night. It's tough to lay low when you're on every guest list this side of the Hudson, you know? And some of us got into that lifestyle more than others. A staple at every hardcore and punk gig in the tristate area, Ed stood taller than almost everyone else at any given show, a trait that would eventually be what did him in.

The staff was invited to cover the record release party of a small punk band called Covered in Puke. It was a sweltering New York summer night, and dozens of people were packed into a DIY basement space known as the Butcher Bin. The squatters that ran it had recently installed stolen industrial ceiling fans to try to keep the air moving. The addition of the fans to the already-low ceilings meant there were exposed metal blades spinning precariously above the heads of drunk punks looking to slam dance their problems away. My brother, Ed, was one of those drunk punks.

We were all a bit out of control during the early years of *The Hard Times,* but on that night Ed was on another level. Ed was known for his unique mosh pit moves, his most famous being "The Salmon," where he'd rush through the pit, jumping sporadically, like a salmon swimming upstream. I believe it was a mixture of the heat and alcohol that night that led him to forget the low fans spinning just inches overhead. Covered in Puke launched into their most famous track, "Puke, Puke, Puke," and the crowd went nuts. Ed started making his way across the pit, predictably launching into The Salmon, and then everything went red--literally. Bill and I watched from the side of the stage as Ed's head separated from his body. I rushed over, but the damage was done. Bill tried reattaching the head, but that just led to more panic as punks scrambled around. As I clutched my brother's limp body, I knew *The Hard Times* needed to change.

Following Ed's funeral, Bill and I reevaluated our lives. Straight edge was becoming a more popular force within the hardcore scene, so we decided the entire staff needed to go edge to avoid future tragedy. Since that day, we have lived by the code of being drug- and alcohol-free. Well, kind of--Bill has made exceptions for "special occasions" over the years, such as turning twenty-one. He'll even tell you that drinking at a wedding or after a breakup shouldn't count as breaking edge, but I say it does, and this book is the best place to reveal his secret. Ed's spirit and dedication to the truth have been a driving force behind *The Hard Times* since his untimely passing, and for that reason I feel it's finally time to out Bill as a secret sipper. He'll try to deny it, but the skeletons in his closet all carry a six-pack.

GG ALLIN ESCORTED OFF "WE ARE THE WORLD" MUSIC VIDEO SET AFTER SPITTING BLOOD ON DAN AYKROYD

BY DAVID TYLER

LOS ANGELES--On Tuesday, punk rocker and violent psychopath GG Allin was removed from a chorus taping of "We Are the World" after spitting blood on Dan Aykroyd, sources being tested for blood-borne illnesses confirmed.

"We were starting to feel the groove of the chorus when all of the sudden I heard the Pointer Sisters start screaming," said recording artist Kenny Loggins. "When I turned to see what the commotion was about, there was this fully naked man cutting his chest with the top of a tin can, puking blood all over Aykroyd."

Reports from those present paint a picture of creative differences between Allin and the other musicians in the studio leading up to the grotesque incident.

"That one fella with the infected tattoos and bad attitude didn't seem to like the direction of the song and suggested we change the name to 'We Are the Turds: American Nazi Anthem,' but Bob Geldof stepped in to try to get things back on track," said musician Al Jarreau shortly after disposing of his blood-splattered shirt in a hazmat waste bin. "He also wanted to add a bunch of lines about dog cum and having relations with dead hookers, but we all felt that might distract from the underlying message."

Witnesses claim that shortly after Allin's suggested changes were shot down, he became irritable.

"We all believe in this project and want to do what's best for the people of Africa. When we didn't accept GG's changes, he flipped out, ripped off his soiled underwear, and zeroed in on Dan," said John Oates. "Aykroyd was simply in the wrong place at the wrong time. Thankfully he was wearing those eyeglasses--who knows what sort of diseases that naked freak has."

Quincy Jones, the song's coproducer, explained his choice to invite the controversial punk rocker.

"I know he's a little off the wall, but this is the sound of the youth, and we wanted to show the world who's making music in America right now," said the legendary producer while washing smeared feces off the studio wall. "I'll never make that mistake again.

"And I just informed Mr. Allin's management that I won't be able to produce his next album with the Scumfucs," Jones added.

As of press time, the artists still present at the scene planned to reconvene at the studio the next morning, and all agreed not to inform Huey Lewis of the rescheduled session.

JELLO BIAFRA'S SUIT WORN ON "OPRAH"

RETURNED TO STORE AT FULL PRICE

By Bobby D. Lux

CHICAGO--Dead Kennedys frontman Jello Biafra returned the suit he wore on Oprah Winfrey's top-rated afternoon talk show to the store in time for a full cash refund, attested sources close to the situation.

"It was a nightmare--the audience kept bursting into applause every time I said something. I was thinking, 'OK, jeez, I really want to take this uptight suburban mom to task over censorship, but I've got a suit I need to return. The more you clap, the longer I have to be here,'" said the singer of his heated exchanges with Parents Music Resource Center (PMRC) cofounder Tipper Gore. "I knew Chicago traffic was about to get bad, no thanks to Reagan cutting the budget for federal oversight of traffic safety. Check that out sometime."

The Dead Kennedys are currently embroiled in multiple lawsuits over their most recent album, "Frankenchrist," which features an insert poster of H.R. Giger's "Penis Landscape."

"Winning in the court of public opinion is great," said Dead Kennedys guitarist East Bay Ray. "But that suit cost $180, and we needed that money to pay our lawyers. Jello said

he'd make it in time, but he also promised we wouldn't get into trouble for selling an album with a bunch of dicks on the insert, so . . ."

Harmony's Menswear is known for having a notoriously unforgiving same-day return policy.

"I bought a men's kimono to wear on 'Donahue' back in 1984, and when I tried to return it the next day, they told me they could only give me store credit," said Ministry frontman Al Jourgensen. "I ended up writing 'My Possession' about the experience."

Biafra explained how he was able to cross town before the store closed.

"I gave myself two hours to get there," Biafra disclosed. "I know these starched-suit business types tie up all the cabs after work so they can drink themselves into oblivion just to get through another day. They talk about creating artificial intelligence someday? Well, look no further than the American workforce--we have plenty of robots with brains willing to do mundane tasks endlessly."

As of press time, Biafra was entering the fifteenth consecutive hour of recounting the suit's return.

WARZONE WOMEN VHS WORKOUT TAPE TO FEATURE FLOOR PUNCHING, CREEPY CRAWLING, FIGHTING JOCKS

BY BOBBY D. LUX

NEW YORK--A new workout tape from the Warzone Women, arguably the most badass fans of the hardcore outfit, promises to give viewers a chiseled six-pack, increased endurance, and the lean muscle mass needed to combat preppy frat jocks, sources close to the production confirmed.

"Some experts are trying to tell me that the VHS exercise market is oversaturated," said Warzone vocalist and the tape's de facto executive producer, Raymond "Raybeez" Barbieri, at the Lower East Side premiere of the "Warzone Women's Original Fuck Off Workout." "But who else besides these chicks can show you how to work your lower abs and floor punch a jock in the balls at the same time? Keep the faith."

The tape aims to target an untapped demographic of skater wives and youth crew moms.

"The girls in the scene need to get ripped too, more so than those suburbanite moms praying at the altar of Jane Fonda," said Warzone Woman CC Dagger. "These authentic, pit-tested mosh moves will give women the strong core they need for fighting off skuzzy punk guys, grabby bouncers, and the Wall Street goons who want to bust you just because you threw a brick through some Volvo. Fuck that Volvo."

Traditional fitness experts haven't been as welcoming to the unconventional newcomer.

"I don't see the appeal," said Jake "Body by Jake" Steinfeld. "You have these women with shaved heads and tattoos everywhere, just punching everything in sight. And have you heard the language coming out of their mouths? How this can be motivating to anyone is beyond me. The only thing this tape motivated me to do was walk to my garbage can and throw it away. They have decent delt striations, though."

As of press time, "Warzone Women's Original Fuck Off Workout" has reportedly become the most stolen workout tape of all time, with every copy having been shoplifted from Times Square retailers within hours of its release.

NAZIS CHASED OUT OF NEW YORK HARDCORE SCENE RELOCATE TO ARGENTINA

BY BILL CONWAY

BUENOS AIRES, Argentina—New York Nazi skinheads recently expelled from city limits have relocated to Argentina and are said to be living comfortably, sources in the area confirmed.

"A few weeks back, we started seeing more and more young men with shaved heads, combat boots, and Youth Defense League shirts showing up and starting fights at local music venues," said poet Diego Gutierrez. "Nobody knows where they're from or why they came here, but they seem to be mad that everyone speaks Spanish."

Experts believe the sudden influx of New York Nazis is part of a plan to kick-start a hardcore scene under the new government.

"Many officials have expressed solidarity with the messages of bands like American Blood, United Welfare, and Burden on Society, who sing about loving their country, unity, and blood on the dance floor," said Argentine music expert Camila López. "They don't want an influx of ska music like Central American countries have experienced the last few years."

Hardcore fans in New York City report that shows have been much more peaceful since the Nazis left, and that they look forward to rebuilding the scene.

"It would have been nice to publicly shame them, but a lot of those skinhead cowards took off at the first chance available," said "Posi" Collin Brady. "We now have a lot of work to do to make shows safer for everyone. We plan on instituting no-stage-dive policies citywide, and outlawing any images with the iron cross."

"Big" Tommy Lincoln, singer of Oi! band The Bowery Bruisers, believes Argentina was the right move for his band and adopted hardcore family.

"In New York, we were being persecuted simply because we expressed not wanting to live near Puerto Ricans," explained the clean-shaven frontman, "but here in Argentina, nobody seems to know what we're saying. Plus we get to set up a lot more shows here, so my band can finally headline."

Despite the recent calm at shows, leaders of the New York scene warn that many Nazis didn't flee but remained in the area, the majority of whom have reportedly grown out their hair and assumed identities as construction workers.

The First Musician to Try to Kick Our Asses

AS REMEMBERED BY BILL CONWAY

Anyone who runs a zine knows they're going to get their ass kicked eventually. It's an unfortunate reality of the job, and The Hard Times was not immune. We knew our in-depth reporting would result in broken bones for one of us--we just didn't know when it would happen, or how bad the beating would be.

In 1981, Matt, Ed, and I were reporting on a local New York punk band named The Blood Donors. They were a skinhead act with an aggressive sound and, apparently, a complete aversion to criticism. We'd heard rumors that their bass player tended to consume an entire foot-long Italian sub from Jerry's Deli during each of their sets, and we set out to write the story confirming these antics. Unfortunately for us, their bass player, "Emergency Room" Ray Lapointe, caught wind of the article and immediately set out to make sure it never saw the light of day.

On the evening of the ass-kicking, the editorial staff was in our small office space on the Lower East Side when we heard an aggressive knock on the door--if I'm being completely honest, it sounded more like someone taped a cooked ham to a baseball bat and was trying to break through. As it turned out, it was E.R. Ray and his pumpkin-sized fists, scarred and battle-tested from years of street fights. Matt opened the door, saw Ray, and sprinted past him as fast as he could; he weaseled his way out of the building and never looked back. For all I know, he ran to New Jersey that day. Ed and I were left alone with a 300-pound borderline-illiterate bruiser who was intent on teaching us a lesson in journalistic integrity.

I would love to say Ed and I fought valiantly, but that would be a lie. I was choke-slammed through a desk, and you can still vaguely see the impression of a size-14 Doc Martens tread on my back. That being said, I consider myself the lucky one. Ed fought back, landing a couple solid punches that Ray ate like one of his beloved foot-long subs before Ray put him through each of our office walls. The beating was so severe that it became New York hardcore lore and eventually led Youth of Today to release Break Down the Walls, an entire album based on the incident. To this day, I still tense up when I hear the opening notes of "Make a Change."

CONGRESS PASSES NEW LAW REQUIRING EVERY PUNK IN EVERY MOVIE TO BE NAMED "SPIKE"

By MIKE CIVINS

WASHINGTON--Congress passed a law Tuesday morning requiring Hollywood to name every vaguely punk-looking character "Spike," from starring cast members to background extras, sources confirmed.

"Spike is clearly a bad person's name, and it's also easy to remember if the character is wearing spikes in some way, particularly on their head or face," said Representative Mitch Branquist (R-1A). "Therefore, all characters should be named as such, in perpetuity."

The legal blockbuster will apply to every spiky-haired ne'er-do-well, low-budget biker, and playground bully depicted in any movie, scripted TV drama, commercial, and/or after-school special to further improve viewer experiences.

"Regardless of format, this bold new law will help audiences quickly identify punk rockers on screen, so elderly viewers can easily follow their favorite programs' story lines," Branquist explained. "By leaving no question whether Spike is 'the bad one,' our nation's older folks will have more opportunities to ask more pressing questions, such as 'What did he say?' and 'Doesn't she look like the girl who works at the Fotomat on Saturdays?'"

This baffling new requirement will also benefit the nation's squarest audiences, including parents, teachers, law enforcement, and convenience-store owners, many of whom seek to spot misguided youths as quickly as possible to maintain order in society at all costs.

"These days, with the hairspray and the denim, it's hard to tell who's a bad seed just by looking at them, so this helps," said Denver resident and concerned parent Leslie Hoff.

Hollywood executives are reported to be perplexed by the announcement, yet willing to cooperate.

"If the nudniks in Washington want the next no-good ruffian who crashes his motorcycle into a dweeb's party to be named Spike, then I guess that's what they're going to get," said Motion Picture Association of America President Jack Valenti. "We're gonna be saying goodbye to a lot of perfectly good Johnnys, Aces, and Pukes, but that's just the way things roll in this fickle bitch of an industry."

Sweeping changes to the nation's screenplays are expected for any fictional character wearing combat boots, cartoonishly large chains, leather jackets, and/or metal studs, as well as anyone lacking a desire to be a positive contributor to society, like "that nice Jamie Watkins boy up the street."

GEAR THIEVES HAVING TROUBLE SELLING GWAR'S 20-FOOT SPIKED PHALLUS

BY JEFF CARDELLO

TRENTON, N.J.--Local criminals report they are having "a hell of a time" trying to sell a 20-foot representation of an alien penis they stole from GWAR's gear and prop trailer early yesterday morning, increasingly anxious sources confirmed.

"When we cracked open the back of the trailer, we expected a bunch of nice equipment we could fence for top dollar, but all we saw was a bunch of freaky masks. I figured it was for a haunted house," said one of the thieves, who wished to be identified as "Frank." "But when we found the gigantic dick, I knew we were dealing with a bunch of sickos."

At this time, the 20-foot Styrofoam phallus covered with latex spikes has not garnered any interest from potential buyers.

"Frank and his boys do a lot of business here. I don't ask no questions, and they keep bringing me top-notch goods," said Mike Corley, owner of Mike's Fast Exchange Pawn Shop. "But when those goons came in here trying to sell something that looked like Godzilla's dingdong, I was like, 'Oh hey, buddy, this isn't that kind of store.'"

In addition to the spiked alien member, the criminals have allegedly had difficulty unloading other items stolen from the trailer.

"Nobody wants to buy a bunch of loincloths covered in blood, or a guitar shaped like a piece of rotten meat. My girlfriend wouldn't even take the spear-tipped bra. In fact, she made me burn it," said Frank. "The drama teacher at a high school a few towns over was interested in a few things for their spring production of 'Little Shop of Horrors,' but that's still up in the air."

GWAR frontman Oderus Urungus sent a harsh message to the thieves.

"We will travel to the ends of this feces-infested filthdump of a planet searching for these pilfering maggots and disembowel them in front of their friends and family," said the singer. "Also, if anyone has any information, please call the Trenton police department and reference case number 8629."

As of press time, GWAR have announced plans to continue their East Coast tour by performing a stripped-down stage show with acoustic versions of their songs, and encouraged fans to bring their own buckets of fake blood.

The HARD Times

The First Musician to Travel Long Distance to Kick Our Asses

As remembered by Bill Conway

The Hard Times' fearless scene coverage wasn't without backlash. Local threats could be dealt with easily: We had a network of informants who tipped us when someone was pissed off, and we'd often defuse the situation before it got too out of hand. But in one circumstance, Matt and I underestimated how far some people would go to express their displeasure.

The California hardcore scene was taking off, and every week freelance reporters sent us stories about up-and-coming bands. Time to Fight 88 was a skinhead group from LA that had been making news because of their infamously violent shows, aggressive sound, and strange obsession with Ronald Reagan. We reviewed their 1985 release *Right, White, and Blue,* summarizing it as cheap knockoff of the New York hardcore sound. This did not go over well with the band's drummer, Donny "The Noose" Nickerson.

We'd received word that members of TTF88 were angry, but because they were 3,000 miles away, we lulled ourselves into a false feeling of security. Then one day the sound of an ox trying to break down our door interrupted our peaceful editing. Matt opened it, recognized the danger of the situation, and sprinted to safety. This left me alone to face a California meathead with a battery of steroids swelling his muscles and poisoning his brain. Once again, I'd like to say I fought valiantly, but that would also be a lie.

In a concussed daze, I managed to reach under my desk for a padlock-filled tube sock. Clumsily, I swang it at The Noose, but he ripped it from my hands and beat me so thoroughly you can still make out the impression of the Master Lock logo on my skull. Then he smashed all our equipment and left me bleeding on the floor. Hours later, Matt returned from his impromptu afternoon off armed with Korean takeout and the knowledge that The Noose had taken a train all the way from LA for the sole purpose of breaking our bones.

Later, reports came in that TTF88 had played a series of benefit shows to raise money for The Noose's train ride. The shows were so successful that he'd been able to travel first-class and stay in a high-end hotel. As a result of this intimidation, we abstained from reviewing their next album, *Blood on the News Desk.*

AGNOSTIC FRONT CONCERNED BY INCREASING LACK OF VIOLENCE AT SHOWS

BY IAN FISHMAN

NEW YORK--New York hardcore outfit Agnostic Front is growing increasingly concerned by a startling lack of violence at their shows, band members admitted following an otherwise well-received set last week.

"We have a real problem on our hands," said singer Roger Miret. "Our last few shows, we've gotten nothing but applause after our songs from a bunch of pansies who just sing along instead of fight. We're a skinhead band; we expect violence and our fans want violence. Or, at least, we want violence."

The issue came to a head with the recording of Agnostic Front's latest album, "Live at CBGB."

"It didn't matter what we did--we just could not get people to beat the shit out of each other like they usually do," guitarist Vinnie Stigma said. "We wanted to do a live album to capture the absolute brutality of our live shows, but we ended up overdubbing all the sounds of the pit."

Bassist Rob Kabula added, "We had to punch each other in the face while shouting along to our own songs in the studio. I've got no problem laying my brothers the fuck out when it means something, but for our own record? We may as well just end it now."

Sadly for some, Kabula may get his wish: The album is likely Agnostic Front's last for some time, as Miret is facing an upcoming prison sentence.

"Maybe it's for the best I'm going away for a bit. The streets just aren't as rough as they used to be," Miret said wistfully. "If this is what unity looks like, I don't want any part of it."

Surprisingly, Agnostic Front has found an unlikely ally in outgoing New York City mayor Ed Koch.

"Look, I've done a lot to clean up this city," Mayor Koch said. "But maybe we've gone too far. No one wants a return to the murders of the '70s, but we certainly didn't want to lose the crowd kills that put New York hardcore on the map. Too many of these idiot kids still have all their teeth. I mean, really--why even fuckin' live here if everyone is going to stand around like it's fuckin' California?"

TIPPER GORE PROPOSES CENSORSHIP OF ANY BAND THAT DIDN'T LET HER PLAY DRUMS

BY ZACH RAFFIO

WASHINGTON--Social issues advocate Tipper Gore announced today that the Parents Music Resource Center (PMRC) will be implementing new censorship measures for the music of any act that prohibited her from hopping behind the kit and playing drums for them, irritated sources confirmed.

"At first I assumed her interest in censorship was for the sake of the children," PMRC cofounder Susan Baker said of the new policy. "But all she talks about is getting back at the bands who wouldn't let her 'beat the boom booms,' whatever that means. I think her judgment is clouded."

Bands such as Twisted Sister and Mötley Crüe, both of whom turned down Gore's request, will be forced to add a "Parental Advisory" sticker to their latest releases to warn of the violent or sexually explicit nature of their music, along with what Gore refers to as their "inability to chill and let me hit the skins."

Black Sabbath guitarist Tony Iommi, who was also affected by Gore's censorship, relayed his frustration.

"I mean, we let her sit in on one session, and she just kept adding these insanely long solos to every song. At one point, she asked for a mic so she could sing harmonies while drumming, but, it's like, we can't be here all night. Some of us have kids to take to school in the morning," Iommi explained. "We told her it just wasn't a good fit, and then the next day, our manager said her committee would be censoring our next record."

While many on both sides of the issue were taken aback by Gore's reasoning for the new policy, her husband, Senator Al Gore, quickly rushed to her defense.

"Tipper is an artist--she needs to express herself," claimed Gore. "And if these bands cross her, so help me God, I will tax the crap out of every single tour, to the point where Judas Priest can only afford to play hometown bar mitzvahs."

At press time, a PMRC spokesperson stated that AC/DC will be allowed to release their song "Let Me Put My Love Into You" without restriction provided Gore is allowed a monthly two-hour jam session for the next 30 years.

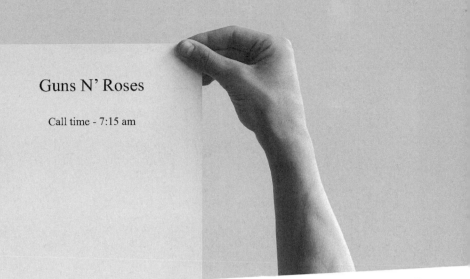

Guns N' Roses

Call time - 7:15 am

AXL ROSE NOT FALLING FOR GUNS N' ROSES LISTED SET TIME OF 7:15 AM

BY GREG HELLER

TOLEDO, Ohio--Famously petulant Guns N' Roses frontman Axl Rose became suspicious when a handwritten flyer taped to the band's dressing room announced the headliners should take the stage "no later than 7:15 a.m.," sources confirmed.

"Something about it just smelled fishy," said the waiflike singer, midway through his afternoon bandanna fitting. "Very few gigs begin at that time. Plus, it was already 4:30 p.m. and nobody was begging me to get to the stage."

The botched ploy was the brainchild of promoter Dan "Clumpy" Masterson, who'd hoped to subvert GnR's recent spate of offensively belated start times, but now admits his tactic was a bit undercooked.

"In retrospect, I probably should have gone with, like, 5 or 6 p.m., but desperate times call for desperate measures," said Clumpy. "I thought removing all clocks from the venue would help, but Axl just seems to operate on some weird circadian rhythm that is heavily influenced by alcohol."

The hard-charging Angelenos' current North American run has seen Rose take the stage with increased disregard for listed start times, something he chalks up to "being a megalomaniacal piece of shit."

"Listen, I know when I am ready to rock and I am not gonna force it. When you've done this as long as I have, you know when your sha-na-na-na-na-na-na knees, knees are ready to shimmy across the stage," said Rose. "See, that vocal tic tells me that I'm getting close, but it'll probably be another six hours before I know for sure."

Complicating matters was the fact that GnR drummer Steven Adler failed to recognize the scheme and, upon seeing the flyer, flew into a panic, assuming he'd missed the gig.

"I figured I had somehow slept through it," said Adler. "I have a tendency to get very, very sleepy. I got to the venue around 10 in the morning and nobody was even there to let me in. But I got to hang out with some dudes under a nearby overpass, and we had a hell of time."

Following their current tour, the band is gearing up to release an EP of covers and acoustic tracks that Rose promises everyone will love, "with the possible exception of persons newly relocated to this country, homosexuals, cops, and African-Americans."

The HARD Times

The Hard Times Finally Repays Loan It Took From Hardcore Crew Death Crush Boys

AS REMEMBERED BY MATT SAINCOME

Something had to change. Bill's complete inability to defend himself and our office space led to a loss of thousands of dollars' worth of inventory and equipment. After his second face-altering beating, he demanded that we figure out a way to protect ourselves and our business. That forced us to make one of the most difficult decisions we ever made as a company: We took out a loan from the infamous street crew Death Crush Boys to restock our offices and hire them as our personal security.

We borrowed $750 from DCB in late 1984. They had a made a fortune selling bootleg Adidas tracksuits all over New York and were looking to expand their unsavory portfolio. The terms of the loan were never defined. At the end of each month, the crew's de facto accountant, a portly man named "Brass" Bobby Vicente, came to collect our payment, with "interest." The interest varied every time: Sometimes it would be an extra $100, other times he would force us to write a positive review of his sister's new wave band. We never knew what to expect.

As the 1980s progressed, *The Hard Times'* popularity grew. Our circulation was higher than ever, and real money was flowing in. This didn't escape DCB's notice, and they demanded more and more interest each month. And as long as we kept paying, the crew took care of us, providing real protection. Bill was never again beaten up by an angry frontman, and I no longer had to hear him whine about how hard it was to eat with a broken jaw. But, ultimately, I felt like they were taking our lunch money, and it was time for *Hard Times* to stand on its own two feet, even if Bill couldn't. Then, in 1989, we finally got the break we needed.

Once every year, Bill and I would treat ourselves to some fine dining in Manhattan. We decided to try Diane, a recently opened upscale eatery known for its high-end seafood. The food was some of the best I'd ever tasted, but Bill had an adverse reaction. As soon as he started eating, he became violently ill and was escorted out back behind the restaurant. Management feared the potential bad press from Bill's sickness might harm Diane's reputation, and so they quickly offered him $3,500 to keep it quiet. Bill's glass jaw had been part of the reason why we were in debt to DCB, but his even weaker stomach is what got us out.

We paid off our loan with the restaurant payout and, as a result, washed our hands completely of any affiliation with DCB. Things were looking up, though Bill remained hospitalized for weeks after--doctors said he'd contracted a foodborne illness that nearly destroyed his stomach lining and almost cost him his life. As far as I know, he still owes thousands of dollars in medical expenses from that month he spent clinging to existence, but at least *The Hard Times* was thriving, free of debt, and ready to make it to the next level.

GEORGE BUSH: READ MY LIPS, NO NEW BLACK FLAG FRONTMEN

By Brad Skafish

NEW ORLEANS--GOP hopeful George Bush promised a crowd of supporters at the Republican National Convention yesterday that he would usher in major reforms of the hardcore scene.

"Keith Morris, Ron Reyes, Dez Cadena, Henry Rollins . . . the American people have had enough! Read my lips . . . no new Black Flag frontmen," boomed Bush, before uproarious applause. "Should a seminal hardcore band be required to pick a frontman, and stick with him? My opponents say no, but I say yes!"

Black Flag fan and newly-minted Bush supporter Travis Martinez embraced the platform.

"I've never voted before, on general principle, especially for a Republican. But finally, the politicians seem to be paying attention to my issues. The revolving door of frontmen needs to end. I hardly know what to expect when I show up to a Black Flag show anymore."

Bush's message wasn't universally welcomed. Senator Bob Dole expressed skepticism.

"What exactly is he proposing? Federal intervention on the personnel decisions of a punk band? It wouldn't work, and I for one would never support that sort of big government overreach," said Dole.

Despite the criticisms, Bush carried on unabated.

"Some say that a band can sustain itself, and even prosper, with a new frontman every few years, but you know what I call that? Voodoo rock 'n' roll! It doesn't make sense, and this will not stand, this aggression against the great fans of Black Flag," said Bush.

Black Flag founder Greg Ginn weighed in, indicating confusion at Bush's plan.

"Bands change members, you know? We had four different drummers in the space of a year, and nobody cared. The second you change singers, everybody gets their panties in a bunch," said Ginn. "Personally, I like to think of all the different Black Flag members--past, present, and future--like a thousand points of light in a narrow and violent sky. Kinda poetic, right?"

"The choice is yours, America," stated Bush, as he brought his remarks to a close. "Vote for my rivals, and get four more years of constant lineup changes. Or join me, and call for a kinder, gentler Black Flag. But to be clear, I expect they'll be neither kind nor gentle . . . it's just a figure of speech, really."

SLAYER UPSET ANTHRAX WEARING SAME EVENING WEAR TO HEADBANGERS BALL

BY MIKE CIVINS

NEW YORK--Attendees of MTV's "Headbangers Ball" were aghast late Saturday night as both Anthrax and Slayer arrived wearing the same leather jacket-denim vest combination with puffy white high-top sneakers.

"Two of thrash's Big Four showing up to the same event wearing the same ensemble is like going to a cemetery without vandalizing any graves, or using the wrong spoon for your consommé," said host Riki Rachtman. "It's a faux pas of the highest order."

While the outfit worked wonders accentuating the figures of all nine musicians, no one could deny the damage done to the metal world's rich yet delicate social tapestry.

"The Ball is more than just a party, it's a weekly celebration of how a dedicated metal performer has blossomed, for the world to see," explained a visibly shaken Kerry King. "And goddamn it all to hell if the world is going to see us looking any less special than the nasty, face-melting guitar riffs we wrote to make it here!"

In addition to offending nearly everyone present, members of both acts expressed equal parts embarrassment and resentment over the glaring gaffe.

"Never in all my life have I been so mortified," said Slayer frontman Tom Araya. "If I had even suspected that other metal dudes would show up wearing the same outfit every other metal dude wears every day, I would have put a little more consideration into my accoutrements."

When questioned about the sartorial misstep, Anthrax frontman Joey Belladonna was inconsolable.

"It's just not fair," declared the vocalist while stress-eating a handful of meticulously adorned canapés from the corner of the men's bathroom. "I always dreamed I'd be the Belladonna of the Ball. God, fuck this stupid night."

At press time, Anthrax guitarist Scott Ian was seen retrieving a DRI cap so he can reportedly flip up its bill in an attempt to distinguish himself from his similarly adorned peers.

BERLIN TEARS DOWN
LEGENDARY GRAFFITI SPOT

BY ANDY HOLT

BERLIN--A landmark graffiti location separating West and East Germany was destroyed by residents last night, erasing decades of street art with no regard for the immense suffering such an action would cause in the punk community, outraged sources reported.

"I grew up bombing that spot every weekend. Last night, I had to watch thousands of people hack the whole thing to pieces. Nobody tried to stop them, not even the police," said local punk and graffiti artist Mia Weber. "It's just another victory for The Man."

Reports indicate that countless revelers mobbed the wall from both sides, dismantling the concrete barrier and the oppressive political regime it represented before celebrating the reunification of their homeland until dawn.

"Hard to believe how selfish people can be," said Trench Mannheim, frontman of industrial band Die Frettchen. "Our street team just put up some fresh tags promoting our bar show this weekend, and those yuppies erased all that hard work like it was nothing. They could at least have had the decency not to cheer while they did it. Such disrespect."

When reached for comment, those responsible for the demolition were quick to apologize.

"I can't tell you how sorry I am about this," said Paul Meyers, an East German activist who spent the past decade in a Soviet prison for running an underground pro-democracy publication. "We've been so caught up trying to free our people from a fascist police state, I guess we got carried away. We never thought about the culture. Boy, do we have egg on our faces."

These statements appeared to fall on deaf ears, however, as punks insisted that the destruction of such a local legend could never be forgiven.

"A scene died today," said Weber, staring wistfully at the rubble. "I think I speak for a lot of punks when I say that this day will never be forgotten."

FOOD REVIEW:
Horrible Customer Service Holds Back Potential of DC-Area Häagen-Dazs

By Phil Matthews

I do not scream for ice cream—I request it in the respectful but firm tone that denotes the importance of the situation. Unfortunately for the proprietors of this new DC-area Häagen-Dazs, their teenage employees do not seem to understand the core concepts of customer service.

For starters, an ice cream professional's hands should be clean and ready for proper scooping. But one teenager named Ian scooped my triple chocolate in a waffle cone ($2) with visible Sharpie marks smeared all over the backs of his fists. Later, I witnessed him handle a filthy skateboard without washing up. Then right back to scooping!

His coworkers weren't much better. Another employee, this one a brooding bodybuilder type, did nothing but grimace when I requested extra sprinkles. When I asked again, he dunked my entire cone in the jar, over-sprinkling the scoops to an absurd degree and hurting their structural integrity in the process. He wasn't wearing a name tag so I didn't catch his name, but at least he had his shirt on. I then saw him remove it for a 15-minute break he spent doing push-ups in an area clearly blocking the fire exit.

The ice cream itself was serviceable. A bit better than store-bought, but nothing special. Unfortunately, what little enjoyment I had was periodically interrupted by the teens behind the counter arguing over what ear-assaulting music to play.

As remembered by Bill Conway

When we saw this review of the Häagen-Dazs where our friends Ian and Henry worked, we had to put it in our zine. We were later sued over it because we didn't have permission to use the clipping. However, since our squat didn't have a mailing address, we didn't learn about the lawsuit for over a decade, and by then the writer had died. Problem solved.

What's wrong with the classics? Would it hurt these kids to listen to anything with a melody? The loud, aggressive noise led me to cut my trip short.

As I was leaving, the duo, oblivious to my discomfort, begged me to take some photos of them. I shot a few pics just to get out of the situation, but these two ruined what could otherwise be a delightful ice cream shop. I will be writing a letter to ownership and will update readers if I get a response.

The HARD Times

FROM THE

VAULT

The 1990s: The Golden Years

In the 1990s, *The Hard Times* was unstoppable. By the end of the decade, high-gloss editions of the magazine, shrink-wrapped with CDs and posters, flew off newsstands at circulation rates that stunned the industry. First it was 200,000. Then 500,000. Then a few million. For a couple weeks, the reported readership of *Hard Times* beat out *Rolling Stone* and *Spin*--combined. The editors relocated from their Lower East Side squat to a voluminous office in a Lower Manhattan high-rise.

The entire expansion was powered by an injection of cash from an undisclosed angel investor. Rumors circulated it was a billionaire south of the border, but no one--not even those in the back office--knew for sure. Regardless, the marching orders were clear: If it had anything to do with music or alternative culture in any format, Hard Times Media LLC was going to take it over.

And take over they did. Books, radio shows, and numerous movie scripts were developed. A concept sketch for a theme park was drawn, and a lot purchased. Seemingly the only thing Hard Times didn't invest in was an internet presence, something the founders dismissed as a "nerd trend."

Inside the office, management purchased anything they wanted: state-of-the-art printers, beepers, prostitutes. They even bought beepers for the prostitutes. A hiring frenzy brought an entire new group of writers and editors to the magazine; now-famous names like Krissy Howard and Jeremy Kaplowitz both got their start in the nineties. Mark Roebuck, Mike Amory, and Eric Navarro splashed the pages with in-depth reporting and reviews. And of course the unique stylings of "Dirty Hand" Dan Rice would be imitated in the writing world for years to come.

That new blood was necessary because there were several periods during this era when the team

suspected Matt had broken edge and gone off the deep end. He would take weeks-long trips then return claiming the company now had satellite offices in Shanghai, Thailand, or a rural Siberian province. He returned from one foray in such a state that immediately upon entering the office, a brutal fistfight broke out between him and Bill. According to eyewitnesses, no words were spoken before the first blows were thrown, it was just two bulls locking eyes and going for it. The result was a stunning defeat for Matt, who had developed a thousand-dollar-a-day cocaine habit and had ballooned to well over 300 pounds.

"Frankly, it looked like he'd never been in a fight in his entire life," one staffer would later tell a documentary crew who filmed material for seven years, but never released anything. "I couldn't tell if he had a spasm or tried to pull out 'The Salmon' to defend himself, but it was a lopsided beating the likes of which we hadn't seen since skinheads charged

the office in the eighties and changed Bill's jawline." (The Salmon, of course, referencing the dance move coined by long-dead *Hard Times* founder Ed Saincome.)

As was tradition in *The Hard Times* offices, the victory officially put Bill in charge of the editorial teams, which he brilliantly led to new heights of reporting, circulation, and spending. Matt was exiled to ad sales and business development--an area that quickly started showing signs of trouble.

Accountants pleaded for Matt to stop hemorrhaging money, but by that point the whole staff had grown too accustomed to being treated to the latest high-end electronics. It seemed he spent most of his days tending to the mysterious and often hush-hush nature of the company's investors, or at the race track, living the life of a media tycoon.

These were the golden years. *The Hard Times* was untouchable, and that would never change.

ON THIS DAY IN PUNK HISTORY

February 9, 1991—
Aging punk is born

Anchorage, Alaska, resident Josh Corman began his 28-year journey toward becoming his hometown scene's Aging Punk. Corman has reportedly been preparing for the position as Aging Punk from the age of 25, at which point he'd replaced his usual two hoodies for an actual winter coat and began declaring that he "just can't rage like I used to and not pay for it the next day, that's for fucking sure."

November 1, 1992—
Abandoned pot of vegan chili successfully rebranded as "compost bin"

A nearly five-month-old pot of vegan chili was finally passed off as a Lancaster, Pennsylvania, punk house's new "compost bin" thanks to equal parts creative/lazy efforts by local riot grrrl and house resident Maria Brent. The new eco-friendly waste management system was reportedly used to eliminate organic material exactly twice before being poured over a fellow scene member's head "like how they do with the Gatorade at football games" during a hilarious, albeit not terribly well-received stunt at a party.

March 16, 1994—
700 millionth eighth grader gets into photography

Tonopah, Nevada, middle-schooler Magdalia Tovar officially became the 700 millionth angsty teen to have gotten "really into photography lately, or whatever." Tovar joins the other 699,999,999 eighth graders before her to have become inspired by the "stark contrast between light and dark that tells a story without saying a word," and lists Ansel Adams as her favorite and the only photographer whose work she is aware of.

August 22, 1997—
Smallest piece of merch sold to largest man in scene

A startling ratio was reached at a Hattiesburg, Mississippi, show when local screamo kid and 235-pound adult man Alex Ambrose purchased a piece of merch "at best" three sizes too small for his body. The Youth XL i hate myself T-shirt reportedly went on and came off of Ambrose's body with relative ease, yet met its end a mere two days later when Ambrose's mom unknowingly washed it in warm water.

December 4, 1999—Deep part in emo bangs started

An excessively deep part marking the beginning of a set of bangs was started on emo scene kid Raj Gulati. While originating just past the top of Gulati's ear, sources confirm it was further pushed back over time, finally reaching its last-known origin somewhere near the nape of the neck way over on the other side of his head in the spring of 2002.

Corrupt Grunge Band in the Pockets of Big Flannel

BY ROB STEINBERG

SEATTLE--Local grunge band Queen Dingus has shocked and disappointed fans after allegations of receiving donations from Big Flannel lobbyists were made public this week, bummed-out sources confirmed.

"This is a travesty, and it totally sucks. They used to be about the music, but what am I supposed to believe now?" lamented longtime fan Megan Owens. "Any unbiased statement they could've made about self-loathing and apathy is now meaningless."

Fans are now giving the band a second look after leaked documents from C/Z records reveal that most of their revenue is not from CD sales but rather from Big Flannel contributions.

"They've been receiving kickbacks ranging from black watch tartan boxers to buffalo-plaid-lined work boots--there's no limit to how far they'll sell out," said label founder Chris Hanzsek. "These people are so rich, they have a flannel tied around the waist of another flannel. It's a disgusting abuse of trust, and I cannot stay silent about it any longer."

The documents in question revealed that the contributions not only impacted the band financially but also artistically, as evidenced by their latest double-disc release, "Standard-Fit Cotton, Size XL."

"I've seen this happen so many times, but I never thought they would take the bait," said L7 frontwoman and longtime friend Donita Sparks. "I know everyone is just doing what they gotta do to get by, but the truth is, you can't be in the pockets of a soulless machine like Big Flannel and stay true to yourself. You just can't."

Despite the damning evidence, Queen Dingus denies the accusations.

"We assure you these claims are false, dude," said frontman Jack Eder. "We're from Washington; it's cold out here so we wear layers. It's not corruption, it's just how people in this town have lived our lives. Flannel is comfortable, it's stylin', and, for such a reasonable price, it looks good on any occasion!"

At press time, the Big Flannel payments to Queen Dingus have included 200 pounds of plaid, 500 pounds of tartan, and a shocking 900 pounds of Pendletons.

Used Toyota Corolla Comes with Complimentary Bikini Kill Cassette Stuck in Stereo

BY COURTNEY PAIGE BARNETT

BRICK, N.J.--A used 1988 Toyota Corolla with 120,000 miles and a faulty timing belt was listed for sale early this morning and features a complimentary Bikini Kill tape that its current owner cannot remove from the cassette player, multiple sources confirmed.

"I have a lot of good memories of this car, but now that I'm moving to New York, it's time to say goodbye to Kathleen," said seller Diana Haggerty, who named the car after Bikini Kill's frontwoman. "The biggest thing I'll miss about her is that cassette, but it's impossible to get it out."

In addition to the car's many features, which include antilock brakes and "windows that roll mostly all the way up," Haggerty is including her "Pussy Whipped" cassette as an added perk.

"The only negative features are the faulty air conditioning and the fact that at no point can you switch out the tape for a different one. You can either listen to the radio or to Bikini Kill," she explained. "But $1,800 is a pretty reasonable asking price when you consider what a good album 'Pussy Whipped' is."

"Besides that and a couple other weird things, it's a total steal," she added.

Due to the mature content on the album, Haggerty also stated that it may not be an ideal family vehicle.

"I promise that, unless you're super lame, whoever buys this car will find side A, and only side A, of 'Pussy Whipped' to be the soundtrack of their summer," said Haggerty, "and every season after that until they also sell this car. I mean, it's really lodged in there. At least it's not Pearl Jam."

Prospective buyer and fellow music fan Donnie Telson expressed interest when he spotted the flyer during his lunch break, but ultimately found the busted stereo to be a deal-breaker.

"Uhh, you mean I'd have to listen to nothing other than angry women whining?!" said Telson. "No thanks; I hear enough of that driving my girlfriend around. Talk to the hand, Shelby!"

At press time, Haggerty's father was seen jamming in a wire hanger to remove the cassette by any means necessary, which Haggerty has declared as "an extremely violent anti-feminist attack."

Corporate Sellout Jello Biafra Seen Sporting Sponsored Vest Patches

BY KYLE SEKAQUAPTEWA

SAN FRANCISCO--Punk legend Jello Biafra has been spotted wearing corporate-sponsored logo patches on his vest, leading many in the scene to suspect that the former Dead Kennedys frontman has officially sold out, sources confirmed.

"It started off with a little Suncoast patch, but none of us thought much of it," said local punk Ian Marshall. "But over the last month, he's been wearing weirder and weirder shit. I know for a fact that that guy has never stepped foot inside of an Applebee's, and now he's singing that fucking baby back ribs jingle? Dude is a full-blown shill now."

Despite the accusations, Biafra insists he's just as true to the scene as ever, and that the patches say nothing about his punk credibility.

"All of these armchair critics and holier-than-thou punks don't have any idea what they're talking about," Biafra said while conspicuously opening a Snickers bar. "The kids these days don't truly understand what punk is about, just

like I don't understand how they fit so much delicious Coca-Cola flavor into just ten calories with new Diet Coke. If you don't believe me, go ahead and try one in a Big Mac combo for $3.99, available for a limited time only at McDonald's. And tell 'em Jello sent you!"

While Biafra's sudden change has angered some in the punk scene, others believe they know the reason behind his corporate turnaround.

"I mean, let's face it, those spoken-word tours can't be pulling in much cash, and that band with the Ministry dude didn't exactly top the charts," said Cass Weaver, a barista at Biafra's favorite local coffee shop. "If he wants another paycheck on the side, I guess I don't really mind. I just wish he'd stop trying so hard to get me to invest in Enron."

Biafra continues to insist that he hasn't sold out despite his recent purchase of a NASCAR-style jacket, which he claims is strictly for "more space for patches of my favorite brands . . . I mean, bands. My favorite bands."

Drug-Addled Musician With History of Depression Probably Murdered by Courtney Love

BY KYLE ERF

SEATTLE--Kurt Cobain, the Nirvana frontman with a history of suicidal ideations and drug abuse, was found "almost definitely" murdered by his wife for a list of increasingly complicated reasons, convinced sources confirmed.

"The 27-year-old singer was found dead in his home this morning along with a suicide note and discharged firearm," said Seattle Police Department spokesperson Emily Hess at a press conference earlier today. "Which could have easily been planted there by a spouse looking to steal his fame, or money, or really anything else, by killing him. We just can't rule out anything yet."

Hundreds of thousands of fans were deeply shaken by the news.

"I just can't believe someone could write a song like 'Rape Me' and then do something like this," 14-year-old Nirvana fan Marlon Tate said through a stream of tears. "There's no way this could have happened without being masterminded by the woman who loves him. At least that's what my stepdad says."

Fans and law enforcement officials alike have already called foul play, pointing to inconsistencies in the handwriting on the suicide note.

"It's possible that his wife, Courtney Love, added details about suicide to a note that was about quitting music," Hess explained. "What's the alternative? That someone's handwriting might look different if they were on drugs or in a deep state of terrifying sadness? Baloney."

The medical community has also thrown its weight behind the "Love" theory.

"It's a common pattern," said research psychiatrist Edward Garcia of the University of Washington. "Someone suffers a lifetime of mental illness and drug addiction, gets pushed to the limits of their sanity as a result of worldwide fame, and then gets murdered by a loved one. It's actually in the DSM-IV, if you want to check it out."

Seattle police are still promising a thorough investigation before initiating an arrest.

"We may never have all the facts," said Hess. "All we have is evidence of multiple mental illnesses, a family history of suicidal behavior, some really dark song lyrics, active addiction, excruciating stomach ailments, and a note explaining exactly why he's going to kill himself. It's just not enough to rule out the wife at this time."

The Hard Times Hiring Frenzy

As remembered by Matt Saincome

The nineties were a boom time for Hard Times Media LLC. In the early months of 1991, I was approached by a team of investors who enjoyed their privacy and needed a hand investing in American businesses. *The Hard Times* was doing well, making enough money to buy ourselves two meals a day and support one stray cat near the office, but this sudden influx of foreign capital led to massive opportunities for expansion. In hindsight, I realize putting our names on documents allowing a Czechoslovakian bank to commit real estate fraud across multiple continents might have been a bad idea, but if I could do it all again, I wouldn't change a thing.

Our financiers were very hands-off, communicating only via encrypted messages and direct threats of violence. Their only requirement of us was that each issue of the magazine had to have a small ad on the back page that listed a new foreign phone number every month. Occasionally, they would send stoic Russian men to our office to use our phones and eat whatever was in the mini fridge, but we didn't ask questions--we were practically swimming in money and had the hand soap in the bathroom to prove it.

After the first check cleared, we got to work hiring a staff of real writers. For over a decade we'd relied on barely literate friends to craft stories for us, but now we had the chance to pay actual music journalists a full-time salary. That meant telling most of our freelancers that we would no longer need their services, which led to some tense moments. One frequent contributor, who went by the name Pinecone and only accepted payment in cigarettes, was particularly outraged. One night when Bill was locking up, Pinecone came out of nowhere and attacked him with a stack of flaming newspapers, leaving him with some small second-degree burns on his neck and chest. Bill also claims the attack damaged his spine, but honestly, he'll whine about anything as long as people are paying attention to what I refer to as "The Bill Show."

The new staff made a difference instantly. Having a college-educated copy editor gave the zine a sudden vibe of sophistication that was difficult to describe. In addition, we now had a team of designers, helmed by an art director who finally convinced us to evolve from our trademark black-and-white newsprint style to a glossy full-color format. And our team of reporters was able to attend most shows in New York City on any given night, from gritty hardcore matinees to industrial Long Island City raves. No matter when or where, we had someone on the beat.

Our growth wasn't limited just to New York. Hard Times Media began opening satellite offices in key markets across the country. We had spaces in Seattle, San Francisco, and Los Angeles, as well as a Singapore office that our investors insisted on for reasons still unknown. We sold out our zines at every show we went to, and our mail-order subscriptions were through the roof. The go-go nineties were upon us, and it was our time to shine.

Poser Spends Entire Show Staring at Beeper

DOORS 7:00
GUT BUSTERS 8:00 - 8:25
KNUCKLE PUNCH 8:40 - 9:05
BUCK HARD 9:20 - 9:50
SAVE FACE 10:00 - 10:30
HANDIE MAN 10:40 - END

NO PUNK TIME!!

BY MARK TURNER

CLEVELAND--Technophile and noted poser Eric Parish spent the entirety of Force of Destruction's show glued to his brand-new pager, according to firsthand reports.

"Most beepers can only receive alphanumeric messages, but this one can both send and receive alphanumeric messages. It's pretty revolutionary," said Parish of his slate-gray PageNet. "I picked it up at RadioShack last week, and I've been giving out the number ever since. I just don't want to miss it when I finally get my first page."

The device, primarily used by medical professionals and criminal enterprises, relies on knowledge of "codes" for common words.

"I saw him send '321' and '883' about 37 times over the last hour," said eyewitness Claire Ingridsen from her position behind a merch table selling anarcho-vegan zines. "I'm more a fan of traditional note-passing myself, but if you need to reach someone that badly, why not just walk six blocks and use a payphone at the bus station like a normal person?"

Parish's absentminded obsession with his new device did not go unnoticed by the band he was supposedly there to see, as FOD often uses its regional platform to speak out about the ills of a technologically fixated society.

"If I spot another one of you posers on a fucking beeper, I'm going to slap it out of your hand!" shouted frontman Mick Davidson. "All I see nowadays is people walking around like zombies, eyes down, waiting for a page. You're playing right into Big Beeper's hands--you're just another cog in their machine!

"I've got a page for you: You're a 7735, 606," he continued before launching into the band's next song.

Parish was reportedly unsure how to respond to the criticism.

"I understand that this technology is pretty mind-blowing for people who don't 'get' it, but I can watch for a page and be an active participant in the scene," he said, stealing a glance at the device. "Just give it time; pretty soon everyone is going to have one of these things."

Sonic Youth's Stolen Guitars Found Tuned to Standard, Otherwise Unharmed

BY JASON VANSLYCKE

LOS ANGELES--New York-based noise rockers Sonic Youth reclaimed a trailer full of stolen equipment, including two dozen guitars that were found safe and unharmed aside from being adjusted to a standard tuning, relieved sources confirmed.

"So many nights were spent worrying about these babies," said guitarist Lee Ranaldo while strumming on a Gibson Les Paul. "It's good to be reunited, but their time away has seen a lot of change, both in us as musicians and them as instruments. This guitar used to roar out 'Brave Men Run,' but now I can only strum 'Three Blind Mice' on it."

Well known for their unorthodox tunings, Sonic Youth relied on the unique properties of each customized guitar as inspiration for different songs in their repertoire.

"These instruments were foundational to our sound. We messed around with them for years until we got just the right tone," said guitarist/bassist Kim Gordon. "Of course, we're happy to have them back home, but I would be lying if I said playing on them feels the same. There will definitely be an adjustment period as we learn to live with each other again."

The stolen equipment was recovered behind a popular UCLA fraternity and was reportedly used to play soft-rock covers for drunken undergraduates at parties.

"An anonymous envelope was mailed to our studio with a grainy videotape of drunk frat dudes playing 'Every Morning' by Sugar Ray on beat-up Jazzmasters. Turns out those were our Jazzmasters," said guitarist Thurston Moore. "It hurt seeing them handled like that, but I imagine their pain was even worse."

Law enforcement officials say cases in which gear is returned in good condition are increasingly rare.

"We are happy to see the instruments back with their rightful owners," said Chief Oscar Franklin of the LAPD. "All across the country, there are hundreds of acoustic guitars that are missing, and we fear they're being used in college dorms to serenade uninterested potential sexual partners."

Columbia House Goons Will Collect Payment for Hootie & the Blowfish CD the Easy Way or the Hard Way

BY KRISSY HOWARD AND MATT SAINCOME

TERRE HAUTE, Ind.--Earlier today, hired hands from mail-order music distribution service Columbia House reportedly reached out to local punk Carrie Roberts over nonpayment for a Hootie & the Blowfish CD, assuring her they will collect it "the easy way, or the hard way--your call," according to terrified eyewitnesses.

"I got one of those 'pay one penny and get 15 CDs' brochures in the mail and figured it'd be a sweet way to get copies of 'Dookie' for me and my friends, but then I had to order a ton of other stuff," Roberts explained. "I thought it was going to be a one-and-done deal--I mean, it says no purchase necessary--but since I placed the order, weird things have been happening."

Roberts says attempts to claim the $24.95 plus shipping costs for Hootie's debut release, 'Cracked Rear View,' have included numerous letters, phone calls, and other "creepy shit."

"The calls started out like normal collections, so I just hung up or let it go to the machine. That's when the ransom-note-looking letters started showing up, but with no postage or anything, like someone put them directly into my mailbox. And I haven't seen my cat in two weeks . . ." she continued. "Honestly, I don't even wanna think about it."

According to sources who are consistently icing their knuckles in preparation for a fight, Columbia is known to hire independent contractors to pursue collection of the outstanding debt by less-than-savory methods.

"Listen, I'm a reasonable, ordinary music fan, and I like hearing my favorite bands for the low, low price of 1 cent with no obligation as much as the next guy," said hired goon Tommy "T-Bone" Briggs. "But daddy's gotta put dinner on the table, and it ain't gonna happen by giving away 10 copies of the same Tori Amos album to 13-year-old suburban kids.

"Now, I'm not saying this is something I'd do, but I will say that it sure would be a shame if someone's mailbox became . . . 'accidentally' filled with seven copies of Meat Loaf's 'Bat Out Of Hell II: Back Into Hell' and invoiced with interest in perpetuity, now wouldn't it?" he added.

At press time, in an attempt to retrieve payment for a copy of the "Pulp Fiction: Music From the Motion Picture" soundtrack, Briggs was seen sealing an envelope containing a collection letter and several human teeth.

Special Hour-Long "Beavis and Butt-Head" to Tackle Topic of Boners

BY TOM KRASNER

NEW YORK--The subversive world of Mike Judge will enter new territory this season as his animated brainchild, "Beavis and Butt-Head," will air an extended, commercial-free "very special" episode covering the topic of boners, sources confirmed.

According to an MTV press release, the show will deviate from its standard comedic tone to address the issue.

"Boners are a part of everyday life, and we consider it a civic duty to present them in an informative and professional way," read spokesperson Janine Alvarez. "While the average viewer may tune in for Cornholio or jokes about Cher's buttcheeks, a glimpse at the softer side of our dynamic duo will have audiences looking at chubbies in a whole new light."

While MTV is keeping details under wraps, complaints are already being registered about the rumored plotline of Beavis getting called up to the chalkboard at school while trying to hide an erection in his gym shorts.

"This time they've gone too far," wrote Chester Rossing, head of parental watchdog group Youth Decay, in his bi-daily newsletter. "How are par-

ents supposed to talk to their kids about pocket rockets when Beesman and Bus-Tooth [sic] are on TV carelessly blabbing away about a topic that should be saved for family discussion?"

"I think [creator] Mike Judge and company should stay in their lane and stick with the crass, sophomoric fart and poop jokes that made them famous," Rossing added. "Leave the boner talk to the professionals."

Judge, who also voices the duo, defends the network's bold decision, saying he feels obligated to use his platform to raise awareness about the billions of stiffies that pop up all over the country every day.

"Nobody wants to talk about it. It's a difficult subject, but I feel fortunate to have direct access to today's youth," Judge said. "We have an opportunity to educate kids, especially young boys, who wouldn't otherwise talk about their woodies without making a 'boing' sound effect, or some other such misguided remark. Hopefully we can facilitate some tough conversations."

NBC officials have since announced the production of "A Very Special Blossom" episode in which the cast deals with the aftermath of watching the hour-long "Beavis and Butt-Head" boner episode.

The Hard Times Goes Tech

As remembered by Bill Conway

Given our analog past, Hard Times Media LLC had always been somewhat wary about emerging technologies, but now that our investors were providing us with unbeliev-able sums of money, we started to make some changes. Payments arrived in the form of a Russian money order that we were allowed to cash at only one particular bank, at a set time every month, and with a designated bank teller. In hindsight, this should've rung some alarm bells for us, but we were too busy enjoying the cash to really question their motives. Instead, we looked the other way and figured we could invest the extra cash into tech improvements.

Starting small, we purchased computers for all our employees across the country. For a cool $2,900 apiece, we were able to equip everyone with a top-of-the-line Dell 486P. This computer had it all: email capability, a 230-MB hard drive, and three different floppy disk ports. These machines streamlined our editorial process. No longer did the writers in the New York office have to wait to use the typewriter to write their stories--everyone had their own state-of-the-art workstation.

We needed more than just computers, though. With the Soviet payout, we were also able to invest in a phone system with cordless headsets. Staffers were no longer bound to their desks by oppressive cords--with the headsets, they could conduct their business anywhere up to 100 feet away. We were on top of the world.

The crown jewel of the Hard Times' expanding empire, however, was the break room in the Manhattan office. Sparing no expense, we purchased a surround-sound LaserDisc projection system with a full video library. There were also two big-screen televi-sions, each hooked up to a brand-new Sega Genesis with top-of-the-line turbo con-trollers. It's amazing we ever got anything done because during the rare times when there weren't twelve Russian men smoking, gambling, and getting into loud yelling fights, you could often find our staff clowning around and having a blast.

For Christmas in 1993, Matt and I gave each staffer a Discman branded with *The Hard Times* logo. Matt was content with the standard features like bass boost, but I fought to pay extra for advanced skip protection--I felt our hardworking employ-ees deserved more. These were the small choices that endeared me to them while Matt drifted further away by spending hours endlessly doodling on his Apple Newton.

Noel Gallagher Regrets Leaving Guitar, Tiny Red-Tinted Glasses on Liam's Side of the Studio Before Painting Line Down Center

BY PATRICK COYNE

MANCHESTER, England--Oasis guitarist Noel Gallagher made the crucial error of leaving his guitar and tiny red glasses on his brother Liam's side of the recording studio before painting a white line down the middle, exasperated sources revealed.

"We couldn't stop fighting, so I grabbed a can of white paint from a utility closet and told Liam, 'You stay on your side, I'll stay on mine, and maybe then we'll finally finish this fucking album,'" reported the elder Gallagher. "But afterward I realized I left the one thing I can't record without on Liam's half: my tiny little John Lennon glasses."

Noel then spent several hours trying and failing to convince his brother to turn over the guitar and glasses. The petty standoff has cost their label $325,000 in studio time.

"I was pleading with him, but the daft bastard kept shouting 'Potato!' at me and smirking like that's a brilliant bloody insult," said the exhausted singer. "I thought I was being clever because the studio bathroom was on my side, but I should've known Liam would be willing to shite in the middle of the floor."

The younger Gallagher sibling provided some context for the brothers' frequent quarrels.

"Noel thinks he's so fuckin' brilliant just 'cause he writes the songs, is the more talented musician, and 'cause Mum used to say he could hold his liquor better," said a slurring Liam. "I was just eight then, Mum, you bloody wanker! I'm way better at drinking now."

The brothers later entered a tense negotiation that ultimately failed due to a communication breakdown.

"Noel was going to trade Liam five tambourines, a Kangol hat, a 24-pack of Carlsberg, and [rhythm guitarist] Bonehead for his guitar and spectacles," said drummer Alan White. "But at this point they were speaking only through intermediaries, and Liam passed out before we could relay the message to him."

Bassist Paul McGuigan stated that this sort of in-fighting was common.

"They've gotten into these wee squabbles since they were lads. Like when Liam pissed all over Noel's stereo, and Noel stabbed him in the throat with a pencil. You know, normal little kid stuff."

As of press time, Blur is in a studio across town recording a groundbreaking genre-defining album with relatively zero drama.

Frontmen Fear Drummer Uprising as Dave Grohl Starts Own Band

BY LAUREN LAVÍN

SEATTLE--Punk frontmen across America are reportedly growing anxious over the possibility that former Nirvana drummer Dave Grohl's new project, Foo Fighters, may inspire their drummers to quit and start their own bands, nervous sources, including Sunny Day Real Estate frontman Jeremy Enigk, confirmed.

"It's a scary time. We're a working-class band, and we believe in supporting each other--you know, unity and all that shit," said Rancid's Tim Armstrong. "But if your drummer quits and starts a better band, then he's a fuckin' cop."

To prevent what they see as a potential uprising, some frontmen are working to inspire loyalty in their drummers.

"[Drummer] Brett Reed is younger than us," Rancid vocalist/guitarist Lars Frederiksen explained, "so we're keeping him happy by catering to his tastes. We've got a cooler stocked with Zima at every practice. We all drink that shit now."

Others are resorting to more drastic measures.

"We've lured Tré [Cool] into a storage shed until this thing blows over," said Green Day's Billie Joe Armstrong. "He's perfectly happy in there. I poked air holes in the walls, and installed a mail slot to feed him through."

However, not all frontmen are afraid of Grohl's influence.

"Yeah, it's all love and good vibes," said Bad Brains' H.R. of drummer Earl Hudson. "Earl's my younger brother. We care about family, bless. And he won't go anywhere unless I fuckin' tell him to. Jah is love."

Despite high tensions in the national punk scene, Jawbreaker drummer Adam Pfahler has refuted rumors that he's considered leaving the band.

"That's completely untrue. Do most of our fans hate us right now because of 'Dear You'? Yeah. Is Dave Grohl a genre-hopping charismatic gem of a human being? Sure," Pfahler explained. "Do I hate that Blake [Schwarzenbach] makes me carry a beeper and checks in every two hours, morning and night, so he knows where I am at all times? Not really; I'm used to it by now."

At press time, multiple pamphlets were found under Pfahler's mattress, bearing slogans such as "Drummers of the World, Unite! You Have Nothing to Lose but Your Chains!" and "Drop Your Sticks and Pick Up Chicks: Learning to Play the Dave Grohl Way."

Danzig Uses 10-Hour AOL Free Trial to Anonymously Bitch About New Misfits Lineup

BY PATRICK COYNE

LODI, N.J.--Former Misfits frontman Glenn Danzig used his 10-hour America Online free trial to praise himself and complain about the band's new lineup anonymously, several annoyed chat room attendees confirmed.

"I've always been jealous of regular people who get to admire and love me," said the singer. "But this AOL CD-ROM I received in the mail lets me enter a chat room and pretend to be one of the millions of fans who adore my new band [called] Danzig, and absolutely despise the current Misfits lineup."

Although Danzig was certain he was doing an excellent job concealing his identity, several users, including Ann Beekley, were quick to identify the "incognito" complainer.

"I was in a punk and metal chat room when I saw someone with the screenname 'xXAmIDemonXx' write 'A/S/L/FMLS.' I later found out that meant 'Age/Sex/Location/Favorite Misfits Lead Singer,' which made me suspicious," said Beekley. "When he wouldn't stop gushing about Danzig

and shitting on Michale Graves, I started piecing together who it was. I mean, I agree that the Misfits suck now, but the only person who could love Danzig that much is Danzig."

Fellow chat room user and Misfits fan Patrick Yurga also noted Danzig's lack of proficiency in navigating the information superhighway.

"He ranted about how Dr. Chud doesn't even have a medical degree. Then he must have thought he exited the chat room and was using a search engine because he typed 'pics of Danzig shirtless + muscle hunk hot bod' followed by 'Jerry Only sucks' and then 'removing cat pee smell from leather pants,'" said Yurga. "Then, a full 10 minutes later, he wrote, 'Oops, my cat walked on my keyboard! Haha.'"

As of press time, Danzig is using his remaining AOL hours to build a website on the domain Misfitssucknowdanzigrulesandishandsome.geocities .com. But so far he has only been able to add a visitor counter, a single picture of a Maine coon kitten, and an animated dancing Ally McBeal baby.

Aspiring Metal Band One-Ups Metallica by Scalping Themselves

BY MICHAEL LUIS

PANAMA CITY BEACH, Fla.--Members of local metal band Demon Warfare had their scalps surgically removed early last week, allegedly in an effort to imitate the publicity boost Metallica received for their new short haircuts, horrified sources confirmed.

"When Metallica came out with their short hair, it was all anybody in the metal scene could talk about," said Lester Brock, Demon Warfare's bassist and lead vocalist. "We're always looking for ways to push the limits and differentiate ourselves from other bands. Now that we've scalped ourselves, we have a whole new crop of fans who constantly point at us and scream, or cover their kids' eyes, when they see us on the street. Fame sure is a funny thing."

Despite their excitement over the newfound notoriety, those close to the band have voiced their skepticism.

"I told the guys I thought it was a terrible idea, as did multiple doctors, and Lester's girlfriend," said Mindy Guzman, the band's manager and booking agent. "Sure, everybody is talking about the new Metallica record, but I guarantee it's because of their new 'hard rock' sound and shiny production, not because James Hetfield has a mullet."

"With the money they spent on these operations, we could've hired a top-flight producer for the new record," she added. "Now we're gonna spend the next six to eight weeks just trying to keep their bandages dry."

Demon Warfare's new album, "Loud," is set to be self-released this November and will be followed by a full U.S. tour, during which the band is excited to showcase their new music and controversial aesthetic.

"This is just the beginning for us," said drummer Rex Yates while wincing and adjusting the gauze covering his skull. "We saw a photo of Lars wearing eyeliner and Kirk with nail polish, so we're toying with the idea of adding makeup to our image too. Think somewhere between campy drag and Kabuki theater. Factor that in with the scalping, and yeah, we're pretty much gonna be unstoppable."

Despite the concerns for their health and desperate pleas from everyone around them, the group assures they are steadfastly happy with their life-altering choice.

"I don't even miss it," added Yates of his scalp. "I had really bad dandruff for years, so good riddance. We also might sell those things as a VIP merch item. I can see them meaning a lot to a diehard fan."

At press time, Demon Warfare's upcoming tour has been canceled as all members have been hospitalized with bacterial infections. Ticket refunds are available at point-of-purchase.

How The Hard Times Got Its First Racehorse

AS REMEMBERED BY MATT SAINCOME

I have two passions in life: The first is reporting all of the news that punks need to know, and the second is the beauty and spectacle of horse racing. When *The Hard Times* was still just a twinkle in my eye, I would often fantasize about owning my own stallion and watching him gallop around a dusty track in search of glory. Thanks to our growing revenue and ever-increasing Russian credit line, in 1995 I was finally able to make my dream a reality.

No expense was spared in finding the steed that would represent the Hard Times empire. Eventually I found a four-year-old Appaloosa, sired from a former Preakness Stakes runner-up and a mare used in late 1980s Marlboro Cigarette ads. I named him "Trust Your Mechanic" after one of my favorite Dead Kennedys songs. The next step: finding the perfect jockey.

When I started the search for Trust Your Mechanic's jockey, I thought it would be easy to find someone from the scene who was small and smart enough to handle our biggest investment to date. I was dead wrong. The only punks diminutive enough were the unfortunate souls whose growth was stunted because they'd started smoking and using drugs before puberty. Though they had the stature, their brain capacity wasn't up to par with the natural instincts of Trust Your Mechanic, whose grace and poise were outmatched only by his sheer athleticism and raw masculinity. Eventually, I settled for an established pro jockey named Victor Lespardeux. He was a Frenchman whose punk credentials were limited to accidentally watching a Green Day music video on MTV, but goddamn if he couldn't ride like the wind.

In an attempt to bring further glory to the Hard Times Media empire, we began entering Trust Your Mechanic in every race we could. Despite his strong pedigree, he simply could not win a race. The best he ever placed was a measly eighth, and that was only because four other horses had trampled one another. In terms of money, Trust Your Mechanic was easily our highest-paid employee. He was not only the unofficial mascot of *The Hard Times*, he was my reason for writing. I'd spend hours in his stall singing David Bowie songs to him, but people just didn't understand the bond we shared. It's tough to describe, but so easy to feel.

Punk Doctor Performs Experimental 26-Second Operation to Separate CD From Plastic Anti-Theft Device

BY BILL CONWAY

BOSTON--Controversial punk doctor Russ Klein successfully performed an experimental operation to remove a large plastic anti-theft device from an Anti-Flag CD in the back corner of Newbury Comics late last night, surprised sources report.

"This is the first time on record that this procedure has been completed without damage to either subject," said medical historian and Newbury Comics loss prevention lead Sheila Bailey, who discovered the discarded anti-theft device during her normal rounds. "In the past, we've typically found these efforts produce severe damage to the CD, often resulting in permanent scratching, but this operation was clearly handled with dexterity and skill."

The clandestine effort reportedly took place during the last few minutes before the store's closing, when the staff was distracted with other duties.

"Russ has a very steady hand, and if there is anyone that could make this happen, it's him," said designated lookout Terry Gorgees. "Only retail professionals have the proper tools to remove those huge plastic things, but Russ constructed his own instrument in shop class in order to open them without causing any stress to the CD. If I hadn't witnessed it with my own eyes, I wouldn't believe it."

Experts believe this procedure could facilitate shoplifting for an entire generation.

"For years, the only option for stealing CDs was running out the door with them and then smashing them with rocks in order to get to the sweet reward inside the jewel case," said small-time criminal Kyla Baron. "This new technology is a huge improvement."

Klein admitted to being happy with the results of the operation and hopes to perform similar procedures in the future.

"This project has been years in the making, and before today I had so many failed attempts that I was starting to feel like a butcher," he said. "I hope to expand my research to find a way for anyone attempting to leave a store with a pair of jeans hidden under oversized cargo pants not to trigger the alarm with the security tag. It's an ambitious goal, but I think we'll be well on our way with the right pair of scissors."

Report: 75 Percent of NYC Fire Escapes Now Blocked by Alternative Rock Singers

BY ANDY HOLT

NEW YORK--The Fire Department of the City of New York has determined that 75 percent of fire escapes citywide are being actively blocked by alternative rock singers, according to recent reports.

"Once these stubborn little pests find a spot and start dancing, they become difficult to remove. They appear to be shooting music videos, although we've been unable to ascertain who would enjoy watching them," said FDNY fire inspector Butch Daniels. "These efforts pose a grave safety hazard to our residents, and at this rate every building in the city will be unsafe by the turn of the millennium."

Although the FDNY admits that fire escape blockage is far from being a new problem, firefighters insist that this latest influx of alternative crooners poses an unprecedented risk.

"You expect a folk singer with an acoustic guitar on the stairs, maybe a rapper in Brooklyn leaning over a railing," said Daniels, a 30-year veteran of the department. "But when you walk down the street and every fire escape is full of shirtless guys from Los Angeles mouthing the words to songs they probably didn't even write, we've got a real problem."

Emergency rooms throughout the city have experienced an uptick in fire victims who attempt escaping their apartments through hallways after finding the windows impeded by gyrating frontmen.

"I heard the alarm and tried to get to my fire escape, but that guy from the Goo Goo Dolls was sitting out there with a thousand-yard stare. So I decided to just brave the flames," said local punk Cheez Williams, who was later hospitalized for smoke inhalation.

Until a more effective solution is found, officials advise that evacuating residents simply strike the obstruction in the face with as much force as possible.

"It's hard to imagine that any of these guys can take a punch," Daniels said, pointing to a poster of a singer with frosted blond tips and a puka-shell necklace. "But we have spent a lot of time imagining it, and it seems the most appropriate option at this time."

FTC Approves Rap and Rock Merger

BY ROB STEINBERG

WASHINGTON--A $54 billion merger of music genres Rock and Rap was officially authorized this morning by the Federal Trade Commission in a move that is expected to bring together the worst artists of each genre, experts close to the situation confirmed.

"Rap and Rock will be forming an official company known as Rap-Rock. The two conglomerates were previously rivals for a place on the top of the Parental Advisory list," said FTC Chairman Robert Pitofsky. "We started noticing a lot of unregulated rap-rock mixing in the mid-'80s, but this official merger will allow the genre to flourish among young men with stained tank tops and eyebrow piercings."

Opponents of the merger have questioned its legality, but due to Congress' new Anthrax-Public Enemy Act, barriers have been removed, allowing the FTC to approve the motion.

"Rap-Rock is creating excitement among United States citizens who have been charged with a DUI," said Andrew Parker of the government watchdog group The Watch Dawgs. "And profits among suburban white males are already tripling. Record labels are also seeing substantial returns on new assets such as Limp Bizkit

and Kid Rock faster than we ever could have imagined."

The FTC instituted measures that specify Rap and Rock must both retain their original properties and only synergize when appropriate in order to avoid saturating the market, in accordance with Section 7 of the Clayton Antitrust Act.

"To maintain variety, Ice-T will swing back and forth between the two genres, but rarely perform in both at the same time. Rock will divest its ownership of the Beastie Boys to Rap altogether," said Pitosfky in a brief. "This will also allow festivals being held in the parking lots of abandoned dog tracks to finally set a lineup worthy of their customers."

Congresswoman Susan Brady, who voted against the Anthrax-Public Enemy Act, is a vocal critic of the merger.

"This monopoly is going to create higher concert prices and lower-quality products. Vanilla Ice's 'Hard to Swallow' is exactly why antitrust laws were created," said Brady. "If Rap and Rock become one, then we will no longer have a division of shelves for CDs at Tower Records."

As of press time, dads around the country were decrying the decision and vowing to "never let that shit in my house."

It looks like your taste in music is trash. Can I help you with that?

Clippy the Paperclip Desperately Trying to Stop College Freshman From Writing Term Paper on Dave Matthews Band

BY PATRICK COYNE

STATE COLLEGE, Pa.--Microsoft Office 97's much-maligned digital assistant Clippit "Clippy" the Paperclip is desperately trying to stop college freshman and Sigma Chi pledge Bobby Mazonwicz from writing a term paper on Dave Matthews Band, sources confirmed.

"I typed my term paper title, 'Ants Marching: The Unexpected Depth of Dave Matthews Lyrics and the Sociopolitical Effects of the Nicaraguan Revolution,' into Word," said a nervous Mazonwicz. "And then that dumb paperclip said, 'Looks like you're writing about DMB. You sure you want to waste your parents' money on this drivel?' How'd it know my parents pay my tuition?"

While some dismissed Mazonwicz's story as a glitch or hoax, University of Delaware sophomore Daisy Flannery experienced a similar intrusion from the anthropomorphized office supply.

"I started writing about Phish for my American history class when Clippy said, 'Hi, I'm Clippy! I'm the Office Assistant, and my job is to stop you from wasting your time on this crap band. Do you need help?'" said Flannery. "I tried to X him out, but he popped back up and suggested

Sleater-Kinney, Archers of Loaf, and a bunch of other bands I should check out."

When questioned, Clippy stated that it views these incidences not as intrusions, but as a learning opportunity for college students.

"Look, I get it. I'm annoying--I correct people's grammar, and I startle elderly users by popping up at inopportune times. But you know what else is annoying? College kids' music taste," said the perturbed paperclip. "The students need me. They're away from their parents for the first time and have no one to tell them that turning in a paper on Moe. for their macroeconomics class is an F."

Clippy admits its attempts to expand the music tastes of America's college students may be futile.

"If you want to get drunk and listen to Rusted Root or O.A.R. with your frat brothers, go for it. But don't write about it for class. But if you insist on somehow connecting these bands' lyrics to the global impact of the Cold War, just don't make me edit it. Buy a Mac instead."

As of press time, Clippy is still hoping for at least one opportunity to help write a term paper on Fugazi.

The Hard Times on Every Newsstand

As remembered by Bill Conway

Even though *The Hard Times* had a sizable following throughout the nineties, we had always distributed everything ourselves and managed all our subscriptions in-house. Our investors thought this was a waste of resources, so they began helping us in our push to go national. One major backer owned a distribution company called Red Decade Publishing Representatives. The people at Red Decade were excited to have another magazine to distribute, and working with them took our small show to the big time. Every magazine seller across the country would now have the latest edition of *The Hard Times* on its shelves.

Our readership doubled overnight. We had trouble meeting demands, but delivering magazines to all our new retailers wasn't our only dilemma. Strange things started happening at Red Decade. On more than one occasion, a delivery vehicle was hijacked and the driver held hostage. The worst incident was when the entire Red Decade warehouse was mysteriously firebombed. They ended up losing half their fleet of trucks, most of that month's magazine inventory, and four workers due to smoke inhalation and inexplicable bullet wounds. We chalked this up to the competitive publishing market trying to elbow out some hungry young upstarts; our investors told us not to worry and keep our mouths shut.

The feds took notice of our lost merchandise and the damage done to the Red Decade shipping facility. Men in black suits started showing up at the office to ask our writers what they knew about our investors. In our eyes, this was just government overreach, trying to keep a punk zine down because they didn't like our politics. At one point in the mid-nineties they even parked an unmarked van across from our office for weeks on end. One day Matt dared me to slap a *Hard Times* sticker on its back window, and as soon as I smacked that baby on, two large goons in sunglasses hopped out and chased me down. Matt, who had been hiding across the street, ran into a subway station to avoid getting stomped. I was not so lucky--I made it about ten blocks before being put in a choke hold and savagely beaten.

Despite this minor setback, nothing could stop *The Hard Times*. We were on every newsstand, and we were pushing to be in every home. The golden times were finally upon us, and we thought they would never end.

"Tony Hawk's Pro Skater" Soundtrack Pulls Surprise First-Round Draft Pick Over "Punk-O-Rama" With Goldfinger's "Superman"

BY DUSTIN MEADOWS

WOODLAND HILLS, Calif.--The soundtrack to "Tony Hawk's Pro Skater" shocked the well-established Epitaph Records compilation series "Punk-O-Rama" by selecting Goldfinger's "Superman" as their first-round draft pick, officials confirmed.

"We built our label on the strength of skate punk, and then this video game comes out of nowhere and upsets the apple cart by going ska right from the rip?" said Epitaph founder and owner Brett Gurewitz. "Fuck, man. We figured they'd take NOFX or Ten Foot Pole or one of those other bands on our label that hadn't been doing super hot for the last few years."

Draft analysts closely monitoring the selection process applauded the unorthodox selections.

"The first few rounds had Epitaph following their standard practice of picking their heavy hitters, such as Bad Religion, Pennywise, and Rancid," said punk expert Jerry Blythe. "Backstage in the media bay, we never thought the Pro Skater franchise would double down on their ska decision. But then they grabbed The Suicide Machines' 'New Girl,' which was projected to go in the sixth round. This is risky, but at least they're not using the same 15 bands with songs that all sound the same."

THPS general manager Tony Hawk explained the logic behind the picks.

"We wanted choices that reflect the current state of skateboarding, so naturally we led with a powerful ska track that can really get stuck in your head. And I'm thrilled we were able to get a Primus song that's nearly ten years old. Songs like these go perfectly with skateboarders like Chad Muska."

Epitaph management reported that they won't get caught off guard again, and they're already looking toward next year's draft.

"Our draft board ended up falling apart to the point where we ended up with a Tom Waits song," said Gurewitz. "Maybe we got complacent when Rancid and The Offspring blew up back in 1994. We're going to do a lot more scouting, and next year you can expect us to make a strong play for Voodoo Glow Skulls and Cherry Poppin' Daddies."

Punk IT Guy Doesn't Give a Fuck About Y2K

By Louie Aronowitz

NEW YORK--Technical support worker Ben Gilbert announced to coworkers at his mid-level record label that he "doesn't give a fuck about Y2K" and will not be updating any computers to prepare for the potential data disaster, concerned sources attested.

"See if I give two shits," said the longtime Deploy Records help-desk lead in regard to the impending resetting of all records. "Information technology is dead anyway. Let's introduce a little mayhem and set everyone back to zero. Erase all debts. Erase all records. Let's burn this motherfucker down!"

Gilbert's colleagues expressed a very different perspective, as they mostly valued the data stored on the company's computer network.

"It makes me extremely anxious that not only will all my work-related information be erased, but we could also lose our money," said coworker Erica Fielder. "Personally, and maybe this is just me, but I feel we should not 'burn it

down.' I think maybe we should see if there's something simple we could download to fix this. Maybe? There has to be something."

Alice Cantor, the creator and current head of the label, as well as the only staff member to have a retirement plan, was especially vocal about the need to fix the possible bug.

"I swear to Christ, if this fucks with my goddamn 401(k), I'm going to lose my mind," Cantor said just before storming into her office and slamming the door.

As a result of Gilbert's insouciance, many in the office have begun passing around a "bootleg" Y2K fix on an unmarked floppy disk.

"I'd only heard the rumors; it had become legendary," commented recently hired intern Beth Cameron. "Then finally one day, an unlabeled blue diskette in an unmarked envelope appeared on my desk. No instructions, nothing. But I knew what to do with it. We all know what to do when it arrives: Insert, open MS-DOS, type 'run a:/ y2k.exe,' and smash that motherfucking carriage return!"

The HARD Times ON LaserDisc AD

As remembered by Matt Saincome

At the height of the cash-rich tech-crazed nineties, Hard Times Media LLC pushed out its biggest flop ever. Bill will say I was the one who came up with it, but ultimately it was his job to filter my ideas, so it's mostly his fault. The infamous *Hard Times* laser disc project rests solely on Bill's shoulders, and may he be burdened with its failure for the rest of his life.

All of our articles converted into easy-to-read scrolling text on 12 laser discs in one box set

Do you love reading but hate not being able to stare at a TV? Like learning but don't have a free hand to turn a page? Seek better picture quality to help bring your stories to life? Well friend, you've just hit the fucking jackpot! Now, for the first time ever, *The Hard Times* is proud to offer all of our articles converted into easy-to-read scrolling text in a 12-disc box set, all for the low, low price of $279.99.

LASER DISC

On the cutting edge of technology!

Welcome to the future of reading with laser disc! Everyone knows that reading at your own pace is BORING AS SHIT, and now, with *The Hard Times* on laser disc, those days are over! With bottom-to-top scrolling text, you can turn perusing your favorite zine into a source of entertainment so intense it'll make you never want to pick up a book ever again. Show's over, *Reading Rainbow,* you smug fuck!!

Quality audio—perfect for reading!

Laser disc also offers CD-quality sound, which doesn't apply here because it would have cost us twice as much to record audio. But hey, at least it doesn't sound worse than CDs, which our public-relations team begged us to mention after we ignored their numerous attempts to keep us from dumping most of our money into this idea. Which has the potential to sound great!

Convenient

Every year, paper zines are reported to take up over 6 percent of precious kitchen table space in punk houses all over the world. Now, with *The Hard Times* on laser disc, you can store all of your favorite articles in one place, assuming that this place is out of direct sunlight and is large and sturdy enough to hold 12 laser discs.

"Basically the vinyl of zines"

The Hard Times on laser disc has been described by industry expert, *Hard Times* founder, and person who came up with this idea Matt Saincome as "basically the vinyl of zines," in that it's similar in size to a 12" vinyl record. Get yours today!

The 2000s: The Collapse

"The sunken faces of those fleeing the napalmed buildings, climbing over dead bodies . . . Jesus, you just can't forget these things you see."

--A Vietnam War veteran describing his time in the Hard Times Media offices in 2002

Eventually, all things must pass. The mysterious investors who had rocketed Hard Times Media to mainstream success turned out to be what the staff would later call "total posers," in that they were Kremlin-connected oligarchs look-

ing for ways to launder money and move drugs and illegal arms around the U.S., all under the guise of a newspaper delivery service. In fact, about 90 percent of the copies were merely driven around the block and incinerated. Pick-up rates, circulation numbers--everything was fabricated in order to increase the amount of money investors could wash through *The Hard Times*. Staff did not respond well to the news.

The day *The New York Times* ran the story "Hard Times Implicated in International Criminal Conspiracy Money Scam, Business Fraud," Matt disappeared. The FBI had raided the office prior to the article and interrogated Bill, who said he didn't know anything. A report from inside the bureau would later call him a "hapless fool" and questioned his mental fitness.

With rumors of the company's demise swirling, all hell broke loose in the office. Employees ripped copper wiring out of the walls, and we're not just talking about freelance contributors; these were upper-level editors meant to be overseeing the "transition period" and calming the lower ranks. Panicked and confused, editor Mark Roebuck was even seen eating the copper. To this day, there are many conflicting reports of what happened, but we do know it was when "Dirty Hand" Dan Rice earned his nickname.

It seemed as if Y2K didn't hit anywhere in the world besides the Hard Times offices. It was total bedlam.

Singapore office. Investigators later discovered that the "relocated" employees were those who got too close to understanding the true nature of the company and asked too many questions.

This trail of bodies ultimately led a multi-departmental task force to investigate Hard Times. Eventually detectives were able to piece together the complex web of shell companies that made up its criminal empire. These included a trucking company, an offshore sports betting site, and an obscure business that was described in court files only as "rat stacking."

With Matt in the wind and a near-catatonic Bill refusing to talk, the remaining staff scrambled to prepare a response and, regrettably, a final edition. This task was made difficult by most computers having been confiscated by feds.

Within weeks, the company had announced bankruptcy. Office printers, chairs, and even the company's beloved racehorse, Trust Your Mechanic, were auctioned off. Intellectual property like movie development projects were seized but ultimately deemed worthless. Even the *Hard Times'* name was sold to an Alabama mug shot

Soon, details of the money-laundering scheme started to emerge in follow-up stories in the *Times.* There were exorbitant spending accounts, a myriad of shell companies, and a complex collection of trout-farming operations, all listed under the Hard Times corporation. The whole company was technically owned by an "import/export" business with ties to a Russian rubber tycoon, but there was so much criminality happening that it was difficult to decipher. Most important, though, was that several people and hundreds of millions of dollars were missing.

Throughout the years, an assortments of accountants and HR reps had been "relocated" to the Singapore office. The problem? There was no

publisher for pennies on the dollar, while the archives were confiscated as evidence. Rough drafts of the final issue, a rambling apology and deflection of blame, were also confiscated and never released.

Hard Times Media officially closed up shop on November 15, 2007. The company left behind a shell-shocked staff, a tattered name, and more legal problems than readers. Though there were several failed attempts to get the magazine back up and running in the years following, for all intents and purposes, *The Hard Times* was dead.

In this chapter, you will read articles and memories recovered through a complicated legal process, from an era when most believed the publication would never release another issue.

ON THIS DAY IN PUNK HISTORY, 2000S

JANUARY 1, 2000--
ALPHABETIZED RECORD COLLECTION REVEALED TO BE GIGANTIC WASTE OF TIME

Furiously preparing for the inevitable Y2K crash expected to end life as we know it, Barnhart, Missouri, man Steven Edwards promptly realized that the weeks spent alphabetizing his extensive record collection were a "fucking huge waste of time--what the fuck was I even thinking?" at exactly 12:01 a.m.

MAY 19, 2003--
GUY BUSTS 200TH WOMAN UNWILLING TO SPEAK WITH HIM LONG ENOUGH TO NAME FIVE SONGS

Dutiful punk and self-described "devil's advocate" Ricky "Dicky" King reportedly "caught" his 200th woman at a show not knowing at least five songs written by the band featured on the shirt she was wearing, as clearly evidenced by her absolute unwillingness to talk to him for more than one second.

SEPTEMBER 23, 2006--
BOX OF SHOW FLYERS CELEBRATES 10 YEARS UNDER CHILDHOOD BED

Tucked securely under a Las Cruces, New Mexico, bed since 1996, a shoebox filled with old flyers celebrated 10 years of being vacuumed around, getting shoved out of the way, and serving as the subject of countless "when are you gonna come home and clean out all this junk?" phone calls from its owner's aging mother who "would love to make room in here for a treadmill someday."

APRIL 4, 2007--
FIRST SHOW TO START "ON TIME"

A Duluth, Minnesota, show projected to start at 8 p.m. shocked showgoers and performers alike when it started exactly 45 minutes after, marking its place as the first-ever show to start before punk time. The show pushes the former record holder, a matinee that started only one hour and fifteen minutes after its intended start, and has yet to be matched.

JANUARY 9, 2009--
ANGRY, YOUNG AND POOR FOUNDER TELLS EMPLOYEES THEY WILL SELL THIS MANY STUDS AND SPIKES FOREVER

Elizabeth Shuba, founder of the online punk merchandise shop Angry, Young and Poor, told her cofounders and employees not to worry, that pyramid studs and bondage pants would sell at this same rate for the rest of time.

Blink-182's Future in Question After Tom DeLonge's Chest Cold Clears Up

By Steve Fiorillo

LOS ANGELES--Superstar pop punk band Blink-182's future is in serious jeopardy after the revelation that guitarist and singer Tom DeLonge's 11-year chest cold has finally cleared up, confirming fans' worst nightmares.

"Yeah, I finally went to a doctor and he gave me some antibiotics. I feel way better. I just hadn't gone to one in, like, twelve years," DeLonge told reporters at a press conference in a voice that fans online would later describe as "distressingly not nasally and completely free of any unnecessary affectations."

DeLonge's new voice, two octaves lower than usual, has put fans into a frenzy that the band will never be the same if he's now a polished, easy-to-understand vocalist.

"Goodbye forever to the Blink we knew and loved," wrote absolutepunk.net user JOsie-SOmbrerOS. "I heard him interviewed on KROQ yesterday and it just sounded so . . . pleasant. He said the word 'I' and it actually sounded like the word 'I' instead of an unholy combination of every vowel twice over. Once I heard that, I started crying. I just knew it was the end."

Music experts shared the concern of Blink-182's longtime listeners.

"Usually it's fans just being stubborn, but I absolutely think Tom DeLonge turning into a competent, possibly even above-average singer would be an absolute death knell for Blink-182," said musicologist Rob Sheffield. "I heard him singing on the way out of the press conference and it was actually cool and beautiful, like Frank Sinatra meets Mick Jagger. You just hate to see that happen to a band."

Blink-182 bassist Mark Hoppus downplayed the situation.

"Blink fans have absolutely nothing to worry about," he assured devotees. "We are not breaking up and we are not changing, and neither is Tom. Just yesterday we laid down two tracks he wrote. One was called 'Confessions From a Divorce Victim,' and the other one was called 'Finger in My Grandpa's Butthole.' We're still the same old Blink-182."

"Though," Hoppus wistfully added, "I will miss being the Blink singer with even the tiniest bit of range."

Terrified Gerbil in Pet Store Avoiding Eye Contact With "Jackass" Crew

BY KRISSY HOWARD

WEST CHESTER, Pa.--A local gerbil was seen actively averting her eyes as the cast and crew of MTV's "Jackass" entered the pet store she lives in, uneasy sources confirmed.

"Fuck," muttered the $8.99 Mongolian gerbil while attempting to build a pile of cedar chips in a far corner of her cage to hide in. "I've heard about these guys, and the things that they put in . . . places, just for giggles. But I never thought this day would actually come."

Other longtime pet store residents were spotted suspiciously eyeing the raucous crew.

"It's not the first time I've seen this happen," recalled African gray parrot and unofficial store mascot, Hank. "About two years ago, these same boys came barreling in here and bought a blue-tailed skink that couldn't have been more than a few days old. It wasn't even two minutes before that poor thing ended up on the wrong end of Brandon DiCamillo's dickhole, and the cameras weren't even rolling or nothin'."

"I didn't speak up then and I've regretted it every day since. I'm not about to make that same mistake twice," he added.

Tensions were further heightened after crew member Chris Pontius began chasing Steve-O around the store with a toilet paper tube while screaming, "Squeal like a pig, oink oink!"

"Oh wow, OK, this might really be it, huh? Best case scenario, I end up swimming around in Preston Lacy's back sweat," the gerbil said. "I didn't survive being one of four in my litter who weren't eaten by my fucking dad just to have Steve-O's ass tattoo be the last thing I witness. I mean, I haven't even seen 'The Wire' yet. There's so much left to do."

At press time, the gerbil was seen running past an elderly ferret on her way into a circular hamster ball, which she intends to use to "make a break for it, sorry Mom."

Saddam Hussein's Abandoned Spider Hole Now Iraq's Most Popular Punk Venue

BY PATRICK COYNE

BAGHDAD--Punks in the Iraqi capital's burgeoning underground music scene transformed former president Saddam Hussein's "spider hole" bunker into the country's most popular punk venue, U.S. intelligence sources confirmed.

"When we first saw the squalid, dank hole where that murderous bastard spent his final weeks, we immediately knew it would make an amazing place to host shows," said local punk Kasim Antar. "Hell, it already had a great name: the Spider Hole. If that's not fate, I don't know what is. So we grabbed some speakers off a burnt-out Humvee and got to work booking the first show."

The rebellious music, and by extension the new venue, are very much at odds with the country's staunchly religious leadership.

"We're literally risking our lives playing punk rock, so obviously the venue is very hush-hush. Unfortunately, some here use religion as an excuse to punish people over trivial things like that, or even their hairstyle," said guitarist Yazen Khouri. "But on the flip side, knowing I could be killed for this gives me a shit-ton of scene cred, man. The worst thing that can happen to American punks is when their dad calls them a loser. Those pussies would never survive here."

Coalition forces quickly became aware of this repurposing of Saddam's bunker, which proved divisive among active-duty troops.

"I'm proud to have helped liberate the Iraqi people; it's just a shame they're using their freedom to be no-good punks," said U.S. Army Lt. Col. Donald Bateman. "Just last night I saw a bunch of youths with dyed hair giving our boys the finger. I guess it's our fault for not, like, dropping a couple Kenny Chesney records between all the carpet bombings or something."

Despite being a secret, and literally a hole in the ground with poor ventilation and terrible acoustics, the venue has proven incredibly popular, attracting attention from outside of Iraq and even playing host to American punk band Sick of It All.

"The bathrooms in the Spider Hole are the cleanest of any venue I've played," said bassist Craig Setari, "whether it's a former despot's hideout or otherwise."

Members of Crazy Town Can't Believe Strip Club DJ Hasn't Heard of Them

By Randy Scope

LOS ANGELES--Members of the rap-rock band Crazy Town were stunned this week by the revelation that a Los Angeles-area strip-club disc jockey had never heard of them or their hit single "Butterfly," Pink Jaguar Management confirmed.

"Seriously, bro? Two years ago, every stripper in this place would've been dancing to us, and this guy has never heard 'Butterfly'?" asked the band's bewildered vocalist, Shifty Shellshock. "Dude, we were all over MTV and K-Rock. The dude must be from Canada or something. It just doesn't make any sense."

A staff member who identified herself as "Crystal" witnessed the exchange.

"The guy in the stained tank top, with all the tribal tattoos, seemed angry that our DJ didn't know the song he wanted for his lap dance," she said. "So he called his friend over to the booth and started singing while his buddy beatboxed. I have seen a lot of things happen inside these walls, and that was easily the most disgusting."

The DJ in question admitted to not being aware of the chart-topping 1999 single.

"It sounded kind of familiar, but their performance didn't ring any bells for me," said DJ/webmaster DJ Blayze. "They wanted me to look it up on Napster but our DSL kinda sucks in the afternoon. So I told them I couldn't do it, hoping that would be the end of it. Then the dude ran out to his car and grabbed a CD. I had to tell him my rig doesn't play CDs. He finally left me alone once I gave him a drink ticket."

As of press time, members of Crazy Town were overheard insisting girls from the club join them at an after-party with the dudes from Buckcherry.

The Hard Times Goes Bankrupt

As remembered by Bill Conway

The end came very fast. Our offices were raided and thousands of pages of documents were removed from the special "Red Room" in the back. Repo men had taken all our computers, laser disc players, and high-end cordless phones, leaving us with nothing. Dozens of angry journalists, finding themselves suddenly unemployed, took off with items from their former workplaces. During the last week of operations in the Los Angeles office, staff rented out the space to pornographic filmmakers in order to make a few extra dollars. We didn't hear a single peep from the Singapore office, and still haven't.

Matt and I were able to avoid jail time because our court-appointed lawyer used something that is now known as "The Hard Times Defense." Our attorney asserted that we were far too dumb to comprehend what was going on, and this ignorance was so overwhelming that we couldn't be held criminally responsible. He was right. The judge took pity on us (a first for punks on trial), and we were free men. We bought back our name from the Alabama mug shot company, but the Hard Times Media operation was in shambles.

Our once-great empire had crumbled: Our money was gone, our distribution network taken from us. Even Trust Your Mechanic, the horse that cost us hundreds of thousands of dollars and never won a single race, was confiscated by animal welfare. I have never seen Matt cry so hard. The only thing he had to remember the animal by was a pile of photographs and four crates of horse tranquilizer he had scored from a shady Canadian vet. It was the end of an era.

We soon discovered that *The Hard Times* wasn't the only magazine that was struggling. The internet was becoming a major player in news coverage and print media was declared dead. But we weren't buying in. We'd learned from Y2K that computers are frightening and untrustworthy, and readers still wanted hard copies of magazines delivered monthly to their doors.

Although Matt and I had drifted apart during the boom period, necessity brought us back together. We became roommates again, and with the $800 we had left, we moved the Hard Times office back to its original squat on New York's Lower East Side. We were returning to our roots, filled with a revived DIY punk spirit. *The Hard Times* would not be defeated.

Dixie Chicks Obliterate
Flock of Bald Eagles Live on Stage

BY JUSTIN COX

DALLAS--Country trio Dixie Chicks once again found themselves at the center of controversy following their outspoken critique of the Bush administration after "absolutely beating the fucking life out of" 13 endangered bald eagles at a show last Sunday evening, horrified onlookers confirmed.

"One eagle for each stripe on the American flag," declared lead singer Natalie Maines. "The ultimate avatar for capitalist American depravity, from the slaughter of the Native Americans to the Florida recount."

Audience members report that 50 armed roadies and crew members lined up along the stage with guns hoisted, ready to slaughter additional birds during the chorus of "Cowboy Take Me Away."

"We're on the brink of a war that will define us for decades," Maines added while wiping blood and loose feathers from her brow. "If Toby Keith thought we crossed the line when we said George W. Bush wasn't an exemplary Texan, wait till his simple ass hears about this."

Backlash over the stunt has been immediate, with radio stations across the country refusing to play Dixie Chicks' music and countless Bush sup-

porters slinging "Wide Open Spaces" CDs into the sky like clay pigeons and decimating them with their own shotguns.

"I brought my daughters to this concert to show them some strong female role models, but my youngest won't stop crying from the horror we witnessed," said former fan Hector Davis. "At one point Emily Robison threw a dead eagle into the crowd and its blood splattered all over me and my kids. I have half a mind to ask for a refund."

The Dixie Chicks' path to radicalization has reportedly been slow but steady.

"Emily and Martie [Maguire] were raised on contemporary bluegrass, but found their way to the New Deal socialist anthems of Woody Guthrie, which you can hear on tracks like 'White Trash Wedding,'" explained music historian Clark McGregor. "By the time 9/11 happened, the two were listening to nothing but Dead Kennedys, early Rage Against the Machine, and Chumbawamba deep cuts, so it's no real surprise that they ended up here, when you think about it."

At press time, the Dixie Chicks unveiled the art for their latest album, which features the women dressed as members of the Taliban, beheading Uncle Sam.

Bush Fires Chief of Staff After Being Spin-Kicked During Combatwoundedveteran Show at Florida VFW Hall

By Bill Conway

TALLAHASSEE, Fla.--George W. Bush fired his chief of staff following a scheduling mishap that resulted in the president being spin-kicked directly in the face during a Combatwoundedveteran show at a local VFW post, sources within the administration confirmed.

"Andrew Card will be stepping down as chief of staff effective immediately," White House Press Secretary Ari Fleischer announced to reporters earlier this afternoon. "President Bush is still recovering from injuries sustained at what he believed to be a charity event for America's heroes. He wants to thank everyone for their support, and stressed the need for neutral spaces at shows where people who don't want to mosh can watch bands play without fear of bodily harm."

Card admitted that his mistake put the leader of the free world in direct danger.

"This was entirely on me. I saw the words 'combat wounded veteran' and 'VFW' and thought it would be a perfect photo opportunity for the president," he said. "I got a feeling from the unsavory people hanging out in the parking lot that being there was a bad idea, but the president insisted on staying because he is a man of the people. I don't want to blame the Secret Service, but they should have seen that tall guy throwing the high kicks coming."

Members of the Florida hardcore scene were reportedly surprised by the sudden appearance of the 43rd president of the United States.

"There were a ton of dudes in black suits and sunglasses surrounding the venue, and we just figured some new grindcore band was pulling a gimmick," said show attendee Tamara Craig. "Then, out of nowhere, President Bush walked in and just kinda stood by the merch table acting super awkward. When Combatwoundedveteran played 'Assassination Attempt Part 2,' Tommy Crute just started going nuts, and the next thing I know Bush was down and Tommy is being dragged out the back door. Fucking killer set."

The event marks the first music-related injury to a sitting president since Bill Clinton passed out from heat exhaustion in the middle of a Fishbone pit in 1994.

Dude Wears Bowling Shoes

By Louie Aronowitz

CHICAGO--Potential trendsetter Pat Benson was spotted wearing footwear generally relegated to bowling alleys as if it weren't noteworthy or at all out of place.

"At first I wasn't sure if they were real bowling shoes or regular shoes made to look like them for some reason," began confused roommate Jessica March. "But confirming they were actual bowling shoes just raised more questions than it answered. Like, did he forget to trade them in after bowling? Did he steal them? And why? Are they comfortable?"

"Is he the one person in the history of bowling to actually stumble upon a pair that fits right, so he refused to surrender them?" she added. "Maybe he wants to be prepared for an impromptu pickup game? Does that even exist? Someone please explain this to me!"

Benson alleged the shoes in question are part of a current trend, and quite common.

"I've seen so many people wearing them--it's definitely a thing," he explained. "And no, I have no idea why the size 11.5 bowling shoes at the Fireside Bowl are now swapped out with a pair of four-year-old Chuck Taylors, and I don't appreciate the implication."

Reactions to the shoes have been largely negative, with even those closest to Benson vehemently opposing the style.

"They look ridiculous!" commented his mother, Shay Benson-Kiehl. "You know, I buy him these nice clothes and expensive shoes, and what does he do? He steals filthy bowling shoes instead! Do you know how many feet have been in those things?"

"Not to mention he's going to have back problems from their lack of support," added Benson's sister, Danisha. "He needs decent footwear. No 35-year-old man should be walking around like that. I don't care if they go with that shirt with flames up the sleeves."

Though Benson was determined to "make the bowling shoes thing happen," he reportedly switched back to sneakers almost immediately after "Brittany from work" was overheard saying that they "look like something a clown would wear to a funeral."

Howard Dean Returns to Former Job as Most Enthusiastic House Show Audience Member

BY GORDON SCHMIDT

BURLINGTON, Vt.--Howard Dean is expected to return to his former role as the most enthusiastic attendee at Burlington punk-house shows following his failed bid as the Democratic candidate for the 2004 presidential election, campaign staff confirmed.

"You know how you can be playing a show and everyone is drinking and talking among themselves, and totally ignoring you?" asked Fuck Flatlanders lead singer and Dean supporter Amanda Fassett. "And you're about ready to give up, but then a lone voice from the crowd belts out a hearty 'YEEAAAAAH,' giving you this wave of adrenaline that powers you through the rest of the set? That was all Howard--so glad to have him back on the scene."

Burlington scenesters say Dean was not only a constant presence at shows, but that he also acted as an intermediary when band conflicts broke out.

"I remember the weeks of mediation he did with The Worst Five Minutes of Your Life back in 1999. Those guys were so close to breaking up, but Howie was in their practice space every night, helping them talk through their issues. He even did backup vocals for two tracks on their EP," recalled Rufus Thatcher. "I have to admit, I wondered if he was missing any essential governor duties while doing that. Still, it was huge for the scene."

Local punks admitted they were supportive of Dean's presidential bid, but had some questions about his priorities.

"We had a house show the night before the Iowa caucus, and Howard was there tearing it up," recalled Marcy Naramore. "I thought he should maybe be in, like, Iowa, but I don't know that much about politics, I guess. The next day I saw him skateboarding downtown and getting chased by security guards with the dudes from My Revenge!"

Dean was unavailable for comment on his next steps, but campaign sources report that he'll be filling in on bass tonight for local act Punk Peepers at a secret show at the abandoned syrup mill.

The Hard Times Goes Back to Basics

As remembered by Matt Saincome

Losing our office was tough. When we started out and it was just Ed, Bill, and me in our tiny NYC squat, I was used to living that punk lifestyle: I had nothing, I hated everything, and I didn't care about anything. But over the years I became accustomed to certain amenities, not least of which was the decadent bathroom I had all to myself; it was the only place I was truly comfortable taking a shit. Being back in that squat with nothing but a curtain separating Bill and me was demoralizing. We were back to where we began, worse off than ever.

Since the 1970s, the Lower East Side had been given a complete face-lift, but miraculously the hole-in-the-wall where *The Hard Times* was born still stood. The graffiti had changed, but the smell was the same. We were home again, two punks trying to produce a zine for people exactly like us. Some would argue that during the time we were spending money on lavish tech investments and racehorses, we may have lost touch with our founding principles, but I firmly disagree. I hate the government and its tyrannical capitalist system like any other punk, so it was always my goal to spend my money as I got it so I wouldn't be a part of the revolving cycle of interest, retirement funds, and whatever other bullshit they try to sell you.

We were ready to get back to work, but we no longer saw eye to eye on how to run the company. I wanted to make zines the old-fashioned way, while Bill insisted that we try going online. Reluctantly, I agreed, and he used what very little cash we had left to start our first website. It was another disaster in a long line of them. Within days, hackers took it over and turned it into a porno page for people with a fetish for mud-covered feet. As a result, our email was flooded with photos of muddy feet and we had to shut down all web activity. Even worse, our only working computer was infected with a virus from our own website, which forced us back to using our trusty typewriter. The old girl had been in storage for a while, and time had not been kind. If you typed for more than ten minutes, smoke would randomly start billowing out even though there was no electricity involved. It wasn't great, but it was all we had.

Things weren't looking good, but we couldn't let *The Hard Times* die. There was too much that needed to be reported on, and we were the only ones who could do it right. We got back to work typing, cutting, pasting, stapling, and getting back out to shows. We had survived so much, had come so far, we couldn't let it end now.

Mail-Ordering Both "Rock Against Bush" Compilations as Involved in Election as Punk Plans to Get

BY BRIAN POLK

AKRON, Ohio--Local punk Jack Walker recently mail-ordered both "Rock Against Bush" CDs, an act he believes is "more than enough" political activism for one person, sources confirmed.

"I know the comps I ordered are about the election, but, like, why should anyone vote when the whole system is rigged?" asked the 22-year-old who's been checking his mailbox daily for his CDs. "I'm just excited to have over two hours of punk music to listen to. I can ignore the stuff about turning political thought into any sort of feasible action--I've done my part already."

Although Walker detests the idea of participating in a democracy, he considers himself extremely politically minded, a trait he learned from listening to a number of the bands on the compilations.

"Look at this lineup," said Walker, pointing at an advertisement in "Punk Planet." "Anti-Flag, NOFX, Bad Religion, The (International) Noise Conspiracy . . . those are the bands that sing about how fucked up everything is. If I hadn't grown up listening to that kind of political and social commentary, I'd probably be just another moron who salutes the flag and thinks this country is perfect."

When questioned about Walker's support of his musical output but not his political guidance, "Fat" Mike Burkett--the driving force behind both the compilations and the organization Punk Voter--expressed frustration.

"Walker is the exact kind of young, passionate voter we're trying to influence," said the Fat Wreck Chords founder. "He's already a liberal punker who relates to the music and message on the comps, so I'm not really sure why he thinks sitting this one out is a good idea. I don't know, maybe he wants to get drafted and fight another war for oil?"

Walker claims his free time is at a premium and that he already has concrete plans for election day.

"I'm probably going to sleep in for a bit because I've had a lot of late nights playing 'Tony Hawk's Pro Skater,'" he said. "Then I've gotta cash the birthday check my aunt sent so I can pay off my late fees at the video rental place. With a schedule that packed, I couldn't find the time to vote even if I wanted to."

Hot Topic Employee-Training Videos Include Both Seasons Of "Invader Zim"

By James Webster

FAIRFAX, Va.--Recently hired Hot Topic employee Carson Woodward was stunned to learn she would have to watch the entire series run of the Nickelodeon cartoon "Invader Zim" as a part of her employee training, multiple heavily pierced sources report.

"Ten hours for an employee training video seems like a lot. I watched the first three episodes with her, but it wasn't for me," said John Woodward, father of the newly employed 16-year-old. "I'm glad she got the job, but two entire seasons of a TV show? When I worked at Wendy's back in the '80s, the training videos were basically just 'put the meat on the grill and don't cut off your fingers.'"

Upon her hiring at the Tysons Corner Center store, Woodward was given the standard-issue employee materials: a Senses Fail sweatband, a My Chemical Romance hoodie with thumb-holes in the sleeves, a ceramic jar that reads "DEADLY NIGHTSHADE," and the two-season "Invader Zim" box set.

"I was expecting to have to watch some videos about sexual harassment in a shitty supply closet in the back of the store, but I guess this is better," admitted Woodward. "I remember kinda liking this show when I was 13 so it'll be cool to refresh my memory. Plus, this DVD set looks expensive, so that's rad."

Close acquaintances have begun to express concern about the effect Woodward's new employer has had on her.

"Since she began watching 'Invader Zim,' conversations with her have changed. She'll start yelling at the top of her lungs out of nowhere, as if sheer volume is some kind of joke," said longtime friend Michael Groth. "Plus there's those god-awful non sequiturs. You ask her how her day's been, and she just shouts 'toast!' like it has any kind of comedic value."

In a follow-up conducted via AIM, Woodward seemed unbothered by the complaints.

"I'm still new at the store, so I'm always trying to make a good impression. The way I see it, saying 'pork muffin' completely unprompted in conversation is a way of taking my work home with me," said Woodward. "Besides, 'Invader Zim' is just a stepping stone. I've heard that they teach the managers 2 tAlK liKe ThIs iN rEaL LiFe. XD."

The Postal Service to Cease Playing Shows on Weekends

By Nick Ortolani

SEATTLE--Indietronica group The Postal Service announced that they will be terminating their services on weekends, citing low record sales and growing disinterest in power-pop medleys, officials close to the band confirmed.

"We've done everything we can," said lead vocalist and guitarist Ben Gibbard as he mopped up spilled cider with his striped scarf. "We tried raising the price of 'Give Up' by three cents, and most of our music is computer-automated, but nothing's made a dent. We want to keep delivering our music to every household in America, but in order to do that, we need to scale back."

Financial woes have largely been attributed to a recent decision at Sub Pop to reallocate Postal Service funds toward pensions for other acts on the label.

"The Postal Service has been a staple of mix CDs and college radio since 2001, and we understand that people have come to depend on them to help with late-night ennui," said CEO Bruce Pavitt, "but someone has to provide for The Shins in their golden years. These 'Garden State' royalties aren't going to last forever."

Employee morale is reportedly at an all-time low following the series of cost-saving measures.

"Those fuckers cut my benefits; I have a solo career I'm trying to support. This is just another blow to working musicians of the world," said contributing vocalist Jenny Lewis. "Now I'm only considered part-time, and I'm afraid I might have to return to acting to support myself."

In an effort to help save The Postal Service, numerous musical acts have combined forces to release as many covers of "Such Great Heights" as possible.

"It'll be a renewable source of income," said Sam Beam of Iron & Wine. "No one will ever get sick of that song."

Despite the grassroots enthusiasm, The Postal Service remains unsure about their future.

"Thankfully I can always fall back on Death Cab," said Gibbard, "but I'm not sure what Jimmy [Tamborello] will do--maybe he'll go back to programming robots or something. I have no idea what he actually does."

New iPod Holds 29,000 Street-Punk Songs Titled "Fight Back"

By Matt Saincome

CUPERTINO, Calif.--Earlier today Apple announced a limited-edition MP3 music player that packs up to 29,000 street-punk songs titled "Fight Back" into an ultraportable 6.5-ounce design that fits in your pocket.

"Apple has invented a whole new category of digital music player that lets you take your expansive collection of street-punk songs, all with the same exact title, wherever you go," said Steve Jobs, Apple's CEO, ditching his trademark black turtleneck for a denim vest and bondage pants. "With iPod Fight, listening to lyrics written by guys with nicknames like Puke Bucket, Rat, or Skinny Pete will never be the same."

Apple executives assert the iPod Fight represents the next generation of portable music players.

"This revolutionary 21st century Walkman doesn't just hold songs titled 'Fight Back' from Discharge, The Exploited, or Clit 45, it actively searches for and downloads tracks with the same title by high school bands practicing in garages and basements around the country," said Apple SVP Tim Cook. "With our patented technology, we will have an entirely new generation of young punks ready to fight the system."

Bay Area punks who have been asked to beta test the yet-to-be-released device have given it largely positive reviews.

"I can't believe how simple this has made things for me," said 16-year-old mohawked rebel Davey Henderson. "I used to have to carry around 200 to 250 CDs to even get close to this many songs about sticking it to your oppressors, whether it be your boss or your shitty parents who won't let you go to the mall even though everyone else will be there. This is so much easier."

However, some older members of the scene were not as enthusiastic.

"This is just the same bullshit iPod they try to sell to everyone's mom and dad, but with a plaid case," said Gilman volunteer Teddy Perez. "It has the same storage as a normal model, but the fat cats at Apple figured out they could inflate their numbers by exploiting punk's notoriously short songs. I'm not buying it."

iPod Fight will also feature a 160-by-128-pixel display, allowing customers to view hundreds of nearly identical album covers featuring stencil font and guys in studded vests in Apple's trademark green-toned screen color.

killed.By.Synth

KiDSTaTiK

Luis Lohan

Prime Territory on Myspace Top 8 Opens Up After Breakup

By Courtney Paige Barnett

DAYTON, Ohio--Prime territory opened up in the Top Friends section of high school sophomore Desiree Hallenbeck's Myspace page since dumping boyfriend Colton Donahue this Friday, ecstatic sources report.

"Everyone knows that your Top 8 is like the official ranking of the people in your life," said local teen and "secondish best friend" Ellie McElhenney. "Just ask the weird horse girl who only has Christian bands on hers. Being Desiree's number one basically makes you vice scene queen of the fucking world."

Sources believe the breakup was ignited after Hallenbeck noticed another girl listed too close for comfort to her number-one position on Donahue's Top 8.

"That girl is my cousin from Tampa and she was only, like, number six, but whatever," Donahue affirmed. "I'm keeping the My Chemical Romance fan page as my number one, I don't care. If Des can't handle that, then it wasn't meant to be, just like my friends said the first three times we broke up."

When asked who's in the running for her top spot, Hallenbeck responded via AIM so her Myspace profile wouldn't show that she was online.

"I'm constantly being hounded with messages; this is more pressure than deciding on my page layout theme and song," she said. "But considering the demand, I might just sell it to the highest bidder, or even rent it out like my realtor dad would do."

Eager hopefuls believe that being in Hallenbeck's Top 8 would grant social access in a scene where becoming popular is often the result of years of ass-kissing or having a cool older sibling.

"I'd kill to be in her Top 8," said another sophomore whose name no one can remember and who Hallenbeck doesn't even know exists. "That kind of acceptance is something you carry with you for the rest of your life."

Tensions ran high among the high schooler's besties as they tried outdoing one another with gifts like concert tickets and lip gloss, given in hopes of being promoted to the penthouse of online social statuses.

"For right now, I'm just enjoying the attention," said Hallenbeck. "The internet is so great. I hope it never goes away and that my parents never get on it."

At press time, Hallenbeck's top spot was being held ad interim by her pet chinchilla's account, while half of the Beacon High sophomore class had her as their number one.

Punk's "American Idol" Audition Praised by Simon Cowell as "Vile Chorus of Dying Sewer Rats"

BY DOM TUREK

LOS ANGELES--"American Idol" judge Simon Cowell took a break from his harsh criticisms Sunday to commend one punk contestant's audition as a "vile chorus of dying sewer rats," sources confirmed.

"This has to be the first time an audition has triggered my gag reflex," said Cowell. "Two years ago I listened to a woman play 'We Are the Champions' on a flute through her stomach, but that was nothing compared to what I witnessed yesterday."

American Idol hopeful and Florida resident Nick Landin recalled his excitement leading up to his performance of "The Star-Spangled Banner," during which he set an upside-down American flag ablaze, a stunt that audiences are hailing as "the most unpatriotic and unnecessary fire hazard in recent memory."

"I came all the way from Gainesville for this," explained Landin, who recently quit his band to embark upon his own music career. "After seeing what going solo did for legends like Sid Vicious and David Lee Roth, I had to give it a chance, and it's clearly paying off, big time."

The memorable audition also drew critical acclaim from fellow judge Randy Jackson, who said, "That's gonna be a 'fuck no' for me, dog," which quickly became the network's first use of censorship on the show.

"The entire performance was spastic," raved Jackson. "It was like watching a fly that had been sprayed with Windex. Just being in the same room with him has left me impotent, if not totally infertile."

However, not everyone was impressed. Sparing no emotion, Paula Abdul called the performance, "truly adorable" and gave Landin an "A for effort." In between incoherent ramblings, the diminutive singer and dancer even went so far as to call the contestant "mainstream material."

"It went better than expected," Landin said upon being eliminated from advancing to the next round. "Getting that sheet of yellow paper would've undermined my whole nonconformist and anti-authoritarian performance. I can't wait to come back and not make it again next year."

Emo Ex-Girlfriend Wants Her Pants Back

BY BILL CONWAY

PROVIDENCE, R.I.--Local emo music devotee Sandra McKenna is in the middle of a vicious custody battle with ex-boyfriend Doug Hoover over a pair of heavily distressed skintight Diesel jeans, sources close to the young woman confirmed.

"Doug wasn't even into skinny jeans before he met me. He would either wear these dumb-looking cargo shorts or dumpy khakis like he worked at Dunkin' Donuts," said McKenna while briefly looking up from her Sidekick 3. "It drives me insane to think he's strutting around town showing off his ankles and hip bones to all these Hayley Williams wannabes."

The couple broke up after Hoover was found to be sending flirtatious Myspace messages to numerous emo chicks.

"I was over at his parents' house and asked him if I could use his computer to update my away message," said McKenna, who is known across multiple online platforms as TakingBackSandy. "When I logged on, I saw he'd left a browser open, and there were all these messages with Brand New lyrics sent to a bunch of different girls. Those were the same lyrics he used to send me. I ended it right then and there, but I stupidly didn't grab all of my stuff from his room before I left."

Hoover denied any wrongdoing, and claims the pants in question never belonged to his former girlfriend.

"She is straight-up delusional. Like she's the type of girl New Found Glory warns you about, man," he said while adjusting his white studded belt. "I have a friend who works at Diesel and he gave me his discount. She could never even fit into these; she'd blow out the crotch the first time she had to walk up a flight of stairs."

Mutual friends of the former couple say the acrimony over the jeans in question has been a source of strife in their social circle.

"Doug is the only person that's usually willing to drive to shows, but I don't want Sandy to think I'm choosing him over her," said Allie Wilson. "But Armor for Sleep is playing with Hawthorne Heights at the Worcester Palladium and I have no other way of getting there."

"Maybe they can take turns wearing them every other weekend or something?" she added. "I don't know, this whole thing has been so messy, and I'm really sorry to see the pants get caught in the middle--they seem like nice pants."

As of press time, McKenna was scrubbing any mention of Hoover from her LiveJournal entries dating back the last four months.

Sigur Rós Show Delayed While Roadie Sent to Score Fermented Shark and Sour Rams' Testicles

By Jeff Cardello

CHICAGO--Icelandic avant-rockers Sigur Rós delayed their show at the Auditorium Theater while the venue's in-house roadie Rodney Gordon was out retrieving the group's favorite delicacies, annoyed and "sort of grossed out," a source confirmed.

"I went into their dressing room and they kept saying how they couldn't go on without 'hákarl' and 'súrir hrútspungar.' I thought they were working on their set list or something," said Gordon while lining the back seat of his car with plastic. "It turns out they were talking about rotten shark meat and sheep balls, and they refused to play until they had some. Chicago is more of a sausage town, so this wasn't exactly like running down to Murphy's and ordering a few brats."

Band members expressed frustration as Gordon's citywide search of grocery stores, back alleys, and petting zoos stretched on for hours.

"This man must be a moron if he cannot find these common food products. Every shop in Reykjavík has enough hákarl to feed half of Iceland," said lead vocalist and guitarist Jónsi Birgisson through his Hopelandic interpreter. "We are getting desperate. We have combed the carpet hoping to find the littlest of scraps, but all we could find were rocks of cocaine and chunks of hash, for which we have no use."

Moments before venue management was about to cancel the performance and start issuing refunds, Gordon appeared backstage with plastic bags packed with the putrefied shark and bitter reproductive organs demanded by the ethereal musicians. When asked, he elaborated on his quest.

"I finally met a butcher who had a hookup, and after making a small sacrifice to Odin, solving a riddle for someone who identified himself only as Geirmundur the Elf King, and promising my firstborn to a clan of trolls, I finally got some choice cuts of shark and testicle," he said. "Those trolls don't mess around, man. They said they were going to 'gnash upon my bones' for disturbing their sacred quarters, but then I made them my offer. Little do those dudes know that I got a vasectomy before hitting the road with Van Halen in '84."

Cool Kid Won't Stop Until Every Inch of Body Covered in Burton Gear

By John Danek

LAKE TAHOE, Calif.--Avid snowboarder and alleged "coolest kid in school" Jacob Donnelly is on a quest to cover every square inch of his body in Burton Snowboards clothing and gear, adoring classmates report.

"Burton stuff is awesome. It's even cooler than DC or World Industries was two years ago," explained the high school senior. "I don't usually buy into labels much, but this one just really represents who I am: A guy who likes snowboarding and snowboarding-related clothing and accessories, a lot."

Friends recall the swift progression from casual supporter to full-blown Burton devotee.

"It started out with a sticker, which fit right on his Nalgene, but it grew pretty quickly from there. Now not a day goes by that you don't see Jay fully decked out," said best friend and fellow South Tahoe High student Marcus Green. "So yeah, he's basically the Ryan Cabrera of our school, and I don't throw that around lightly."

Donnelly can be seen wearing any combination of Burton-brand T-shirts, zip-up hoodies, beanies, parkas, boots, mittens, and balaclavas on a daily basis, a sense of fashion that has those closest to the teen both impressed and enamored.

"I just feel so blessed that Jacob could see past my Billabong shirts, Roxy jeans, and flat-ironed bangs to discover who I really am inside--a Burton girl," said Donnelly's girlfriend, Jennifer Quigley. "The Burton condoms are sorta weird though . . . I don't know where you even get something like that, but it shows commitment, so that's cool."

Despite the welcome attention, those close to Donnelly report that the teen's loyalty to the brand has led to certain difficulties.

"I know he failed his driver's test, like, five times because he refused to take off his snowboard boots," explained Green when pressed for details. "And he begged an optician to make him prescription snow goggles; I've seen him wear those to a friend's funeral. It didn't go over too well with the parents, but I bet Ricky was psyched to see the coolest frosted-tip motherfucker on Earth decked out in the latest Burton threads standing by his coffin, throwing up one last 'shocker' for old time's sake."

"Man, what a fucking cool-ass dude," he added.

As of press time, Donnelly was rushed to the ER to be treated for heat stroke after refusing to take off his snow pants and parka for gym class.

Missing Teens Found Safely Giggling Inside a Spencer's Gifts

By Courtney Paige Barnett

CHERRY HILL, N.J.--Fourteen-year-olds Dexter Spinelli and Lucas Goddard were safely returned home by authorities tonight after a frantic three-day search ended when the boys were discovered snickering inside of a local Spencer's novelty gift store, relieved sources confirmed.

"We got the call from the Spinelli kid's mother after she noticed the young men hadn't returned from skateboarding," said Cherry Hill Chief of Police Bob Winthrop. "It took three days of scouring parks and riverbeds before we found them in this store, laughing hysterically at an 'FBI: Female Body Inspector' T-shirt and a plastic fart detector. Thank God they're safe."

Cherry Hill Police got the call of the missing boys' whereabouts when the store's manager, Raven Xanthos, saw the report while watching TV on the job.

"I'm used to teens wandering in, but with these dudes, I was like, whoa, you guys clearly haven't had a beej yet," said Xanthos, who was "mostly just relieved" to get the boys out of her store. "Apparently they were hiding in the dressing rooms during closing. It's gonna take me all day to check the inventory for jizz residue, and I don't even want to think about how many cherry-flavored condoms and Smarties thongs they ate just to stay alive."

When questioned, the boys claim they stopped at the mall to grab Sbarro and took advantage of the lack of parental supervision to enter the innuendo depot, where they reportedly lost all track of time and any traces of maturity.

"I guess I'm sorry we freaked out our parents but, honestly, I'd totally do it again," Goddard said. "That store is sick! I saw the same 'Stoned to the Bone' poster my friend Ricky's sister has in her room. This place has everything anyone could ever want."

While the boys' parents are relieved by their safe return, they worry about the impact three days in "that Godless hellhole" may have had on their children.

"We're lucky they're alive, because I just about had a heart attack when I saw the trash they were selling!" said Goddard's mother, Peggy. "Glow-in-the-dark bongs? Pamela Anderson posters? This Spencer fellow is corrupting our children!"

At press time, the boys are no longer allowed at the mall without parental supervision, while there was some concern as their fathers disappeared for 30 minutes, only to be found inside Spencer's squeezing breast-shaped stress balls.

Attractive Emo Singer Really Testing Suspension of Disbelief With These Lyrics

By Eric Navarro

BALTIMORE--Fans of popular emo band Down the Road are reportedly questioning the authenticity of new album's lyrical themes when considering how objectively hot the singer is.

"I was looking forward to this record for months, but after seeing the cover, the lyrics felt really inauthentic," fan Tiffany Hall said. "When all of your songs are about the crushing despair of being unloved and alone, your cover art probably shouldn't be of your perfect-bone-structure singer giving the camera 'fuck me' eyes . . . and I don't even wanna think about how much strategically placed pomade went into that messy bedhead look."

A first look at promotional materials for the album only increased the divide between art and reality.

"In the music video for a song about waiting by the phone hoping any girl will call, there are literally girls all over him," said dubious fan Joy McCauley. "I mean, maybe it's, like, symbolism or something? Because at least one of those girls has to have a cell phone, or at least chirp from Boost Mobile."

While many casual fans were perturbed by the situation, emo purists cited several modern bands of the genre as examples of this being appropriate marketing.

"I'm what you might call an emo snob; I've been listening to emo since Dashboard Confessional created it in 2002," said local eighth-grader Luis Martin. "If Chris Carrabba can cry over girls while looking like a Backstreet Boy, why are people all pissed off now? If you think showing off full sleeves from a white V-neck T-shirt that clings in all the right places is some new thing, then you need to do your homework, bro."

"You know aliens didn't really blow up the White House in 'Independence Day,' right?" he added. "They clearly used special effects. Not everything is meant to be taken so literally."

When reached for comment, Down the Road vocalist Bryden Bastille tossed his bangs from his eyes, mumbled something about the futility of love, and walked off with a fleet of groupies.

Crust Punk Kicked out of Ca$h Cab Before First Question

By Gordon Schmidt

NEW YORK--Last night, crust punk Martin "Meathook" Madison was kicked out of the titular ca$h cab from the popular TV show before the first question was even asked, curbside witnesses and show crew members confirmed.

"We were as surprised as anyone when a cab actually stopped to pick him up," said fellow crusty Momi Alana. "He was on the sidewalk, his pants halfway down, giving traffic the finger when the car pulled over and the door opened. I figured it was a rookie cabbie--Meathook doesn't exactly look like someone who would be a good fare."

"Ca$h Cab" host Ben Bailey reported realizing his mistake almost immediately.

"We had gotten a bit desperate for a contestant, so I stopped at the first person who looked like they were trying to hail a cab," he said. "As soon as the door opened, a rottweiler-type dog wearing a filthy bandanna jumped in. Then I looked back and saw this guy covered in tattoos hoisting in a CVS bag dripping with something foul. He smelled like the dumpster behind a low-budget seafood restaurant."

Producers admitted to breaking format in order to remove the potential contestant from the game as fast as possible.

"We have a strict 'three strikes, you're out' policy," said executive producer Ron Deutsch. "While viewers know a contestant gets a strike for getting a question wrong, a contestant can get strikes for other things too. This contestant got three strikes before the first question: dog peeing on the seat, contestant vomiting in the cab, and contestant questioning if Ben had a taxi license. Actually, forget I mentioned that last one."

Although Madison had been kicked out of the ca$h cab, he remained optimistic in the face of adversity.

"I knew I wanted out anyway as soon as the lights in that cab turned on. Looked like a shitty rave full of posers in there," he explained. "Anyway, this shit isn't new to me; I've been kicked out of plenty of cabs, and game shows, and vehicle-based game shows before. At least this time I was able to steal a headrest."

Hot Topic Closed for Day as Manager Officiates Lavigne-Whibley Wedding

BY GREG HELLER

TORONTO--The Toronto Eaton Centre Hot Topic is closed for business in order to host the wedding of Canadian power duo Deryck Whibley and Avril Lavigne earlier today, overjoyed sources gushed.

"For real Canadian punks, this is like a royal wedding, you know?" said store manager and wedding officiant Gary Bouchard while signing for a delivery of Paramore-branded chain wallets. "I've known the couple for a few years now. This is where they buy all their clothes and hair dye, and since Hot Topic is the church of punk, it made sense to hold the event here.

Among those looking on were Whibley's fellow Sum'ers--guitarist Dave Baksh, drummer Steve Jocz, and bassist Jason "Cone" McCaslin--as well as Lavigne's bandmates, who are legally not allowed to be named.

"Yo, seeing Deryck totally get married was, like, fuck man . . ." said Jocz while adjusting his tuxedo shirt with cut-off sleeves. "It was just so gnarly the way he stormed into the wedding like his name was El Niño--that guy is my bro for life."

At the time of their nuptials, Whibley and Lavigne reportedly strolled down the aisle of the store's screamo section to stand before Bouchard beneath a canopy custom-fashioned from Good Charlotte baby tees. The groom wore ill-fitting slacks, a white shirt, suspenders, and a poorly knotted skinny tie. The bride wore the exact same thing.

"She looked so breathtaking, I could hardly keep my composure. There definitely wasn't a dry kohl-rimmed eye in the house," admitted the officiant/manager. "At one point, I looked into the crowd and saw Simple Plan's Pierre Bouvier wiping away tears. It was a beautiful moment."

Following the ceremony, a reception was held in the Belts & Cuffs section, where the emotional groom thanked Bouchard for a "punk as fuck" ceremony.

"Yo, everything about this was so tight. Thanks to the Hot Topic staff for all you've done," said Whibley to the gathered crowd. "But most of all I need to thank my mom. I don't think I'd be here today if she hadn't ignored that doctor who advised her to have an abortion, 'bortion, 'bortion."

Bouchard says the Hot Topic at Eaton Centre will reopen to the public on Monday and, to honor the newly wedded pop-punkers, he's just announced a 50 percent off sale on H8GEL, Lavigne's signature line of middle-finger nail polish.

The Last Print Edition

As remembered by Matt Saincome

Creating the last print edition of *The Hard Times* was an emotional experience. One reason was that Bill and I had become heavily addicted to horse tranquilizers and our supply was running low. The other reason was that we'd made it to the top of the mountain, then fallen so far. We'd tried our best to keep things going strong, but the internet was more popular than ever, and it seemed people no longer had time for a hard-copy zine. There was now a ton of online competition: Former contributors had blogs, and many of our old staff members were at *Pitchfork* or *Punknews* and scooping us left and right. We couldn't keep up with the fast pace--it was time to say farewell.

Bill and I were in a deep, deep k hole when we put together the last issue. Using our last bit of money, we printed a limited run of 500 copies. It was filled with spelling mistakes and grammatical errors, not to mention bloodstains from the wounds we sustained while trying to staple despite being so high it felt like we were walking on the moon.

Our goal was to sell our remaining stock at the 2009 Black N Blue Bowl. We reserved a table and were ready to say goodbye to the hardcore world for good. It just felt right: We'd be at a show with the bands we had covered for so long, and the people who had been such ardent supporters. Unfortunately, it wasn't meant to be.

Bill and I loaded up my 1986 Subaru Outback that I'd bought for $200 on Craigslist. It leaked about a quart of oil an hour, but it ran like the wind. As we made our way through the dense New York traffic, I suddenly nodded off. I could blame the drugs, I could blame the lack of sleep, I could even blame the car's awful exhaust leak that filled the cabin with carbon monoxide. Whatever it was, it doesn't matter now; the car careened off the road and into a construction zone, flipping over in the process. Bill and I were dragged out moments before it went up in flames. The oil leak mixed with 500 zines turned the Outback into a fucking tinderbox. We watched our remaining inventory burn while being handcuffed to stretchers and thrown into the back of an ambulance.

This fiery end befit our modest beginnings. Soon after, our squat was condemned by the city upon finding the address on a more lightly damaged copy of the zine, and eventually the property was converted into a high-end frozen yogurt shop. Bill and I stopped speaking; we needed time apart. The passion that drove us to create *The Hard Times* and keep it going was no longer there--the world had knocked us down one time too many. But even though our fighting spirit had been nearly extinguished, I knew we would rise again.

Boss Surprises Entire Staff With "In Rainbows" for Christmas

BY GREG HELLER

GREENSBORO, N.C.--Discount Tour & Travel founder Brad Kaiser gifted all 12 of his employees a download voucher for Radiohead's "pay what you wish" release, "In Rainbows, at the conclusion of this year's Christmas party, underwhelmed sources confirmed.

"I know my reputation," said Kaiser while eating a large Italian sub. "I know they call me 'Kaiser the Miser' and also 'that cheap asshole,' but this year, I don't know, something just told me it was time to open up my wallet and give. I've heard great things about this band, and this album seems really special."

Asked if Radiohead's innovative payment option might have factored into his sudden change of heart, Kaiser offered up a small slice of deli ham and suggested trying it "with a little honey mustard."

Belinda Jackson, veteran travel agent and "proud" grandmother to five "gorgeous" grandchildren, was among those most touched by Kaiser's kindness.

"I know the company has been struggling a bit lately. People today are so busy on their computers that they forget to come down to the travel agency and book vacations," said Jackson while trying to figure out how to download the album. "For Mr. Kaiser to be this giving right now is extra special. Compact discs cost about $20 these days, so I can't even imagine how much it costs to buy an internet CD."

Radiohead frontman Thom Yorke admitted to having mixed emotions when he was informed of Kaiser's so-called generosity.

"It would have been nice if he'd thrown a little cash the band's way. We were just starting to come to terms with the fact our fans are willing to rip us off," said the singer, "but then to find out someone used our business model to stiff his entire workforce? That's just wrong, mate. I just hope they enjoy the tunes."

Kaiser was noncommittal when asked if he planned to be equally charitable at next year's seasonal soiree.

"It's just that I spent so much this year, I'm not sure I'll be able to repeat it," he said. "But let's see what happens with the travel market in 2008."

By the 2000s, *The Hard Times* had a reputation as a magazine that could take a joke, but we also received very serious letters posing intimate questions about how to handle punk identity issues. During the early aughts, the question "How do I explain to my partner that I'm into nu metal?" was submitted so frequently we made it a cover story.

EXPLAINING YOUR NU METAL FANHOOD TO YOUR PARTNER

The HARD Times
FROM THE
VAULT

ILLUSTRATIONS BY ANDREW DUBONGCO

Coming to terms with your nu metal fanhood can be a confusing time, and sharing the news with the people closest to you may be an overwhelming, daunting task. While you may feel compelled to hide your Ozzfest tickets and Disturbed hoodie from new acquaintances, disclosing this information is not only the responsible thing to do, but will ultimately dispel any shame or stigma you may be carrying. Revealing your status to new partners, friends, and anyone with whom you plan to share a car for longer than 30 minutes is crucial, as the spread of nu metal may be contagious to those without a solid taste in music.

YOU ARE NOT ALONE

Explaining to a current or potential partner that you willingly listen to nu metal can be embarrassing, but it's important to remember that you are not alone. An estimated half-million high school students and thousands of unemployed adults live with nu metal fanhood every day. Many nu metal fans were inadvertently exposed to the sickness during their formative grunge years, while others reluctantly yet willingly associated with nu metal fans during fifth-period lunch, claiming it's "not ideal" but "still better than hanging out with those weird ska kids in marching band."

HOW TO BREAK THE NEWS

When informing your partner of your nu metal fanhood, it's best to approach the topic as directly as possible. Stating facts like "Creed clearly took hints from early Pearl Jam" and "Limp Bizkit is actually kind of posi, when you think about it" will not only give you the confidence to stand by your decision to disclose your fanhood, it will help you come across as informed and safe to those to whom you are admitting this information. For many, nu metal fanhood is simply something they live with and rarely affects the quality of their day-to-day life. Countless nu metal fans have gone on to have healthy and fulfilling relationships with partners, friends, colleagues, and family members who do not share their interest.

LIVING WITH NU METAL FANHOOD

When left untreated, a nu metal phase can result in piercings of the eyebrow, lip, and tongue, and may cause the formation of facial hair into a goatee ranging in size from "crazy fluffy" to "comically thin." Growing out of the nu metal phase is certainly possible, although for many it will lie dormant, only to recur when least expected. Nu metal phases can be triggered by any number of things, including, but not limited to: cage fights, visits to the mall, Criss Angel's face, a quick glimpse at any show on Spike TV, and commercials for the United States Army.

The 2010s: The Reunion

In late 2014, as the scene was demanding more and more hardcore band reunions, a wild idea started forming. It was first discussed in the back rooms of venues, dive bars, and squats, and then in offices and via phone. This idea was as dangerous as it was bold, as intriguing as it was explosive. The kind of thing that, out of fear of public reaction, could only be whispered among close friends and a trusted inner circle.

"What if we brought back *The Hard Times*?"

It had been five years since we'd published an issue. While the challenges of reviving a dead media entity seemed difficult, piecing together the original lineup proved to be even harder.

Matt had been spotted making wild bets at various racetracks and a few local shows, but people kept their distance. Despite "The Hard Times Defense," rumors swirled that he'd cooperated with various agencies in exchange for immunity from prosecution. And though rumors aren't always true, they were this time. Matt was a turncoat coward with no morals or loyalty who had cooperated with authorities to weasel his way out of jail time.

Bill had broken edge and was on a years-long bender when Krissy found him living as a scuba instructor in the Florida Keys. He had no interest getting back together with "that rat bastard," but Krissy and a core group of die-hard editors urged him to bring the green boot back to life. They knew there was only one way to reunite the original *Hard Times* line-up: get Riot Fest to pay them a ton of money.

Riot Fest balked at the idea of advertising in a defunct magazine, but Krissy told Matt and Bill they'd agreed to an advertising package with a serious budget. They took the bait so she brokered a meeting between the magazine's founders and a smattering of old staffers.

The team had some concerns: *"How involved was Matt in the fraud last time?"*; *"I saw Bill beaten nearly to death with my own cordless phone in the eighties, and quite frankly, I haven't been able to look at him the same ever since"*; and *"I'm still owed $15,000 in back pay and am only here to serve you both."* Somehow, they worked through these issues. The opportunity was too ripe to not reunite—only this time, it would be online.

They posted the first new *Hard Times* article in December of 2014. The response was terrific, with millions of readers storming the new site in the first month, and since then, the small team of DIY punks, comics, and their friends have run the site without corporate backing. In this chapter you'll see highlights from *Hard Times'* first stable website, thehardtimes.net, each an example of the fearless journalism that has made *The Hard Times* a punk-household name.

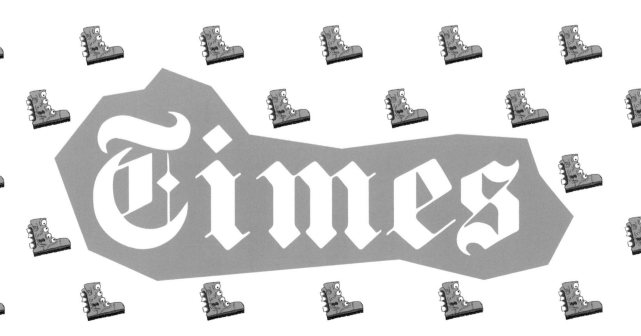

ON THIS DAY IN PUNK HISTORY

June 18, 2015—
Eyebrow ring–wedding ring combo sparks mass confusion; hundreds injured, four dead

Aging nu metal fan John Menahan's simultaneous sporting of an eyebrow ring and a wedding ring led to massive confusion at an Orlando mall. The incomprehensibility of Menahan's neon-green facial jewelry paired with a wedding band seemingly gifted to him by some human person resulted in utter catastrophe, eventually leading to multiple deaths and numerous injuries.

April 15, 2016—
Door guy smiles

Milwaukee, Wisconsin, door guy/security guy/bartender-when-the-other-bartender-is-on-a-bathroom-break Wes McDonald smiled for the first and only time in his 25-plus years working the position, according to shocked eyewitnesses. In addition to the smile, McDonald also suggested that a patron "have a good one," igniting concern from friends, family, and coworkers.

August 11, 2016—
Heaviest studded belt created

A DIY belt created out of no fewer than 200 pyramid studs broke records as the "heaviest belt ever made," thanks to the diligent work of local punk Charlene Sodi. The belt now successfully outweighs the already-heavy jeans it was intended to hold up, thereby rendering itself entirely useless.

February 9, 2017—
Regular-ass trip to CVS inspires eight new Menzingers songs

A quick trip to a Wilkes-Barre, Pennsylvania, drugstore somehow inspired The Menzingers frontman Greg Barnett to pen nearly a full album's worth of songs. The story arc follows a younger Barnett as he ventures into the store in search of toothpaste, but instead found at the cash register a "sad face with a wild heart" with whom he promptly fell in love, looked for shooting stars, drifted apart from, stayed together with anyway for way too long because the fear of being alone is sometimes deeper than the fear of accepting loss for what it is, eventually broke up with, and now recalls fondly any time he sees a kite in a park, all within the span of twenty minutes.

September 29, 2017—
Mix CD responsible for developmental growth during adolescence featured in Instagram story documenting most embarrassing moments of woman's life

A mix CD comprising songs that contributed to the emotional development of San Antonio woman Monse Delgado when she was in high school was dismissed as "embarrassing LOL" in a recent Instagram story. Featuring the Portishead song she lost her virginity to in ninth grade and the Propagandhi track that led to her first four-year vegetarian stint, the CD became the subject of a 15-second video bearing only the inscription "#cringefest #90s."

The HARD Times

Band Pretty Sure It's Safe to Park Van Here Overnight

BY MATT SAINCOME

DETROIT—Embarking on their first tour, members of ClearlyxStraight are pretty sure it's safe to park their van in a dark, crime-ridden alleyway overnight, sources maintained.

"Dude, whatever. I'm tired, and it's getting way too fucking late. Just park the damn thing," said Casey Rodriguez, the band's drummer and soon-to-be Kickstarter manager. "We'll be totally fucked if we park on the street and end up getting a ticket. At least if we park the van here near the dumpsters, nobody will be able to see it from the main road."

Other members of the band were just as enthusiastic about leaving their equipment in a dimly lit alley in a bad part of town.

"In our hearts and in our minds, united, together, the only thing we need to worry about is if all this shattered glass is going to pop our tires," frontman Daniel Morgan preached to the back seat as he pulled into the spot. "Nobody will touch our stuff, keep the faith."

The Detroit Police Department had hoped their "break-in area" signs would keep drivers from parking their cars in areas they deemed dangerous, but the program has seemingly failed to inform one key demographic: touring bands.

"You're basically giving your gear away by parking in this neighborhood. It's probably better to just leave it unlocked so at least you won't have to replace any broken windows," said Sergeant Rick Caldwell. "Once they report their van was broken into, which they most certainly will, the best we can do is just offer them a map with some of the city's more popular pawn shops."

Update: ClearlyxStraight is reporting via Facebook that all of their equipment and merchandise has been stolen. The estimated value of these missing items is around $350.

The HARD Times

Ex-Girlfriend Totally Normal Now

BY BILL CONWAY

OLYMPIA, Wash.—Local punk Kyle Watkins, 33, made the startling discovery that his ex-girlfriend Erin Wallace is now a completely normal and productive member of society, follow-up Facebook searches confirmed.

"Erin and I dated for three crazy years, man. I was kind of drunk and feeling a little lonely so I decided to look her up. I couldn't believe what I was seeing—she was wearing regular jeans without any holes, and a button-up shirt. Worst of all, she had this super reasonable, age-appropriate haircut," said Watkins about his former pit-warrior/lover. "It's completely symmetrical, dude."

Wallace, known as "Bulldogg" during her punk days and a staple of the Olympia scene in the early 2000s, was known for her aggressive dance moves and willingness to mix it up with anyone looking for a fight. The recent discovery that she is now married to a salesman for advanced medical prosthetics and a mother of two young boys has shaken Watkins to his core.

"I never thought I would see the day. This is the same girl who bit the cap off a beer bottle because no one had an opener," Watkins said. "There was even one time when a fire marshal tried shutting down a show in her basement so she hate-moshed the guy till he ran away sobbing. It was nuts."

When asked to comment on the situation, Wallace responded via email from her three-bedroom, two-bath suburban home outside of Oklahoma City.

"Oh yeah, my infamous hardcore days? When I went to college, I sort of unleashed a new side of myself and may have lost control a little bit, but I like my life now. My boys are a handful, but to be honest, I would rather get peed on by one of them than some random guy on stage who thinks he's the reincarnation of GG Allin," the former punk said. "Plus I drive a Range Rover now."

Watkins also confirmed that his Facebook stalking led to the discovery that his high-school best friend is now a cop and "absolutely does not" want to get the band back together.

Deafheaven Bassist Falls Asleep Onstage

BY JOSH FERNANDEZ

PORTLAND, Ore.—Bassist Chris Johnson was lulled to sleep in the middle of Deafheaven's Red Bull Sound Select show in Portland last night, according to music critics raving that he snoozed through the band's ambient shoegaze black-metal bullshit perfectly.

"It was a flawless performance—just absolutely flawless. These guys are creating a new genre," one pundit wrote on his Pitchfork worship blog. "When he started snoring, I knew I was witnessing the best set of the year, possibly of the century."

This was just one of many positive reviews following the seemingly endless set.

"They are just so dark; I've never seen anything like it. I can't even wrap my head around how they get that dark," said journalist Terry Harris.

Johnson explained the cause of his sudden lapse into unconsciousness.

"I was standing there, laying down the bass line for 'Vertigo,' when I felt this warm calmness wash over my body. It was like I was all wrapped up in one of our signature Deafheaven Blankets™, being gently rocked from side to side," he said.

The next thing Johnson remembered was Deafheaven guitarist Kerry McCoy kicking him in the ass and yelling "This isn't fucking funny!" while the band attempted to finish the song.

"I was tired too, but I would never fall asleep on stage," said McCoy. "This isn't a fucking joke. Everyone was laughing, but it's not fucking funny. We're creating a new genre."

Deafheaven is no stranger to controversy. After canceling a tour due to lost luggage containing all of their black clothing, the band's rider was leaked to the public. It stated that each band member requires three lint rollers before taking the stage.

The Hard Times reached out to the Deafheaven vocalist for comment, but his response was too low in the mix for us to understand.

The HARD Times

Crust-Punk House Made Entirely out of Patches

BY MATT SAINCOME

AUSTIN, Texas—Following years of haphazard repairs and DIY construction attempts, a local crust-punk house is now made entirely out of patches, multiple astounded sources confirmed.

"It started out of necessity. We threw a show in the kitchen and someone punched a hole in the wall, so I took a Toxic Narcotic patch off my pants to cover it up. That worked well, so when the ceiling in living room started falling apart, I used my Discharge butt-flap to seal it. Eventually we were patching patches with patches and, well, just look at it," said housemate Derek Garner, motioning to the sloppily stitched-together dwelling that hosts touring bands most weekends. "I've found that hipster D-beat and crust band patches are better suited for the house's exterior than '90s street-punk. We use those ones inside."

Some within the scene have criticized Garner for not having listened to some of the bands whose patches are holding up the modest house.

"Yo, I fucking heard he bought the Graf Orlock patch that's holding the bathroom together off of Etsy," said longtime Austinite Tiesha Kelliher. "The house might be made out of patches, but straight up, it is built on a foundation of lies."

Despite the criticism, Garner is more concerned about the authorities than his fellow punks.

"The city and our landlord are freaking out about us not having any load-bearing walls. But our house isn't 100 percent patches; there are studs in there," he said. "English 77 cone studs—we got 'em off Angry, Young and Poor."

City officials have been in talks for several years about demolishing the house, especially after the election of a more conservative mayor who is allegedly hell-bent on "cleaning up the city's trash." But the 16 punks and 12 bandanna-wearing dogs who call the patch house home remain optimistic.

"Oh yeah, everyone is always talking about kicking us out. It'll never happen. I've been living here for three years and I've never even paid rent," said the ringworm fungus living on the couch. "This is our home, and I'll be damned if I'm going to let the city unstitch the bonds I've made with its residents."

The Hard Times Gets Back Together

As remembered by Managing Editor Krissy Howard

After spending years quietly working as a staff writer in what I would call the "suicidal, at best" conditions of the cramped NYC office of *The Hard Times,* I was finally free to honor my own calling. Thanks to the company's collapse, I was able to pack a suitcase and hit the road to chase my dream of landing literally any other editorial position in the country.

I had barely made it out of Jersey when I got an alert from my bank stating that a home loan I'd never applied for near Bakersfield, California, had been approved. Reviewing my finances, I discovered that I'd been listed as a cosigner on multiple loans, property purchases, and questionable contracts for "experimental equine insemination practices," all initiated by my former boss and weaselly fuckhead, Matt Saincome. Matt had stolen my Social Security number and listed me as a guarantor on several large purchases, leaving me in crippling debt. I cursed myself for not knowing better. In fact, I knew that I should have quit *The Hard Times* as soon as I learned that it was not, in fact, a quarterly journal of literary erotica as I had initially assumed.

I had to get Bill and Matt back together to make this right. As neither even remotely possesses any marketable real-world skills with which to eventually repay me, the only way to restore my credit was to get the zine back on the map, using a little something our youngest and most tech-savvy editor, Jeremy Kaplowitz, referred to as "the internet." The internet--much like emotional intimacy and Indian food--was an unfamiliar and therefore frightening place to me at that time, but I had to get over my fear in order to get my checking account unfrozen. Doing this would eventually lead to the site as it exists today.

Bill wasn't difficult to find, as anyone south of Savannah could recall the obnoxious, albeit effective, jingle he created in an effort at reinvention: "555-2183, call Bill Conway, the Scuba King of the Keys." Immediately following the collapse of Hard Times Media LLC, Bill had reinvented himself as the "Scuba King" of the Florida Keys despite not being certified or even knowing how to swim, and having a debilitating allergy to "the environment."

Finding Matt proved far more difficult; his horse tranquilizer addiction made him a tough man to track down. Luckily, with the help of an aptly named guy named "Guy," I uncovered my former boss cowering in the corner of a squat, talking to a pile of old jeans.

A lie about an unlimited source of tranquilizers let me to lead Matt all the way to Chicago, where another lie about Riot Fest ad packages had Bill awaiting our arrival. This reunion of the zine's founders meant *The Hard Times* was back in business.

BREAKING: Singer Billy Joel Quits Green Day

BY DREW KAUFMAN

LONG ISLAND, N.Y.—Singer-songwriter Billy Joel revealed today that he has quit Green Day and, going forward, will no longer have any association with the band, stunned sources confirmed.

"The rumors are true. It is with great sorrow that after almost 30 years as a fan, I've chosen to leave Green Day behind me. At first, I loved their poppy and punky sound, but this past decade it seems like they've done everything possible to piss me off," Joel said in a Facebook post this morning. "The outfits, the crowd lighting, the musical—this isn't the same Green Day I once loved."

Green Day started as a punk band in 1986. After a few years of playing small clubs, Billy Joel is now best known for playing sold-out shows at Madison Square Garden.

"He may be right. He may be crazy. Either way it hurts knowing he isn't a fan of anything we've done since 'Minority,'" said Green Day bassist Mike Dirnt. "But no hard feelings. I still think Billy Joel is the best songwriter in the world, and he always has a VIP space in our fan club if he wants it."

Since facing DUI charges in the early 2000s, Billy Joel has publicly struggled with his substance abuse. However, the rock icon claimed to be sober and clear-headed long before announcing his plans to leave the band behind.

"Maybe one day I'll be able to listen to those old albums and feel something, but until then, I'm putting *Kerplunk* in a box and keeping it in the garage next to my copy of *River of Dreams,*" the piano man said. "To all the Green Day fans out there, I just want to say keep fighting the good fight. You are stronger than I am."

There is no word at this time on what the Long Islander's next musical infatuation will be.

"It's really tough to say what the future holds," said Billy Joel. "But what I *can* say is that I've really been getting into podcasts lately. If you have any good recommendations, feel free to email them to me."

Male-Fronted Hardcore Band Proves That Guys Can Rock Too

BY MATT SAINCOME

BALTIMORE—Suffrage, a new all-male hardcore band, is a group of radical-minded men intent on proving once and for all that guys can rock too.

"Suffrage plays fast, loud, and aggressive which is not something you might expect from a bunch of dudes," said guitarist "Nasty" Nate Garcia. "We don't care how many times we get stopped at the door of a venue and asked if we're dating one of the women in the band—we're here to shake things up in a scene that has historically been a girls' club."

Members of the guy group are unapologetic when it comes to showing off their bodies on stage.

"If I get all hot and sweaty, you better believe I'm gonna take off my shirt, and if you don't like that, well, get used to it," said frontman "Big" Tim Ramsey, proudly sporting lengthy

armpit hair for anyone to see. "I don't wear sleeveless shirts for you; I wear sleeveless shirts for me. So if you can't handle a full-bodied man in a position of power, then don't come to our shows."

Suffrage has already received glowing praise across multiple social media platforms.

"The vocalist is so good you can hardly tell he's a guy," tweeted @AmandaJames. "And look at the bassist in his cute little shorts. Uh yeah, #would."

During a recent performance with six other all-male hardcore acts, Ramsey had a bold message for the crowd.

"You might not like the thought of men playing in hardcore bands, and it might be tough for you to wrap your little head around, but dudes are here to stay. Guys to the fucking front."

The HARD Times

Man Clearly Yelling Gibberish During Sing-Along Part

BY BILL CONWAY

CHICAGO—Fans of popular hardcore band Without Mercy were outraged this weekend when they discovered that a man was clearly just yelling gibberish during a popular sing-along part of the band's hit song "Time to Die," multiple heavily tattooed sources confirmed.

"I was doing my thing singing it back when, out of nowhere, there was this guy climbing all over my back, yelling non-sense into the mic," reported fan Brendan Burke. "I spent lots of time in my car memorizing these lyrics, so I know for a fact this guy was screaming the wrong words. It really threw me off my game, and I missed a crucial pile-on."

Fans were further bothered when the man started clapping before songs had ended and was caught singing along to a new, unrecorded song.

"This guy was a complete goon. He was even trying to mosh between songs. I kept thinking *Why are you here, man? Do you even know this band?* every time he pulled that crap," said scene staple Mike Hobart. "When TJ, the singer, said, 'If you know the words, get up front,' this guy had the nerve to push past me and start pounding the stage. Ridiculous, man."

Members of Without Mercy were understandably irate at the young showgoer's attempt at participation.

"Sing-alongs are a time-honored tradition at hardcore shows," said guitarist Keith Howard. "Historically they've identified who knows the lyrics the best, which also proves who likes the band the most and has the most credibility. Randomly yelling nonsense like that is an insult to every-thing hardcore stands for."

When reached for comment, the man in question replied, "Argh blarg watermelonwatermelon LIVING A LIE!" adding "test press sundress, TIME TO DIE!"

Merch Guy Puts Off School, Family to Pursue Dream of Tagging Along

BY NICK CONWAY

DULUTH, Minn.—Merch guy Kyle Hook bucked societal norms by putting education and family aside while hitting the open road to pursue his dream of tagging along with his more successful friends in bands, disclose loved ones who wish he would grow up a little.

"I don't mind if the guys force me inside a drum case and put me in the trailer; I know they'll let me out if they need someone to do an overnight drive while they nap," said Hook of his new role with Next To Tomorrow. "It's like they say: 'Behind every great band is a great merch guy, in the trailer, alone.'"

Hook is constantly battling the difficult truth that although the life of a touring band may seem glamorous to "outsiders," it's anything but.

"Do you know how hard it is to sleep on the floor of a van? Last night I used a bag full of burger wrappers as a pillow. Will I wake up tomorrow and want to do it all again? Probably not, but I will," said the hanger-on, who gave up a full scholarship to UM-Duluth to sell shirts and pins. "But ever since I was the water boy on my peewee football team, I knew I wanted to be kind of a part of something great."

"I was watching all my friends following their dreams and their passions. And what was I doing? Sitting in a classroom like a dick, texting my girlfriend and planning my mother's 55th birthday party. I was fucking miserable," Hook added.

Next To Tomorrow guitarist Trevor Simms initially recruited Hook to be their merch guy, effectively changing the young man's life for the worse.

"I just straight up said to him, 'Hey man, we need a merch guy. I totally understand if you don't want to come along—it's kind of a shitty job. We can't really pay you and you'll need to pitch in for gas, but it's yours if you want it,'" said Simms. "Kyle's face just lit up. I know how much he likes to watch others succeed while he just sorta hangs out. You could tell his dream was unfolding before his eyes."

Next To Tomorrow is currently in the middle of a week-and-a-half-long tour of the Midwest. With most members still in college, they have a very strict touring window.

"We're all working toward a degree or have a full-time job. I genuinely have no idea why Kyle quit college and dumped his girlfriend for this. And he keeps talking about getting our logo tatted on his neck," Simms added. "None of us even have tattoos."

Police Use Axe Body Spray to Break Up Crust-Punk Protest

BY JEREMY WHITE

NEW YORK—NYPD officers deployed Axe Body Spray to disperse a group of crust-punk protesters after what they called a "biochemical provocation," sources desperately trying to get the smell out of their mouths confirmed.

"We treated several punks who were exposed to the men's fragrance. Injuries varied based on proximity to the blast," said Dr. Caroline Corcoran of NYU Langone Medical Center. "Some protesters suffered severe side effects such as a sudden affinity toward plaid shorts, uncontrollable use of the word 'bro,' and a strong craving for Coors Light."

The violence erupted after nearly 200 crust- and anarcho-punks took to the streets to demonstrate against a recent city ordinance requiring all dogs be properly vaccinated and identified.

"These dogs live on a steady diet of discarded street food and can often be found in crowded basements where loud, horrible music is played," said New York Animal Control officer Susan Branch. "For the safety of the animals and the residents of this great city, we need to properly identify and care for these creatures. Simply writing the dog's name on a stained bandanna just doesn't cut it."

One protester, who would only identify himself as "Nuggets," claims that he was directly hit.

"We wanted to stand up for our pets' right to remain anonymous, but now I reek like a frat house, bro," said Nuggets. "If I wanted to smell like this, I would've finished my marketing degree."

"To be honest, I'm not sure which is worse, the protesters' body odor or the spray. It's like burning cheap potpourri in a sewer," said area resident Anna Wilson. "I really hope it rains soon so this stink will stop lingering in the air."

A law enforcement official who spoke on the condition of anonymity defended the use of the popular body spray in corralling the protesters.

"We have proven time and again that we aren't afraid of chemical warfare in situations like this. Pepper spray and rubber bullets can't penetrate dreadlocks and Crass patches, so, to restore order, we needed to make these punks smell like a lacrosse team," said the unnamed officer.

As of press time, the public is asked to stay away from the Axe blast area for fear residual scent could cause a sudden interest in longboarding and cornhole.

Hardcore Singer
Accidentally Swallows Microphone

BY BILL CONWAY

CLEVELAND—Live It Down lead vocalist Eric Sarno turned a recent show into an abject scene of horror when he accidentally swallowed the venue's only working microphone, reported witnesses.

"He does the 'microphone in mouth' move all the time," said bassist Jake Mainini. "Nobody saw this coming though. We'd joke about it, but the time for jokes is over. Now we have to pay for that mic out of the band fund, which sucks because we actually thought we might make money on tonight's show."

Reports indicate Sarno was bouncing around onstage with the microphone in his mouth when he was inadvertently struck on the back by a man attempting a stage dive. It then disappeared down Sarno's throat, leaving show attendees scrambling for where to shout the lyrics.

"Some of us started yelling into his belly, as if he were pregnant. Others yelled down his throat. It was sheer pandemonium," said show patron Marie Daniels.

"I had it under control. I knew I just needed a few minutes and maybe some coffee and then everything would be back to normal," said Sarno after the ordeal. "Someone yelled that I should 'pull a GG!' and puke the thing up and keep playing, but I don't know, I didn't want [the mic] to chip a tooth on the way out."

Show promoter Rob Wilford was not pleased with the situation.

"It was unprofessional. We hold these guys to a certain standard, and swallowing a mic is as rookie of a move as playing out of tune or covering the same band twice in one set," he said.

All signs point to the singer making a full recovery, but the microphone was not so lucky.

"We have to throw it out. Most mics are gross enough with spit and other bodily fluids, but I can't justify using one that was partially digested," said Wilford. "Besides, this mic had a good run. The thing survived four shows, which is a new record."

Sarno is currently recuperating at home, spending his time bragging on the internet about being the first vocalist "to finally make this happen."

The HARD Times

Bassist Quits Band Over Unending Group Text

BY MATT SAINCOME

HAVERHILL, Mass.—Greg Feldman, bassist for local hard-core outfit Forever Rises, decided to quit his band following a 78-hour uninterrupted group text between the other four members, sources close to the band confirmed.

"I couldn't focus at work because my phone was blowing up every few seconds with someone saying they found a cheap van on Craigslist, or that Afroman should front Screeching Weasel," said Feldman of the iMessage thread meant to discuss practice times or the band's upcoming EP. "I mean, yeah, a cheap van would be nice and Afroman is certainly qualified, but I have shit to do other than reading texts about who's the hottest member of Destiny's Child."

Feldman asserted that the constant barrage lead to a noticeable dip in his quality of life.

"I was getting bummed out every time I felt my phone vibrate," the bassist reported. "All day, all night . . . unending. Someone would say that we should start color-coordinating for our 'band image,' and then it'd just be three hours of sending each other the poop emoji."

When asked about the group chat, other members of Forever Rises described it as a mixture of personal observations, wrestling GIFs, and Tom DeLonge links.

"I personally thought it was great," said Michael Henderson, the band's frontman. "It was making us closer as a band, sharing laughs and inside jokes. Man, this shit is hilarious. Greg just didn't get it."

"Greg was always a turd boy," said guitarist Lawrence McKenzie through an emoji-ridden text. "I'm breaking out the most prime Barstool Sports links and Gronk GIFs—which I call 'Grifs'—and he's not even responding. Seriously, GRIFS—how good is that?!"

According to Feldman, the last straw came when McKenzie sent a picture of himself brushing his teeth totally naked, with only a head of broccoli covering his genitals.

"It's not just that the text came while I was in a meeting with my boss," remarked Feldman, adding that his decision to leave the band went unnoticed for another 347 texts. "It was that they all thought that shit was hilarious. When people ask, I'm just going to say I left over creative differences."

Local Man Insists Scene Died When He Stopped Going to Shows

BY RYAN CLARK

ASTORIA, N.Y.—Recently retired punk-community member David Gorman insists the scene died at the exact same time he stopped going to shows, and he's been continuously stating this fact to anyone willing to listen.

"This scene is so fucking dead now," Gorman explained from his spot on a barstool at Diamond Dogs, his local watering hole. "I used to go see bands play all the time, but the second I stopped going, it's like the punk scene vanished. The same thing happened when I stopped reading comic books—I never see those things around anymore."

Bar patrons in close proximity to the ex-punk tried explaining that people do in fact still attend shows and that comic books are more popular than ever, but Gorman put his fingers in his ears and chanted, "La, la, la, la, la, I'm not listening to you, la, la, la," in an obvious act of defiance.

When asked to reminisce about the last show he attended, he had a hard time recalling the details.

"God, I haven't thought about that in a while; I quit maybe four or five months ago. It was Drilldriver at The Outhouse," said Gorman. "You have to understand, it was a different time: Music meant something back then. People were terrified because North Korea didn't want us to see *The Interview*. It was winter, so we all wore sweaters, even indoors. Drilldriver was at the center of it all, and everything changed when they broke up."

Drilldriver frontman Victor Alvarez explained the reasoning behind the band's sudden breakup.

"Drilldriver? Oh, that was just a joke band. We only played, like, four shows, and we just fucked around," said Alvarez. "You should check out my new band, Fuzz Top, next Friday. Bunch of people are gonna be coming out for that one."

Although Gorman misses those few months he was involved in the punk scene, he does say things have gotten better. "I'm 21 now, so that's pretty cool."

Mid-Twenties Hardcore Fan Enters His "Liking Hockey" Phase

BY BILL CONWAY

BOSTON—Self-described "hardcore kid" Jared Mahoney came to the realization that he is ready to enter the "liking hockey" phase of his life while watching the recent series between the Calgary Flames and Vancouver Canucks, sources confirmed.

"I was getting drunk with my dad at his apartment while he was watching the game, and these players started fighting like wild dogs. Something just clicked," said Mahoney. "I've put this chapter of my life on hold for so long, but once I saw a dude spit out four teeth and keep going, I knew the time was right. I'm ready to dive into all of the weird last names and violence the game has to offer."

Although Mahoney has watched less than three hours of hockey in his life, it has not stopped him from forming strict, unflinching opinions about his newly adopted favorite team.

"My Bruins might not be in the running for the Cup this year, but I am confident that we'll be back and better than ever next year," he said while perusing a series of Bruins tattoos on Instagram. "All we need is to draft a guy who can get the puck in the net, not like these other washed-up bums who aren't even fit to skate on my uncle's cranberry bogs."

Hockey remains the sixth most popular sport in the United States but is quickly becoming the sport of choice for hardcore kids. Some experts predict it could rise to second most popular for hardcore kids during years without a World Cup.

"If there's one thing hardcore kids love, it's having a deep knowledge of subjects the general public could care less about," said psychologist Dr. Colleen Harrow. "Also, hockey is the ideal sport for hardcore kids of a certain age who are no longer as athletic in the pit, but still have high levels of pent-up aggression."

While Mahoney has expressed deep love for the sport, he does have some criticisms.

"I think the refs sometimes need to just back off and let the guys fight. Also, the puck is hard for me to see a lot of the time," he added. "I sort of wish it was highlighted on the screen like it was when I was a kid."

Kim Jong-un Appoints Himself New Supreme Lead Singer of Black Flag

BY JEFF CARDELLO

PYEONGYANG, North Korea—Kim Jong-un, leader of the Workers' Party of Korea, shocked the Western world when he announced himself as the new supreme lead singer of Black Flag, geopolitical experts disclosed.

"Our most benevolent leader, whose voice shakes the mountains of the fatherland like a mighty drum, shall lead Black Flag to the delight of the North Korean people and everyone in the universe," read an update on the official website of the Democratic People's Republic of Korea. "We will rise above."

The rare press release further stated that "Kim Jong-un could recite every Black Flag lyric from memory by the age of three." It also featured never-before-seen photos of the young leader that reveal a birthmark on his upper right arm that bears a striking resemblance to the punk band's iconic four-bar logo.

"What we know so far is that Kim was installed as the new vocalist during a recent gig in Australia," said CNN reporter Christiane Amanpour. "Fans in attendance told me that with only two songs left in the set, he grabbed the microphone from former singer Mike Vallely and allegedly said, 'You're done—the Workers' Party is taking over.'"

Dennis Rodman, the flamboyant former professional basketball player and unlikely friend of Kim Jong-un, responded to the news.

"Yo, look, Kim loves Black Flag, and I say that America loves Black Flag, so let's start there," stated Rodman. "He's a true fan; he has bootleg recordings of Black Flag shows that most people probably don't even know occurred. He's also a vocal critic of *What The . . .*, and has promised he'll only play songs we all know and love."

This new and presumably final incarnation of Black Flag will reportedly perform all of the classics, with Kim Jong-un contributing his own takes. Comprising their new set list will be songs such as "My War (with South Korea)," "Rise Above (South Korea)," and "In My Head (the Virtuous Words of the Most Exalted Leader of the Most Prosperous Nation, Kim Jong-un)."

The HARD Times

First Person to Arrive at Show Unsuccessfully Attempts to Appear Busy on Phone

BY GREG MCGONAGLE

ORLEANS, Mass.—Earlier today Golden Grave ticketholder Nick Cascarella made a desperate attempt to appear busy on his phone upon arriving to a show several hours before doors were scheduled to open, perplexed venue staff confirmed.

"Of course I got here early on purpose," said Cascarella. "I needed to respond to some work emails and I couldn't do that with all the distractions at home. I'm so happy that none of my friends decided to come to the show with me, that's for sure."

Employees setting up for that night's performance reported Cascarella's charade was one of the most transparent attempts at appearing busy they had ever witnessed.

"I was running some trash to the dumpster when I noticed the dude, phone in hand, scratching his chin like he was making some big decision," said dishwasher Zack Martin. "But when I looked over his shoulder, I saw that the screen asking for his password."

Bartender Brittany Tomkin also was not convinced.

"I glanced over at him and he was silently cracking up as if he was having a funny conversation with someone and thought to myself, *'Why the hell is he here this early? There's a mall four blocks away, you know. Just go hang out there in the air conditioning,'*" she said.

While Martin and Tomkin saw straight through the performance, sound guy Frank Marasco was a bit more forgiving.

"When I first showed up and was talking with the door guy, I'll admit he had me fooled for a second. I was convinced he was sending a text, or at least checking email," said Marasco. "I thought he must be a tour manager, then I remembered the closest thing any of these bands have to a tour manager is their bass player."

During the opening band's set, it was reported that Cascarella was conspicuously absent. However, it was later confirmed that he was charging his phone at the only empty outlet behind a stack of chairs in the back room.

Portland Trash Core Band Outed as Three Raccoons With a Drum Machine

BY JUSTIN LENTZ

PORTLAND, Ore.—Stink Bandits, a heavily hyped local trash core band, were outed as nothing more than three raccoons and a drum machine after their record release party was broken up by police responding to a series of noise complaints, law enforcement officials reported.

"In a joint operation with Southeast Animal Control, Portland Police Bureau investigated an abandoned building in relation to complaints from neighborhood residents," said spokesperson Duff Fallon. "When we arrived, there was an abnormally large pile of garbage on the front yard separating the band from a crowd of punks. After scaling the massive wall of rubbish, officers and animal handlers discovered the discordance was being performed by a small group of feral raccoons, who release music in the form of limited-edition cassette tapes under the name Stink Bandits."

In recent months, Stink Bandits have been the leading edge of the trash core, a movement that, according to a reputable trash core online forum, promotes "musical chaos, dumpster diving, and washing your food before you eat it."

"Part of the appeal of Stink Bandits was that nobody knew who they were," said longtime fan Kerry Lampley. "There were even rumors that Banksy was involved, but now that we know the truth, I can't tell if I like them more or think they're sellouts."

One Stink Bandits fan was particularly upset by the revelation his favorite band was a group of nocturnal mammals.

"About nine months ago, I hit a raccoon with my car. Stink Bandits took a hiatus around that same time, and now I'm afraid I killed a member," said 18-year-old Taylor Allen, blinking back tears.

Authorities are shocked that followers of the group were unaware that the musicians they loved were, in fact, disease-infested scavengers.

"As officers, little surprises us. On this call, we'd presumed this was a typical southeast gaze of raccoons; we had no idea they were actually local celebrities," said Animal Control officer Mike Stephens. "I still don't know how they figured out how to program a drum machine."

Stink Bandits are currently being held at the Multnomah animal shelter but are scheduled to be released into Mount Tabor to complete their citywide Trashcan Tipping Tour.

Tall Guy Finds Perfect Woman to Stand in Front of at Show

BY BILL CONWAY

AUSTIN, Texas—After wandering around aimlessly during the first two opening bands, the tallest guy in the room has finally found the perfect woman to stand in front of for the duration of tonight's show, frustrated sources with obstructed views confirmed.

Witnesses estimate the man stands at a sturdy 6'3".

"This happens at every show," said short-of-stature show-goer Katie Washington, who arrived at the venue early to avoid this exact situation. "I got here 30 minutes before doors and found a prime location off to the side of the stage, but when I went to the bathroom, I lost my spot. Now I'm forced to stare at this guy's sweaty back for the rest of this set. Cool."

The incident is just the latest in one of the most time-honored traditions at live music events. Last year, upward of 75 percent of women of show-going age reported having to deal with views eclipsed by oblivious men who, more often than not, had a beer in each hand and yelled at seemingly random times.

"Honestly, it seemed like he could predict every move I was going to make. If I went to get a drink and then found a new spot, he would slip right back in front of me less than a minute later," said Washington while trying to squeeze around the man in question. "Am I just being paranoid? This seems like a deliberate attempt to block me from seeing anything that happens on stage."

Dave Olsen, another tall man in attendance, easily observed the situation from a distance.

"I saw her too. As soon as I walked in, I knew that was the girl I wanted to stand in front of, but that other goon got there before me. I had to settle for a girl who's awfully persistent and keeps nudging my back," said Olsen as he deliberately stiffened up and stood closer to the man next to him to prevent the young lady behind him from seeing anything. "This chick is really impeding my ability to enjoy the show."

Whole Foods Break Room Becomes Impromptu Band Reunion

BY RICK HOMUTH

OKLAHOMA CITY—A Whole Foods break room, normally reserved for 15-minute shift breaks and minor clerical duties, was transformed into the site of an impromptu reunion of the thrash band Wretched Breath, excited witnesses reported.

"I had just finished restocking the hot bar with this bomb-ass quinoa salad before heading back for a much-needed break," said Whole Foods employee Diego Abreu. "Sure enough, as soon as I open the door, I see my old bass player Pete fucking Leibowitz. We hadn't talked in years, but I guess he started cashiering here after being fired from the post office."

The two along with Matthew Hartwell (head pastry chef and part-time drummer) are all ex-members of Wretched Breath. The band broke up unceremoniously in 2007, citing "personal differences" on their official Myspace page.

"When I walked in and saw Diego eating an egg salad sandwich with that stupid 'I just farted and it smells bad' grin of his, I almost quit on the spot," said Marconi of his former bandmate. "We hadn't talked in so long, I figured he'd moved to Portland like he'd always talked about. He put on a lot of weight, so I hardly recognized him, but his terrible hand tattoos gave it away."

Though all three now work at the same Whole Foods location, sources close to the band say there is little chance of an official reunion.

"I doubt they'll be playing music together anytime soon," said mutual friend and coworker Kathleen Gallo. "Diego once told me that Pete urinated on Brandon's tom-toms when he was drunk before a 'gig.' Is that what you call it, a 'gig?' Or is it a concert? Either way, apparently they haven't really talked outside of a few passive-aggressive Facebook and Instagram likes."

When pressed for comment, Marconi had little to say about Leibowitz.

"Fuck that dude. With his tiny bladder, there's no way he'll last here," Marconi said before leaving to hose down the floor mats behind the deli counter. "Honestly, I'll probably ask to work the early shift so I don't have to see either of those dudes anymore."

Update: Sources confirmed that another reunion, this time of militant straight-edge band Honor Pledge in the store's security department, ended very poorly for a customer who "broke his word" in the dairy aisle.

Legendary Punk Venue Now Just a Normal Basement

BY GREG MCGONAGLE

BRIGHTON, Mass.—Legendary basement venue the Pizza Dungeon is being converted back into a normal basement, leaving a void in the city's landscape of awful-smelling, poorly ventilated DIY venues, sorrowful sources confirmed.

"First CBGB's turns into a bullshit suit store, then The Rat was torn down to make way for a luxury hotel, and now this. Fuck, man, the first time I saw Chain Breakers was at the Pizza Dungeon," reflected frequent attendee Jason Collier. "Some kid kept requesting they play covers, so Mickey Chain grabbed him by the neck and repeatedly smashed his face into the fuse box. All the electricity in the house turned on and off with every other blow; it was like a cartoon. I didn't realize a face was capable of bleeding that much."

The illegal all-ages venue has been a staple of the Boston hardcore scene for the past 24 months, with the exception of a brief period in December when the water heater was broken due to a poorly timed stage dive.

"The Dungeon was the best thing that ever happened to me," said Matt Carroll, the venue's only consistent tenant and primary show booker. "However, in the past few months, Comcast has really been screwing us. They keep raising their rate and telling us it's the cheapest in the area. With football season finally here, I need to move somewhere I can get DirecTV and the Sunday Ticket."

But not everyone will miss the legendary space.

"This place is a mess," said landlord Chris Hanley during the final walk-through. "These assholes can kiss their security deposit goodbye. Thank god the new tenants aren't some punk kids—they'll treat this basement with the respect it deserves."

Despite losing the venue, many regulars remained optimistic.

"I'll miss that place, sure," said Janet Porter, a local squatter who often used the venue as a temporary residence. "But at least it's not being converted into a Dunkin' Donuts."

The HARD Times

Crust Punk Disgusted by Local Dumpster's Lack of Vegan Options

BY DREW KAUFMAN

TUCSON, Ariz.—A local crust punk who asked to be identified as "Tik Tak" was disgusted to learn that the two new dumpsters placed behind the Frontier Village Shopping Center refused to serve vegan options, attested multiple hungry sources.

"We separate glass from aluminum," said the malnourished millennial, who is not forced to live this way but does so by choice. "Why not [separate] meat-based waste from plant-based waste? I'm not being picky, I just don't want to contribute to the suffering of animals while I'm trying to avoid contributing to capitalism."

Tik Tak has adhered to a vegan diet for the past five years, inspired by her friends The Cardbored Boyz, who can often be found licking plastic packages at the recycling bin near the Jamba Juice.

"You know, it's one thing to pick coffee grinds and used ketchup packets off of a killer vegan donut—I'm totally fine

with that," said a local punk known only as Dribbles. "But I'll have to throw out a perfectly good piece of day-old bread if it's sitting next to a quarter-full cup of Matcha Green Tea Blast. When will this mall realize not *everyone* eating out of the dumpster is freegan?"

Mall staff admitted they have no plans to accommodate their vegan-but-not-freegan crust-punk customers in the future.

"Trash is trash, it all goes to the damn landfill. I'm not going to put up with being called 'bloodmouth' just because I won't fill one of these dumpsters with tofu," said Rob Gainly, a mall maintenance worker. "It's not my job to be their personal cafeteria worker—go to the damn Whole Foods and buy some rice already."

As of press time, Tik Tak was seen loudly complaining in a Starbucks parking lot about the complete lack of dairy-free alternatives in the coffee she had stolen from unaware customers.

Straight-Edge Friend Total Scumbag in Every Other Way Possible

BY DAN LUBERTO

BANGOR, Maine—Local man Kyle Matthews has a corrupt moral character that has led many to describe him as "the biggest scumbag walking the planet," despite living a lifestyle completely free of drug and alcohol use.

"He used to be a cool guy back when he listened to, like, Fat Wreck Chords and other punk stuff. But it seems like the day he got into hardcore and claimed edge, he also made a vow to be a gigantic throbbing dickbag on every level possible," said Matthews' brother, Pete, who recently let Matthews borrow his car with a full tank of gas and had it returned empty.

Many of Matthews' closest friends verified that despite the sober lifestyle advertised on many articles of his clothing, he is indeed a terrible human with very little redeeming social value.

"He always suggests ordering pizza and then announces he 'doesn't have cash' once the delivery guy shows up. Then he proceeds to eat more slices than anyone and hogs all the breadsticks," said longtime friend Nicole Nelson. "He justi-fies it by saying we're all getting fat and he's doing us a favor, that piece of shit."

Accusations against Matthews range from the benign to illegal.

"Homie will gamble on anything and then take forever to pay you. I owed him money once after losing a game of Connect 4 and he took a swing at me," said George Smith, Matthews' coworker at Unlimited Screen Printing. "He said I was taking too long to pay him. It had been 45 minutes."

"All those 'one life drug free' tats don't stop him from going to bars and trying to pick up drunk girls," said Tonya Fuller, bartender at The Horse's Mouth. "He acts wasted then gets them to take an Uber home with him, and he always turns and winks at me as he's leaving. He's human trash."

When asked how he related to the lyrics in Minor Threat's lifestyle-defining songs, Matthews callously responded, "Fuck Minor Threat, fuck Ian, and fuck you. I've got better things to do than listen to that bullshit. Money over every-thing, bitch."

Bernie Sanders Launches GoFundMe After Tour Van Stolen Outside Debate

BY BILL CONWAY

LAS VEGAS—Presidential hopeful Bernie Sanders had his Ford Econoline tour van stolen from outside the Democratic debate Tuesday night, sources close to the Vermont junior senator confirmed.

"Let me be clear: It's not just the van I lost. I also lost my acoustic guitar, laptop, all my merch, and a binder that outlines my entire fiscal plan," said an emotional Sanders. "But I don't blame the criminal who did this; poverty is what drives crime, and if the government had been helping our disenfranchised citizens with healthcare and a living wage, then I wouldn't have lost all my damn CDs."

Sanders said he would be starting a grassroots campaign through the popular crowdsourcing site in hopes of recouping the cost of the van and valuables within.

"Honestly, I feel worse than I did the day the Supreme Court upheld the Citizens United decision. We need to get money out of politics and into this GoFundMe account so I can make it to the next debate," said the visibly frustrated candidate. "We need a revolution of millions of people coming together and donating $5, $10, or $20 to my GoFundMe."

Sanders is not the first politician to face a major setback on the campaign trail. Dennis Kucinich famously experienced a delay at a screen printing facility that led to an entire campaign tour with no merchandise, an error that many experts believe lost him the election.

"Senator Sanders will recover from this—it's just a small bump in the road," said political strategist Kerry McGough. "But until he gets a new van, he'll be sleeping on the futon in my living room. My wife is going to be pissed."

The candidate's advisors remain optimistic that he will return to the campaign trail stronger than ever.

"Motherfuckingshitfuck, I just realized my Fugazi tape was in there," said Sanders.

The HARD Times

Scene Historian Recounts Glory Days of Three Years Ago

BY BILL CONWAY

ST. PAUL, Minn.—Armed with a comprehensive knowledge of all punk and hardcore bands within a 50-mile radius of his home, local musician and amateur historian Kyle Adams recounted the glory days of the 2012 St. Paul underground music scene, fascinated sources reported.

"Man, shit was popping off three years ago. All the preppy kids were bumping that 'Call Me Maybe' song, but the scene still had the Bruise Necks wrecking shop, and The Turncoats had just released a demo cassette that basically redefined the genre," said Adams while lovingly scrolling through his Instagram timeline from three years ago. "We had the same energy of New York in '88, probably."

"We all used to go to The Firehouse on Friday nights, which ironically burned down in November 2012 when someone threw a lit cigarette into a trash can. It would've been easy enough to put out but the singer of Underbelly had emptied the fire extinguisher in one of the most epic pits I've ever seen. None of us could breathe—our eyes felt like someone was hitting them with a hammer made of rock salt. It was awesome," said a smiling Adams. "But that fire spread quickly and did a lot of property damage. A homeless outreach shelter was totally destroyed."

When asked to speculate on why the local scene had suffered in recent years, the 22-year-old historian had a variety of explanations.

"A lot of the dudes here broke edge and started playing in cover bands at bars on weekends to make some extra money, and those shows just aren't as fun. You can't really stage-dive to Aerosmith songs," said Adams. "Also, winters here suck, so basically everyone moves away as soon as they can."

He added, "The kids today will never get to see some of the most influential bands of this scene: Blood Diamonds, Chad Briggs and Blackhearts, and the incomparable Hopeless Eyes. I feel bad—they'll never understand."

Old Guy Looking Out of Place at Show Apparently Local Legend

BY ERIC CASERO

PHILADELPHIA—The mysterious old guy seen wandering around aimlessly at a hardcore show last night is apparently a local scene legend of some kind, early reports indicate.

"I saw this guy in super normal jeans and thought to myself, *Who would force their dad to come to this?*" said attendee Jana Moskowitz. "At one point, I overheard him say 'Let's get this show on the road, my dogs are barking' to seemingly nobody."

Sean Statham, lead vocalist of Life On Patrol, expressed concern for the man's safety, saying, "Hardcore shows can get violent. That old dude could end up breaking his hip if he's not careful."

Sources confirm Statham was unaware that the man was in fact Jack Lister, vocalist for legendary hardcore band Western Front, who was rumored to have beaten up both Glenn Danzig and the Philadelphia chief of police in the late 1980s.

"Maybe he has a bracelet with an emergency contact number on it or something," Statham said as he scrolled through his Nextdoor app to see if anyone had reported a lost relative.

The once-mighty Lister went unrecognized despite the ill-fitting hoodie emblazoned with "Western Front Straight Edge." Uninformed attendees were left confused as to why a man of such an advanced age would spend his Tuesday night at a local punk show featuring no established bands.

"He sort of smelled like if you were to boil leather or something, like real musty and old," said Kelly Howland from behind the merch table. "He asked me if I gave senior discounts, then laughed to himself before walking off. I even heard him say, 'How's the weather up there?' to Tall Jason on his way out."

Sources confirm Lister stayed toward the back of the venue for most of the night, until Stand Out frontman Skyler Allen announced, "This one is by Western Front! If you know the words, I want you up here with me. BREAK!"

"I was about to punch that old man," Allen said after his band's set. "He kept trying to steal the mic from me. Who the fuck does he think he is anyway?"

Hardcore Kid Tried as an Adult

BY MATT SAINCOME AND CODY BACKUS

NEW YORK—Officials have confirmed that 36-year-old self-proclaimed hardcore kid Kamal Ahmed was tried as an adult in New York County Superior Court early this morning.

"As you can see, your honor, my client may be old enough to be the father of teenagers, but he is in no way, shape, or form an adult. If it pleases the court, I'd like to call into evidence the fact he wore a Warzone T-shirt to this trial," said public defender David Hankley. "Add to that his Twitter feed, where he obsesses over ideas of 'unity' within a scene full of 15-year-olds, and I think the picture becomes clear."

The judge and prosecutor, veterans of the court system, were reportedly unmoved by the motion.

"Everyone would like to take a couple years off the top, am I right?" mused the charismatic, handsome prosecutor, Geoffrey Brennan, to the jury. "Hell, I know I would. But just because this man belongs to the Die Young Crew and still doesn't have his driver's license, it doesn't mean we shouldn't try him as what he truly is: an adult. He isn't the first hardcore kid to attempt this, and if we don't send a strong message now, he won't be the last."

In his final ruling, the honorable Judge Mike Joge struck a chastising tone with Ahmed.

"Just because you spend all your time arguing with children on these online music forums doesn't mean you are a child yourself," he asserted. "I sentence you to 25 ta life."

Hankley has already begun plans to appeal.

"I think we may need a change of venue. Maybe we could do better in a place like Portland," he said. "I mean, this is a travesty. He might be an adult, but he's a minor at heart."

Before Ahmed was dragged off to his holding cell, he gave a brief statement to the press.

"It's not how old I am, it's how old I feel," he insisted as he writhed in handcuffs. "I'm gonna stay young until I die."

Local Man Gets in Touch With Nature by Relentlessly Instagramming Hike

BY DAN LUBERTO

BURLINGTON, Vt.—Local man Aaron Forks spent the greater part of his day staring into his phone, attempting to post photos of an afternoon hike to Instagram while "just trying to get away from it all," witnesses confirmed.

"I really needed to get back to nature, but nobody told me how shitty the service is out here," said Forks after posing for a photo that would eventually collect 13 likes. "I was Snap-chatting with this girl I met on Tinder, and a quarter-mile in, I'm at zero bars. What if she's trying to send me something right now?"

Forks' main photography subject was close-up shots of himself, not the many impressive views and majestic wildlife he unknowingly walked by while battling nature for cell service.

"If I had known all my problems were gonna follow me out here, I wouldn't have even bothered," sighed the visibly frus-trated hiker.

As the sun began to set, Forks was in full-on panic mode, fearing he had missed out on the perfect shot that proved he was one with nature.

"Why would I even buy these boots and $75 CamelBak if no one can see my whole getup? How in the hell am I supposed to feel at peace with this bullshit?!" shouted Forks from atop a tall rock, waving his phone in the air in a desperate attempt to get a signal.

Upon arriving at his Subaru Outback parked at the trailhead, he reflected on his journey as he treated his 232 followers to a 12-item image dump consisting of selfies and shots of his feet on the trail.

"It really felt good to get away from the city for a bit. I just feel bad for the people that are slaves to their television and never take a minute to appreciate the beauty that's all around us," said Forks. "They're really missing out."

The HARD Times

Local Band Convinced Full-Stack Amps Are Necessary for Show at Doug's House

BY CLAY KALEDIN

MONTCLAIR, N.J.—Local emo group Asthenia Falls defended their decision to bring two full-stack amplifiers and a four-foot bass cabinet to a venue with a standing capacity of 30, sources waiting on the lawn outside the DIY venue fondly referred to as "Doug's House" confirmed.

"I'm just not myself without the stack, ya know?" said guitarist Steven Homer while loading his gear in through the kitchen door. "It's a comfort thing. I think of my amp as a really big security blanket that wraps me up and keeps me warm. Sure, Doug's House might not be the biggest venue we've ever played, but I live by the motto 'If it's too loud, maybe you shouldn't have let us play in your basement.'"

Lead guitarist Richard Horigan, standing a respectable 6 feet tall, fondly patted the side of his amplifier, which stood an inch or two higher than its owner.

"For me, it's all about tone," said the musician as he meticulously picked pieces of lint out of the amp's grill. "What's most important is the sound quality. A really big amp cranked all the way up to 30 percent volume? Can't beat that."

Doug Jefferson, who booked the show to coincide with his parents' trip to the Bahamas, was not fond of Asthenia Falls' decision.

"I have no idea if we have enough outlets to plug everything in. Usually I just have a guy playing acoustic guitar, and maybe he has to plug in a laptop or something. I don't even know how we're going to get it all down the stairs," said the promoter after fetching another extension cord from the toolshed.

Horigan stood by the band's decision, saying, "Yeah, we could probably get away with a half-stack or maybe some practice amps in such a tiny space, but there are some die-hard fans here tonight that came for the full Asthenia Falls experience."

"Besides, I spent my graduation money on this equipment," he added while maneuvering the amp around a low-hanging light fixture. "We need to put it to use eventually."

UPDATE: Local Band Convinced Full-Stack Amps Have Nothing to Do With Power Outages at Doug's House

BY CLAY KALEDIN

MONTCLAIR, N.J.—Emo band Asthenia Falls grew frustrated with the perceived "lack of professionalism and utter disrespect for musical expression" after the third consecutive power outage within 15 minutes at local DIY venue Doug's House, ready-to-rock sources confirmed.

"This is the problem when you do favors for friends and play in their garbage house. The idiots that wired this place must've done it all wrong. What else could be causing the power to cut out?" said bassist Colin Almez as show promoter Doug Jefferson inspected the house's fuse box. "We shouldn't even be playing shitholes like this if they can't support a wall of sound."

To help remedy the problem, touring band The Ruby Blue offered use of their vintage combo amplifier, but the emo act politely declined.

"My guitar just wouldn't have sounded the same," said guitarist Steven Homer while waiting outside for the show to resume. "I didn't come here to half-ass this. If the people who came tonight don't leave here with early symptoms of tinnitus, then I haven't done my job."

West Oakland Punks Hold Vegan Bake Sale to End Gentrification

BY DAN LUBERTO

OAKLAND, Calif.—The West Oakland punk community gathered this past weekend to hold a vegan bake sale fundraiser as part of a series of continuing efforts to combat the scourge of gentrification across their city, beanie-clad sources confirmed.

"It's amazing how much the neighborhood has changed since I moved here a year ago," said Dave Myers, a software developer for Uber. "What first attracted me to the area was its energy. It had this . . . *feeling*. I want to do my part to help bring that back."

The event, sponsored by the Oakland Soul Collective, was particularly successful at bringing in newer members of the community who share their concerns.

"We reserved the [basketball] courts using this new app called Open Spaces. At first the local kids seemed pretty bummed they couldn't play here today, but now I think they understand what we're doing is to benefit the community, so it's cool," said Taylor Houghton, one of the bake sale's organizers and an artisanal vegan soap maker. "Everything here is five dollars or less if you have a valid, government-issued photo ID to prove you're from the neighborhood."

The event brought in bearded vendors from across the city who have benefited from Oakland's reasonable rents and rapidly changing economy.

"We have vegan pies, vegan cakes, vegan cupcakes, even vegan brownies," said Liam Martin, owner of Fresh Batch, an artisanal vegan pâtisserie with a Scandinavian theme. "This is the true flavor of the neighborhood."

In addition to coffee and treats, the collective tabled with reasonably priced zines and pamphlets to promote local culture.

"I'm killing it here with my zines, plus I've gotten exposure for my grind band by playing our demo on loop," said Becky Newman, a local artist specializing in cruelty-free sculpture. "It's just people helping people. Once we decide where to donate the profits, we'll definitely see improvement."

While the event was considered an overall success by those involved, Houghton did voice disappointment toward long-time residents of the neighborhood who didn't bother to show up.

"I'm making a change," she said. "If people can't accept that, then they can leave."

Man's Tattoo a Constant Reminder of Time He Stabbed Panther in Face

BY MARK TURNER

WILKES-BARRE, Penn.—Local tattoo enthusiast Josh Stuart is covered in tattoos that act as constant reminders of his adventures, and the many rare and endangered animals he has mercilessly stabbed through the face, according to eyewitnesses who have inquired about their meanings.

"This one here, the panther? Yeah, stabbed it with a jewel-encrusted dagger I lifted from an ancient tomb," said Stuart, rotating his bicep to show the large image of a black feline. "I didn't want to do it, but there was no way I was letting some big cat ambush our ragtag group of treasure hunters deep in the Amazon."

Stuart's body is a veritable smorgasbord of weaponry piercing various openmouthed animals' heads. On his right calf, a scimitar decapitating an Asian elephant is adjacent to a cobra impaled on a switchblade.

"It's really crazy how many of my excursions abroad have turned into violent exhibitions of man's dominance over beasts," Stuart reflected. "I've stabbed a hell of a lot of flora *and* fauna."

Many have mistakenly thought the adventurer's numerous tattoos were picked from a book of flash or obtained at conventions, but every single piece of art on his body has unique significance.

"When the kraken rose from the depths and ripped our mast from the deck with a slimy tentacle, I knew we were in trouble," said Stuart of the massive shipwreck covering his chest and stomach. "I was stranded on a piece of driftwood for over 48 hours until I washed ashore in Japan."

"Which is lucky for me, because that's where I met my wife," he added, turning his shoulder to reveal a traditional geisha.

In one of many bird-related incidents while on peyote in Joshua Tree National Park, Stuart witnessed an American bald eagle battling a diamondback rattlesnake. The same eagle allegedly stole a quiver of flaming arrows he was shooting aimlessly into the Southern California desert, as depicted on his left thigh. Stuart, however, was incredulous when asked if he had served any prison time.

"Oh, this?" he said, pointing to the spiderweb on his left elbow. "No, I'm just a huge No Doubt fan."

The HARD Times

Punk Mom Embarrassed to Drop Off Juggalo Son at Concert

BY RAY MCMILLAN

LAS VEGAS—Kate Swanson, a local suburban mother and former Plasmatics tribute band vocalist, was "humiliated" to be seen bringing her teen son to a rap-rock concert, sources confirmed.

"Oh, my god, this is the worst," Swanson allegedly muttered under her breath from her minivan, trying to avoid eye contact with any of the face-painted Murderous Detroit Clownz fans lined up outside the venue. "I hope no one recognizes me."

Swanson's son, who prefers the moniker "Tyler Da Knifecutta," smiled at his ashamed parent while exiting the vehicle at what she described as "the pace of a goddamned snail stuck in gum."

"Thanks, Mom. I love you!" said the young Juggalo, enthusiastically waving goodbye as she sped off.

Swanson explained her deep-seated hatred for the subculture.

"These kids think they're rebelling against something, but they're all just conforming to the same tired antiestablish-ment rhetoric sold to them at the mall," she said, glancing into a rearview mirror adorned with a Misfits air freshener. "Did you see all that merch for sale outside the show? When did that start? This is all clearly just an attempt to capitalize on teen angst."

In addition to his "unfortunate" musical preference, Swanson expressed further shame for her son's "vulgar aesthetic."

"What compels a teen to wear makeup to 'shock' people? I mean, just look at the hair on some of these kids! You know it doesn't just grow like that. Their mothers probably dyed it for them," she said as she dug through her purse for a clove cigarette. "It baffles me that necrophilia, face paint, and rude jokes are attractive to kids," she added, rolling down the minivan windows and blasting TSOL's "Code Blue" at full volume.

As of press time, Swanson was seen in a nearby parking lot mentally preparing to pick up her son, who was outside the venue practicing martial arts with a group of heavyset teenagers drinking Faygo.

Drummer Reluctantly Compliments Band's Music Just Before Asking to Borrow Their Equipment

BY GREG MCGONAGLE

JAMAICA PLAIN, Mass.—Silver-tongued punk Victor Gross resorted to complimenting a band he genuinely hated in hopes it would increase his chances to procure the drum set he desperately needed to borrow from them, witnesses confirmed.

"You guys were super tight. I was mad into it, bro," Gross reportedly said multiple times before casually asking to use the gear owned by Sean Fitzpatrick of opening band Beat It. "Do you mind if I play around on those bad boys for our set? I don't know if I can rip as hard as you, but I'll try."

In a textbook display of manipulation, Gross even referred to Fitzpatrick, a complete stranger, as "brother" numerous times throughout their exchange, until Fitzpatrick reluctantly agreed to lend the equipment in question.

"I should've known this was coming when I saw his band pull up in an Acura. The dude spent our whole set trying to make eye contact with me, so when he walked over, I knew I was in for a treat," said Fitzpatrick. "What kind of jackass doesn't bring a kit to a show they're headlining?"

Gross later bragged to reporters about his ability to grift other musicians into lending out their gear.

"Dude! What an idiot. I can't believe he actually fell for the old 'your band ripped' routine," Gross said. "I left my kit in my basement. It's only four miles away, but it takes, like, eight minutes to break [the kit] down. I don't have time for that sort of bullshit."

Fitzpatrick reportedly looked on in horror as the other drummer mistreated and damaged the borrowed gear over the span of his band's 24-minute set.

"After every song, he would get up and kick the toms over and scream about who-fucking-knows-what. He even picked up a cymbal stand and threw it like a javelin straight into the wall for no apparent reason," he said, examining his brutalized kit.

"It just sucks. I borrowed these drums from the butt-rock band we share a practice space with," Fitzpatrick added. "I'm not looking forward to explaining this."

Frontman Makes It Perfectly Clear ISIS Not Welcome in This Scene

BY BILL CONWAY

SPRINGFIELD, Mo.—According to numerous sources, Steady Focus frontman Spencer Wilt made an impassioned declaration to ISIS "and other terrorist groups," clarifying that religious extremists of any creed are "not welcome in this scene."

"Yeah, as I walked in they were finishing up their first song, and their singer was going off about keeping ISIS out of the scene. Don't get me wrong—I agree, but why bring it up?" said Melissa Nguyen of the bold stance that elicited tepid applause from the crowd, along with a solitary "woo." "I mean, is that a thing? I don't think that's a thing, is it?"

Multiple observers report Wilt returned to the topic of religious extremism after nearly every song.

"Hey! Listen up. If you think it's cool to behead people in the name of religion, well, there's the fucking door," said the vegan, straight-edge frontman before making a dramatic gesture to an emergency-exit sign to the left of the stage. "That sort of intolerance has no place within these walls."

"You don't see me going around bombing everyone that gave our demo a bad review, do you?" he added. "No, because that shit isn't what hardcore is about. This song is off our demo, which you can get at the merch table in the back. Bust it!"

Other members of Steady Focus had mixed emotions about their singer's message.

"We've talked with him about this over and over again, but at each show he gets more fanatical about it. I think he really believes that members of ISIS are going to infiltrate the scene," admitted drummer Mark Livingston. "I really don't think that's the case . . . although, hardcore kids are pretty impressionable, so who knows?"

In a post-show interview, Wilt remained unfazed by the criticism of his between-song banter.

"Did you know ISIS has banned listening to music in parts of Syria?" he asked rhetorically while loading his band's van. "It seems like I'm the only one even talking about this. In New York, people stood up to run the Nazis out of the scene—I'm standing up to run out the jihadists."

Skinhead in Red Fred Perry Shirt Accidentally Works Shift at Target

BY MARK TURNER

PEORIA, Ill.—Local skinhead Melinda "Rude Girl" Rodriguez was unwittingly conscripted into service when she wore her favorite red Fred Perry shirt while shopping at the retail giant, witnesses confirmed.

"I was looking for a come-up on some track pants and new hair clippers on my only day off this week, and customers started asking me about sales or if I could find them something in the back. One thing led to another, and here we are," said Rodriguez, quickly putting away a cart of "go-backs." "My new manager, Tanya [Bargazzi], just told me to go round up carts from the parking lot, so I guess I should get used to this."

Target management praised the work ethic of the accidental staff member.

"Ms. Rodriguez is an exemplary employee," said Bargazzi of her unclassified proletarian. "She doesn't ask for much; she just does the job. She seems perfectly built to handle the near-psychotic abuse of retail.

"I don't think she's taken a break yet, unlike Johnson over there," Bargazzi continued, motioning disdainfully to an elderly man eating a sandwich.

Despite looking forward to her one day off this week between swing shifts at the local metal factory, Rodriguez could not refuse the allure of more consistent and tedious work.

"Employment is, like, 60 percent of my identity," said Rodriguez while restocking half of the housewares section by herself. "Plus, I only worked 72 hours at the factory this week and I was starting to get the feeling back in my feet. I'm no slouch; I'm a blue-... well, red-collared American."

Other Target employees admitted that Rodriguez has been working circles around them despite not officially being on the payroll and having no previous knowledge of the store's inner workings.

"She takes this job so seriously," said teen part-timer Caleb Herman. "Who the hell would *run* to clean up a broken pickle jar? For minimum wage? Not me."

Management attempted to reward Rodriguez with complimentary popcorn and coffee from the Starbucks cafeteria but were rebuffed by Ms. Rodriguez's strict "no handouts" policy.

UPDATE: Unconfirmed reports indicate Rodriguez, wearing a blue Ben Sherman and khakis, was spotted manning the register at a local Best Buy.

The HARD Times

Polyamorous Guy Who Brought Ukulele to Party Explains Feminism to Young Women

BY ED SAINCOME III

BERKELEY, Calif.—Local ukulele owner and polyamorist Rick Walcott graciously explained the core concepts of feminism to a group of female undergraduates Saturday night during a house party near the UC Berkeley campus, bystanders reported.

"The thing is, women have been oppressed for so long that it's not even about equality anymore," Walcott said loudly, adjusting his man bun. "It's about actively pushing women to the forefront of the conversation, giving them an easier path to management positions in the workforce."

Christina Lopez, an art history major, attempted to engage with the ukulele player, insisting she "just wants to be treated as an equal to my male counterparts," but was immediately cut off.

"No. No, it's too late for that," Walcott snapped. "It would never work. Men wouldn't let it. Trust me; I know what I'm talking about."

One witness reported Walcott went on to generously explain the feminist ideals of power dynamics in polyamorous relationships.

"Katy and I are in love, but we're also free to explore our feelings with other people. For example, I have another girlfriend, plus I hook up with additional women at parties just like this one. Katy is more monogamous, but that's *her choice*. It all works out just as I planned . . . I mean, it all works out perfectly," he said, tuning his hand-carved ukulele while sizing up the room.

Beth Cunningham, a premed sophomore who was witness to three different renditions of Oasis' "Wonderwall," wasn't buying it.

"It seemed like bullshit to me," said Cunningham. "The last thing I need right now is some douchebag with a ukulele telling me that I'm less of a feminist because I don't want my boyfriend to fuck other people. He says he's bisexual, but I heard it was just one kiss during freshman year, which doesn't count."

Sensing he was losing the interest of his captive audience, Walcott, who moonlights as a self-described "yogi," suggested a group breathing exercise.

"Let's all just take a minute to breathe in deeply through the nose . . . and out through the mouth . . . while we envision a world without the tyranny of the patriarchy," he said.

As of press time, witnesses report seeing Walcott encouraging a group of women on a midnight fun run to remove their shirts in protest of the campus dress code.

Man Enters 10th Year of Searching for Perfect Surface to Apply Band Sticker To

BY BILL CONWAY

HANSON, Mass. Local man Aaron Noble has entered his 10th year of searching for the perfect surface to apply a sticker from beloved Boston hardcore band Blackjack to, sources close to the indecisive man confirmed.

"I grabbed this sticker from their merch table the night they played their farewell show. This is the only thing I have left that will let people know I loved Blackjack," said Noble after 15 minutes of staring blankly at his car's bumper. "If I put it on something I end up throwing away within the next couple of years, it'll be lost forever."

Despite owning many surfaces to which most people could apply a sticker, Noble remains unsure what he will do, claiming that with each passing day, the sticker just becomes "a bigger deal" to him.

"I thought my microwave would be a good spot. Who owns more than one microwave in their lifetime? My guitar case is another good option, but I never take that out of the closet. There's also the carrier I take my cat to the vet in, but people might think he's the one who's into the band," said Noble,

still staring at his bumper. "I just bought this car. It's used, but in good shape. I just worry someone might rear-end me when they see the sticker because they're thinking, *Damn! This guy is a Blackjack fan—he knows his shit.* You know what I mean?"

Noble admits he has changed a lot over the past decade, but his struggle to perfectly place the three-inch die-cut piece of vinyl has been one of his few constants.

"It's weird to think I was straight edge and vegan when I grabbed that thing. Oh man, I was dating Julie back then. She's married with a kid now, and I still can't figure out what to do with a fuckin' decal," he said. "I should post on her Facebook and see how she's doing."

Kevin Horgan, Blackjack's former frontman and current manager of a kiosk specializing in cell phone cases at the Hanover Mall, was surprised to hear about Noble's dilemma.

"I literally have 2,000 of those stickers in my mom's basement," said Horgan while on a cigarette break. "Tell him he can have them all—he just has to pick them up."

The HARD Times

Punk Clears Out Pit to Make Room for Crossing Ducklings

BY STEVEN KOWALSKI

AKRON, Ohio—According to reports, local punk Paul Van-slyke is being declared a hero after he weathered a shower-ing of beer, boos, and fists while clearing out the center of a mosh pit to protect a brood of ducklings crossing the venue in search of a nearby pond.

"I mean, we just finished our first song, and as I'm tuning my bass, this guy is just crashing into people, spilling drinks," said CeCe Kano of opening band Electric Lurker, one of the first to notice the altruistic behavior. "And he just kept screaming, 'Open this shit up, motherfuckers!' At first, I was thinking, *Dick move, guy.* Of course, that changed when I heard the quacking."

Witnesses confirm the distressed mother duck and her five ducklings sought safe crossing to their nest at a small pond just to the right of the stage.

"Look, I don't care if you're human or waterfowl—I'm here to help the helpless," said Vanslyke after the show, as he sat on the stage and fed the duck family pieces of old hot dog buns. "None of these other posers could take 10 seconds to quit scrolling through Tumblr to help these adorable animals. THAT is problematic."

Many in attendance admired Vanslyke's quick thinking and pit-boss antics.

"When I see some hoss out there throwing himself around between songs, it's usually like, 'Who is this jerkoff?'" said Mike Dixon, a crowd member who'd been shoved by Van-slyke. "But then I saw those cute ducks timidly walk across the pit while this dude windmilled into people and yelled, 'Yeah, fucking right, get it goin'! Quack!' . . . *that* was a really beautiful moment."

Vanslyke, however, downplayed his gallant display of kind-ness and potentially litigious behavior.

"You never know what could happen," he said when pressed for a statement regarding potential injuries to fellow show-goers. "There are ducks here now. You gotta be aware or, yeah, you're gonna get hurt."

Venue owner Donna Schlegel may have best summed up the evening.

"The leak in the roof has only been getting worse," she said. "It rained pretty hard last week so there's a good-sized pond by the PA. I guess a family of fucking ducks lives in it now. Between them and the skunks in the basement, this place is turning into a damn petting zoo."

Aging Punk Loses Battle to Comfortable Clothes

BY MARK TURNER

TUCSON, Ariz.—Members of the Tucson punk scene were delivered upsetting news earlier today when, at the age of 34, local mainstay and style icon John "The Don" Bergeron finally succumbed to comfortable clothing, bereaved sources confirmed.

"He fought. He really fought," sniffled longtime friend Joey Staples. "Every time he squeezed himself into his favorite pair of floss-sewn riveted franken-pants, I could tell it took a little bit more out of him."

Friends and family discovered that Bergeron had surrendered to normal-fitting attire when he was seen in what appeared to be a pair of slim-fit slacks from Old Navy and a loose knit sweater, an outfit that was not only sensible for the weather, but took Bergeron fewer than five minutes to assemble.

"I get why everyone is sad: We all put a lot of time and hard work into sewing patches on my jackets and pants," said Bergeron. "But it had become annoying. I sweat a lot more now for some reason, and those clothes were just so restrictive. Turns out wearing leather pants at the gym can lead to chafing."

Bergeron, whose legendary wardrobe once consisted of ratty cheesecloth-esque band shirts and a hybrid leather/denim jacket held together by industrial safety pins and Shoe Goo, had known for several months that his time wearing formfitting clothing was drawing to an end.

"It started last year when I was at Costco with my girlfriend and we walked by the sweatpants," he said. "They were calling to me like . . . like if I just let go, I would finally be welcomed into the sweet relief of coziness."

Bergeron is survived by his family, girlfriend Jenni, and a pair of calf-high pleather combat boots. Some affected by Bergeron's passing have expressed anger along with their grief.

"You think I want to wear all this shit? You see these Docs on my feet? I would rather be dead than put Dr. Scholl's insoles in them," said Staples, sweating profusely but refusing to remove his heavily studded jacket. "It's a rad-as-shit burden. I just can't believe he left us like this. Rest in piss—fucking sellout."

UPDATE: A private ceremony will be held at the local thrift store. Bergeron's family asks that those who wish to contribute consider a donation of used bullet belts.

The HARD Times

Lucky Airline Passenger Wins Free Five-Hour Spoken Word Concert by Jello Biafra

BY KYLE ERF

NEWARK, N.J.—Unassuming airline passenger Peter Monahan was treated to an "energetic" and "unending" spoken word concert from former Dead Kennedys frontman Jello Biafra while traveling on a red-eye flight from San Francisco to Newark late last night, tired bystanders reported.

"When I went to sit down, he was in the window seat fogging up the glass and drawing crude animals," claimed the exhausted Monahan, who had no previous knowledge of the punk icon but has since learned Biafra's opinions on topics ranging from government corruption to what constitutes "authentic New York pizza." "I wanted to be polite and make small talk, so I asked [Biafra] where he was headed. He looked up and told me, 'We're all headed straight down the proverbial shithole,' and it just kind of went from there."

"I asked him what his job was and he said, 'I blow minds for a living.' Later it came up that he was in a popular punk band or something?" added Monahan.

Like many on board the 11 p.m. flight, Monahan had purchased his ticket with the hope of sleeping for most of the five-hour journey, but was instead treated to an avalanche of Biafra's wisdom, wry humor, and radical solutions.

"I kept trying to put my earbuds in, but I didn't get the opportunity," Monahan recalled. "He was on a roll about all the organizations keeping society in the dark: the TSA, NSA, CIA, PMRC, GOP . . . It was a long list. I almost fell asleep once, but he startled me awake by pulling *The Washington Post* out of his back pocket to corroborate a point about minimum wage. He seems like a smart guy, and I actually agreed with most of what he had to say. God, I'm so tired, though."

As of press time, reports indicate that Biafra is preparing a special encore performance for one lucky airport cabdriver.

Adult Band Paid in Pizza

BY NICK CONWAY

BALTIMORE—Touring pop-punk band Facts of Life was thrilled to learn show promoter Mickey Hall wouldn't be paying the band in legal tender, instead opting to compensate them with a delicious "Spicy Italian" pizza following a sparsely attended show, enthusiastic sources confirmed.

"At first, I was a bit taken aback. For real? A pizza? But Mickey assured us that yeah, it was ours—the whole fucking pie," said frontman Ryan Crowley. "I didn't know what to make of it. I'm just a normal 32-year-old guy, so I'm not used to this sort of first-class treatment. It even had the Parmesan cheese packets on the side."

Facts of Life drummer Brett Marks seemed the most excited by this revelation.

"I can't tell you how long it's been since my last authentic Baltimore-style pizza!" exclaimed Marks. "Probably not since my parents brought us here on vacation when I was a kid and we went to Cal Ripken's Strike-CalZone. I'm thrilled. It shows that our hard work is appreciated."

By paying bands with unique items, Mickey Hall has made quite a name for himself in the Baltimore scene.

"Just last week I had a great metal band come through. You should've seen the looks on their faces when I paid them out for the night. Each member got a $5 Old Navy gift card and their choice of any item from our lost and found," he said. "I have a show coming up next week where the headliner is going to get two bathrobes I swiped from a hotel a few years back. I can only imagine how much those things are worth."

Hall remains nonplussed by critics who say he should no longer pay bands in gift cards and cheap food but in actual money so the musicians can sustain touring.

"I put a lot of thought into these payments. Some acts have told me they'd rather have gas money than smoke-damaged promotional hats from the movie *Monster-in-Law*," said Hall. "But I'd rather make my compensation memorable as opposed to valuable."

As of press time, Hall had opted to pay local hardcore band Last Confrontation with a Groupon for a month of CrossFit classes at a gym 30 miles outside of Baltimore.

Supportive Father Fucking Shit Up During Son's Performance

BY DAN LUBERTO

JACKSONVILLE, Fla.—Supportive father Doug Cooper caught parents and students off guard by "tearing shit up" during a performance by his son's punk band, Dog Days, at the Samuel W. Wolfson High School Battle of the Bands, numerous maimed sources verified.

"We were just getting into the swing of things—the crowd seemed pretty into it—and then I saw my dad just wrecking house," said Sam Cooper. "He was windmilling like a madman, and, at one point, he deliberately spin-kicked Vice Principal Rothman."

Witnesses on the scene report that as Cooper patiently waited for his son's band to go on, he showed no signs that he was about to "fuck shit up harder than most people have ever seen."

"My daughter's ska band played and he just politely nodded his head throughout, but then when his kid's band started up, that dude dropped some next-level cartwheels and started winging haymakers at the other parents trying to watch," said fellow father Ben Jacobs. "When he started throwing folding chairs into the crowd, I grabbed my six-year-old and ran outside."

Other attendees who tried to dance were put off by Cooper's pit antics.

"I thought it might be fun to jump around a little, but I was out there for about five seconds before Sam's dad charged at me and pushed me into the bleachers," said freshman Eliza Sharpe. "Then he started punching the stage really hard and doing these weird mule kick things. I was completely over it by then."

Dog Days frontman Eli Clark exacerbated the situation by dedicating a song to Cooper, who'd had to remove his shirt to cool off after the first song.

"I knew Sam was really embarrassed that his dad was going off. I haven't even told my parents I'm in a band for this exact reason. When I said, 'This song goes out to Mr. Cooper,' he started clapping his hands super loud and stomping the floor. Sam was bright red," said Clark, smiling. "He even did a one-man pile-up and sang along for a bit. I was psyched on it."

After Dog Days completed their set, witnesses report Mr. Cooper chanted "one more song" for two minutes and then waited in his pickup truck for the show's remaining two hours before taking the band out for pizza.

Girl Likes Music

BY BRYANNA BENNETT

CHICAGO—Shocking yet-to-be-confirmed reports are coming out of Chicago's underground music scene tonight that Stephanie Cales, a girl, does in fact like music.

According to multiple sources within the DIY world, Cales, a human woman, genuinely enjoys both the recorded and live-performance varieties of music—and sometimes even creates it herself.

"This should be a great show tonight," Cales said as she unloaded her gear into a basement venue. "Really stoked. See you in the pit."

Mark James, frontman of local hardcore band Ironsides, offered the woman a helping hand.

"I asked her if she needed help loading in all that heavy gear for her boyfriend's band and she glared at me," said James just before posing for a crew shot. "I was just trying to be a nice guy . . . would it kill her to smile?"

With this recent discovery, male members of the local scene have become distraught. Not only is Cales physically able to load in her own gear with basic human strength, but she has also proved to have deep knowledge of the music she claims to enjoy.

"My girlfriend stayed home so I asked Stephanie to hold my jacket while I moshed," said perplexed show attendee Tommy Pelligero. "And out of nowhere she strikes up a conversation about this obscure Italian Oi! band from the '80s whose patch I have on my jacket. She started rattling off their whole discography and even asked which demo I liked better."

"What is she even doing here?" he added after working up a sweat by displaying his dominance with a crowd kill to the back of the room. "Socialite."

Reports show an increasing number of female women actively participating in music without ulterior motives. By early 2020, these same reports predict, not a single girl person will be left to stand around just to smell nice and be subjected to unwanted, embarrassing sexual advances by male showgoers.

Opening Band Hopes to Win Over Crowd With 17th Song

BY ED SAINCOME III

CONCORD, Calif.—Opening band Glide hoped to win over an apathetic crowd by launching enthusiastically into their 17th song at tonight's show, largely disinterested sources disclosed.

"'Stick Together, Forever' is the song that's going to set the place off," said lead guitarist Jimmy Kaufman. "I finally convinced the guys to let me solo before and after the breakdown—people need to hear this."

Attendees outside of the garage seemed less than enthusiastic that Glide was still onstage and showing no signs of wrapping up anytime soon.

"Ah, what the fuck?!" exclaimed show attendee Jessica Span upon learning of the seemingly endless set. "Those guys are still playing? I intentionally showed up late so I could miss them. I almost died of boredom when they played with Sinister Sisters. Thanks for the heads up, though. I'm gonna go around the corner and get a beer; can you text me when Mutant League starts?"

The members of Glide, however, seem to think that first impressions don't matter much.

"If they don't like the first song, or the second, or the 10th, there's no reason this one can't be the one that hooks them," said optimistic frontman Drew Axelson. "When we're playing as hard as we can, giving it all we have, and I look out to the crowd and see those faces just absolutely glowing from the screens on their cell phones, I can only think to myself, *We have them right where we want them. Any second now, we're going to win over new fans.* Plus did you hear that our new song has two solos in it? People are going to lose their shit."

UPDATE: Axelson has just informed the crowd that Glide has "four more songs" and "if anyone knows the lyrics, stand up front."

Punk Parents Blame Child's Terrible Taste in Music on Vaccinations

BY BILL CONWAY

DENVER—Punk parents Deanna and Paul Melun believe their 15-month-old son's terrible taste in music is directly linked to the vaccinations he received, sources close to the couple confirmed.

"It's a fucking conspiracy, man. More government storm troopers forcing bullshit down our throats," said the infant's visibly aggravated father. "When Isaac was born, we would play him Leftöver Crack, Aus-Rotten, shit like that, and he loved it. But we got him vaccinated and now he shows no interest in listening to Reagan Youth at all, but he sure as hell goes nuts for the songs on that poser-fest *Yo Gabba Gabba*."

Despite overwhelming evidence that vaccinations are beneficial to society at large, the punk mother still believes having her child vaccinated was a mistake.

"I don't know anyone who has ever had whooping cough, or rubella, or whatever other made-up diseases we're supposed to believe threaten our kids. But what I do know is that whenever we're in the minivan, the only thing Isaac wants to hear is The Wiggles—and I seriously want to drive off a bridge," said Mrs. Melun. "Although, Rubella would be a sick band name . . ."

"Anti-vaxxers," as they are called, believe vaccinations have led to a rise in autism and other health issues, despite fierce opposition from medical professionals. Musical preference among children has not been proven to be affected by these inoculations whatsoever.

"Most kids just don't like loud, politically motivated music. It has nothing to do with modern medicine," said pediatrician Laura Weinhorn. "Isaac will eventually develop different tastes and grow out of this phase. The parents, on the other hand, don't seem like they will grow out of this at all . . . have they been vaccinated?"

Even though their child is only 15 months old, the Meluns have already decided on homeschooling in an effort to control their child's exposure to music.

"We are his parents—we know what's best for him," said Mr. Melun while lighting up a cigarette in the family's kitchen.

The HARD Times

Headlining Band Shouts Out Opening Act They Didn't See

BY ED SAINCOME III

BROOKLYN, N.Y.—Cleveland hardcore legends Dayz of Mizery shouted out local band Massive Gains despite arriving at the venue a full two hours after the openers had finished playing their 12-minute set, witnesses reported.

"I listen to DoM, like, every day on Bandcamp, and I have all their shirts—even the long sleeve that sold out instantly. I had to save up and get that one on eBay and they only had an XXL, but my mom helped take it in a little bit," said Massive Gains' 16-year-old frontman Mark Spence before the show. "It's so crazy we get to play with them tonight. I hope they like our cover of Cliff's first band, Blackened Ghosts. It'll be such an honor to have them watch our set."

On day 27 of a national tour, Dayz of Mizery arrived at The Blast Zone around 9:30 p.m., just in time to catch the final song of Attrition by Subtraction, the co-headliner. With the venue near capacity, sources say Dayz of Misery ripped through the first half of their set to an overwhelming, enthusiastic reaction. Between songs, frontman Cliff Lopez looked

to fill some dead air as the band's guitarists tuned their instruments.

"Yo, big shout-out to Steve for putting on the show . . . this place is sick. Give it up for other bands?" said a seemingly disinterested Lopez as the crowd applauded politely. "Shout out to Massive Brains for opening; support your local bands."

The crowd once again clapped in a lackluster show of support, but one crowd member couldn't help but feel slighted.

"Massive Brains? Really?" asked a dejected Spence. "I mean, it was bad enough they missed our set. I think they would've really liked it. Maybe we could've hopped on their tour if they'd seen us, or at least I might've been asked to do some guest vocals onstage. I don't know, just a disappointing night . . . Massive Brains?"

When questioned about letting down one of his biggest fans by missing his band's set and then shouting them out by the wrong name, Lopez responded with a question of his own.

"Do you guys know where I can score some bud around here?"

D.R.I. Logo Tears ACL

BY JOHN KENNEDY

HOUSTON—D.R.I.'s legendary "Skanker Man" was sidelined with a torn ACL following an injury brought on by decades of touring and the wear and tear of life on the road, doctors confirmed.

"It was a typical night," said the logo. "I was there for the load-in, soundcheck, everything. Then about halfway through the show, I'm in the crowd, like usual, and I just came down on it wrong. I heard the pop and realized something was fucked."

Fans of the logo were shocked to hear that he had suffered what could be a career-ending injury.

"He's held it in that bent position for 34 years straight," said longtime devotee Becky Clayborn. "I don't know that he can do anything else; this has been his whole career. It's heartbreaking. I mean, where do you go from here?"

The logo tried to carry on stoically with a steady dose of pain-relieving patches and bandage wraps but was forced to seek medical attention after his makeshift brace and cane ruined the aesthetic of the band's bass drum.

"He really tried to put it out his head and carry on as much as he could," said D.R.I. frontman Kurt Brecht. "But his knee was so swollen that he almost looked like the silhouette on women's bathrooms. It was tough to see him in that much pain."

Representatives of the band say D.R.I. has temporarily brought in the Circle Jerks logo to help finish out the tour, until their own logo is back on his feet.

"Look, it gets harder as you get older," said the Circle Jerks logo. "I do at least half an hour of stretching before every show and always hit an ice bath afterward. You can learn all about it in my new web series, 'Punk Rock Pilates.'"

Despite the injury, the D.R.I. logo is trying to maintain good spirits. "I guess you could say I'm Dealing With It! You know, like the album?" he pleaded.

Doctors say Skanker Man is expected to make a full recovery thanks to intense physical therapy at the same clinic where Milo, the Descendents logo, was treated for early-onset male-pattern baldness.

Self-Conscious Punk Keeps Leather Jacket on in Pool

BY BILL CONWAY

ORLANDO, Fla.—Self-conscious punk Walter Vaughn was too embarrassed by winter weight gain and excessive body hair to remove his outerwear while taking a dip in a local pool with friends, sunbathing sources attested.

"I won't lie, after I quit smoking cigarettes, I really let myself go," said Vaughn from his position in the shallow end of his apartment complex's pool. "I ballooned up to 160 pounds this winter. Normally I'm at a lean 140. My bullet belt doesn't even fit anymore."

Friends of Vaughn noted that he has been comfortable with his body in the past and is usually the first person to go shirtless at shows. The sudden change caught many off guard.

"We all thought it would be great to hang out in the pool and drink, but then Wally refused to take off his jacket. At first I thought it was a joke, but then he got really defensive and mean," said longtime friend Shelly "Shellz" Romero.

"Nobody would even notice if he'd gained weight, but you definitely notice the one guy wearing a leather jacket while floating on a pool noodle."

Initially Vaughn tried deflecting his body shame with a variety of excuses, but nothing seemed to convince the other pool partiers.

"First, he told me he was a really big Who Killed Spikey Jacket? fan but when I said, 'Oh yeah, pool-punks dress punk,' he just gave me a blank stare. Then he told me he was trying not to get burned and doesn't want to support the sunscreen industry because of its history of animal testing," said Romero. "Whatever. This guy did more cocaine than I thought was humanly possible last weekend, and now he's worried about getting a tan?"

As of press time, Vaughn was approaching a full hour of being "it" in a game of Marco Polo due to his jacket hindering his ability to move quickly through the water.

The HARD Times

iPod Shuffle Treats Party Guests to Noam Chomsky Lecture

BY ERIC CASERO

BOSTON—According to witnesses, a college party underwent an abrupt change in mood late last night after the host's iPod Shuffle launched into a lecture by renowned philosopher and political theorist Noam Chomsky.

"Yeah, I was having a pretty good time, getting down to some Kendrick Lamar," said attendee Rob Williams, encapsulating the guests' collective feeling. "But things got really wild when I became aware that the United States' imperialist foreign policy compromises its democratic ideals."

Other partygoers reported similar reactions.

"The playlist was fine most of the night," said senior Tina Rodriguez. "But the new 2 Chainz track just doesn't compare to the sudden realization that monolithic media conglomerates are marginalizing third-world concerns by monopolizing public discourse."

When asked about the party the following morning, accounts were hazy but the guests, many of whom passed out atop half-finished "Occupy Wall Street" signs, expressed overall positive impressions.

"I don't remember much about last night," claimed Jerry Schaeffer, "but it must have been a good time. When I woke up, I saw that someone had drawn a penis on my face, along with a manifesto for syndicalist resistance to exploitative capitalist labor practices."

Molly Jeffries, the host of the party and the political awakening, was left with a substantial mess, cleanup of which is scheduled to begin sometime today. However, she and her roommates are optimistic that solidarity, collective action, and a shared commitment to fighting puke stains will lead to a brighter future.

"I learned a lot from that two-hour lecture. I realized I need to look in the mirror and start taking responsibility for my own actions, not just make justifications for why the sink is filled with dirty dishes," said Jeffries. "If I could only apply those same ideas toward breaking up the massive concentration of wealth that is ruining an entire generation's chance at upward mobility, then the world might be a better place."

As of press time, Jeffries was reportedly getting pumped for her morning run by listening to her "TED Talks Jamz" playlist.

The HARD Times

Promoter Suspects Guy Loading in Single Extension Cord Not Actually in Band

BY KRISSY HOWARD

HUNTINGTON, W.Va.—Show promoter Mia Lambert began to suspect that the one guy loading in a single extension cord may not, in fact, be a member of the band he was "helping," sources close to the tense situation confirmed.

"You wanna get a friend in or whatever, it's really not a huge deal," said Lambert from her position working the door at the American Legion Post 16. "But when I saw four different people carrying in individual cymbals saying they were playing for Bounce! I started paying attention. I mean, I've known the dudes in that band since middle school. I think I know how many members they have."

Her suspicions were confirmed when scene regular Donny "Ronnie" Jacobs, best known for being "that kid who let that other dude hit him with his own car," attempted to walk in behind the band's guitarist carrying only an extension cord.

"It's just, like, are you fucking kidding me right now, dude? It wasn't even a heavy-duty cord. It was six feet long and covered in cat hair and dust like he had grabbed it from under his bed," Lambert stated. "And not to mention Ronnie is actually banned from this venue because the last time his band played a show here he threw a bunch of live crabs into the audience, some of which ended up in the ceiling, which made the place smell pretty ripe for a month or two."

After members of Bounce! were only able to offer Lambert an unhelpful "I don't know . . ." when questioned about Jacobs' role in the matter, the promoter decided the trouble of confronting someone she describes as having an "arson-y vibe" wasn't worth it and ultimately let it slide. However, she remains dumbfounded by the entire ordeal.

"I mean, I guess I could see if it were some huge sold-out show, but there are 26 people here, and it costs $5," Lambert said. "You know what's fucked up? This is actually a charity event to raise money for a no-kill animal shelter. Whatever."

When asked for comment, Jacobs simply shrugged with an incredulous, "What?"

The HARD Times

LimeWire Download Finally Finished

BY PETER WOODS

PEORIA, Ill.—In a Facebook post that sent shock waves through the local social media landscape, claims adjuster Steve Hurnsman announced today that he successfully completed downloading a file from the peer-to-peer file sharing program LimeWire.

"I just never thought this day would come," said Hurnsman. "After I left for college and my mom switched to DSL, I figured it was a lost cause. I mean, the download paused for three and a half years at one point. But I guess if you just keep the faith and don't give up, good things happen."

The news comes 16 years, 3 months, 19 days, 6 hours, and 22 minutes after he started the process of downloading "Outcast- Stankoniia FULL ALBUM UNCENSORED" to the Compaq computer in his parents' living room.

"I'm not super into this stuff anymore, but I'm still pretty excited to check it out," said Hurnsman while searching for a blank CD to burn the album onto. "I remember that one song about carnivals being pretty good."

Hurnsman posted the eight-word status at 7 p.m. yesterday, simply stating "Nice. Just nabbed that Outkast album off LimeWire." The post had gone viral by morning, with over four million shares and 200 comments from other users offering congratulations.

"Patience is a virtue," said Reddit user Drugz4Sale420. "At any point he could've bought that record used on Amazon for less than a dollar, but instead he showed those greedy musicians that we aren't going to pay for their hard work."

Erstwhile LimeWire users from around the internet appeared to enter a state of shock upon hearing the news.

"I didn't even think that could happen," claimed Mark Gorton, LimeWire CEO. "Every test we ran at the office, the download just got really close and then canceled for no apparent reason. That was really all anyone expected back then."

The excitement generated by the event was unfortunately short-lived. Sources report that after opening the file, Hurnsman discovered two tracks were missing; another track, despite the file name, was, in fact, censored; and that his mother's computer had contracted a virus that corrupted its hard drive.

As of press time, Hurnsman intended to "just stream it later."

The HARD Times

Local Dad Offered Record Deal After Sick Drum Solo on Buick Steering Wheel

BY SARI BELIAK

PHOENIX—Local mechanic and father of two Bruce Harvey was offered an exclusive record deal after he was seen performing a drum solo on the steering wheel of his 2004 Buick LeSabre during his daily commute to work, ecstatic sources confirmed.

"At first I could have sworn I was hearing Rush," said Stan Shiffman, head of A&R at Epic Records. "I haven't heard someone play the steering wheel like that in ages. The way he used his dashboard as an Octapad was insane—clearly this was a musical genius in front of me. I yelled to him to pull over and we signed a contract on the spot."

Shiffman discovered Harvey at the intersection of 7th Street and Osborn while the two were stuck in traffic.

"I mean, this guy was just annihilating his steering wheel, playing high-hat on an empty Coke can and obliterating the glove compartment. At one point, I even noticed one of his air conditioning vents popped out. It was super metal," said Shiffman. "He's is a next-level talent who needs to be exposed to the masses, not just a few stuffed animals in his back seat."

Harvey believes his hard work and passion for in-car drumming, which often embarrasses his teenage daughters, has finally paid off.

"I've been practicing every chance I get. It used to be something I did to pass the time, but now it's my passion," he said while spinning an imaginary drumstick in the air.

Michelle Raskin, a casual-turned-hardcore fan, witnessed the face-melting drum solo while waiting for the bus.

"When he played the ashtray full of coins, I thought, *OK, this guy is pretty good,* but then the smoke effect from his cigarette lighter kicked in and, wow . . . that dude is a powerhouse of an in-car drummer," said Raskin. "I just hope that when he drives by here again tomorrow, he gets stuck at this red light so I can watch him work his magic."

As of press time, Harvey has entered negotiations for his own line of signature steering-wheel covers that prevent finger bruising.

Zine Editor Extends Submission Deadline for Eighth and Final Time

BY DANIEL LOUIS

CHICAGO—Editor Lily Grashin officially set the eighth, and final, deliverable date for all contributing content to her first publication, having previously extended submission deadlines throughout the last 18 months, sources who are definitely "working on it" reported.

"I wanted to release a small run of handmade zines with contributions from friends and other like-minded members of the scene," Grashin explained of her perpetually delayed anarcho-punk journal *Minimum Jazz*. "And I don't want to have some kind of corporate-culture 'deadline,' ya know? Fuck that. That's not what *Minimum Jazz* is about. Well, it's not what we would be about if we could get some copies out the door.

"But I really wish my friends would send me what they promised," she added. "I gotta have everything by this Friday. Seriously. I'm going broke because the rubber cement I bought to glue everything together keeps hardening inside the bottle."

The zine, which may be nothing more than a leaflet by print time, had hoped to skewer the 2016 Republican presidential primary election leading up to the Iowa Caucus.

"My friend Becca was going to write a scathing piece of political satire on Scott Walker and Carly Fiorina. No one gives a shit about Scott Walker anymore," said Grashin. "Maybe I can just have her draw a picture of Trump in a KKK robe or something."

Minimum Jazz was initially intended to act as a voice to report on the local music and art scene, providing sharp, well-informed praise and criticism.

"I was planning on doing a piece about a new DIY venue that opened on the South Side," said potential contributor Gregory James. "But I've been kind of lazy and now it's shut down because someone got hit in the back with a cinder block. It would have been a cool piece, though."

Grashin planned for *Minimum Jazz* to hit online distros prior to Thanksgiving to give readers a different perspective on mainstream American holidays.

"This morning, my roommate Amanda finally handed me her article, 'How to Dumpster a Vegan Thanksgiving Dinner.' Thanksgiving was five months ago," said Grashin. "I'll just revise the headline to 'Memorial Day.' It's basically just eating bread from a bakery garbage can anyway."

If current trends continue, *Minimum Jazz* is expected to be available in the first quarter of 2072.

Hardcore Conclave Meets to Decide Which Pop-Punk Band Gets a Pass

BY PETER WOODS

ROME, Ga.—Various leaders and veterans of hardcore scenes around the world are congregating this Thursday in the basement of squat venue Vatican House to decide which new pop-punk band will officially be "given a pass," clandestine sources confirmed.

"According to traditional hardcore teachings, followers of all subgenres should only listen to pop-punk bands approved by scene elders to avoid having their hardcore credentials called into question," said scene legend Brian Newton. "This list is gospel. Anyone who listens to music not on it risks being blacklisted."

For many, blessing another pop-punk band with scene cred could not come soon enough.

"We are in shambles right now," said Björn Juhlin, a representative from the Zurich D-beat scene. "The old standbys are entrenched and will probably never change. No one will ever call you out for listening to Dillinger Four or that first Taking Back Sunday record, but there are too many bands in the gray area to feel safe. There's a lot on the line here: Listen to the wrong band and you could be classified as a poser, have your stage-diving privileges revoked, or, even worse . . . get called out on my blog."

"Is it OK to listen to Blink-182 now that Skiba is in the band? Does the whole Vegan Reich and Racetraitor thing cancel out that god-awful *Ghostbusters* theme song?" asked tough-guy hardcore pioneer Donny "Devil" Wenning. "And we *still* have no idea what to do with Paramore's new stuff."

With uncertainty at peak levels, experts in the field expect this meeting to be one of the most contentious and unpredictable in modern history.

"I'm betting that Capital Leather is gonna be the one that's approved," claimed scene archivist and leader emeritus, Scott Vogel of Terror. "Dude's vocals are tough enough that the band in no way challenges your masculinity while you sing along, but at this point, I can only conjecture. Anything could happen, and nothing would surprise me."

"[The atmosphere] is eerily similar to the days leading up to the 2002 conclave," added Vogel. "That was the year we couldn't agree on whether The Get Up Kids counted as pop-punk, emo, or both. The scene fractured. I mean, that's why we have Emorthodox sects today."

The conclave will announce the meeting's end by sliding a white-vinyl copy of the Smoking Popes' *The Party's Over* underneath the basement door. Until then, all shows at Vatican House are canceled.

Straight-Edge Elder Celebrates 24th Birthday

BY BILL CONWAY

FORT WORTH, Texas—Danny Lopez, the longest-tenured straight-edge member of the Fort Worth hardcore scene, celebrated his 24th birthday at a small private ceremony with friends and family, sources confirmed.

"When I was 16 and told people I was straight edge, everyone said it wouldn't last, that it was just a phase," said a teary-eyed Lopez as he avoided the smoke from the recently blown-out birthday candles. "But look at me now: still here, still edge. Let me be an example for the younger generation."

In order to remain straight edge, Lopez has battled many obstacles, including alienating close friends.

"Danny and I claimed edge on the same day; we were edge brothers. When I started casually drinking four months later, everyone thought Danny would be next," said ex-friend Rob Merrimack. "Glad to hear he's still edge. He won't accept my Facebook friend requests and I've heard he still wants to fight me, but that's OK, I don't really think of him all that much. I'm usually pretty busy with my nonprofit that helps people wrongly convicted of crimes get out of prison."

Lopez is proud that he has breezed through many life events and milestones with his edge intact.

"When I got a car, I put a straight-edge bumper sticker on it. And I didn't start smoking when I turned 18," said Lopez as he freshened up the X's drawn on his hands. "Twenty-one was a breeze because nobody wanted to hang out with me anymore. Next year I'll be able to rent a car. Can you imagine that? A straight-edge person renting a car?"

However, not everyone in the Fort Worth scene is as excited by Lopez's ability to remain straight edge at such an advanced age.

"That little twerp is such a poser Maggie Daily, the owner of the vegan pie shop downtown, has been straight edge for the past 25 years and nobody's throwing *her* a parade," said show promoter Darcy Lavoix. "He was bragging to me about how he's the oldest edge person in town. When I mentioned Maggie, he just said, 'Girls can't be straight edge' and walked away. Fuck that guy."

The HARD Times

Reuniting Screamo Band to Play Classic Split 7" in Its Entirety

BY DANIEL LOUIS

AMHERST, Mass.—Legendary Massachusetts screamo act Trees and You announced they will be reuniting to perform their only physical release—one side of a split 7" EP—in its entirety, sources confirmed.

"We're super excited to play these two songs," said guitarist Corey Armada, 38. "We had to listen to the record hundreds of times to figure out the chords. It was a long afternoon, but I think we finally got it down."

Forty-year-old vocalist Josh Battel, known for his intense stage performances, worried whether his endurance would be the same as when he was 20.

"I'm not going to lie—I was nervous about getting on the mic again," admitted Battel. "But considering most of the recorded vocals are out-of-breath talk-singing, I think it'll be fine. I don't know if I'll be able to roll on the floor like I used to, and I certainly can't fit into those tight pants anymore . . . but no one should notice I'm completely out of shape."

While some fans see the reunion as an obvious cash grab, others are excited to relive the two months in 1996 when Trees and You was an operating band.

"I honestly never thought this day would come," says long-time fan Ned Perry, 35. "I listened to those two songs on repeat when I was 16. Those two minutes and 12 seconds were the soundtrack to my youth."

In preparing to reunite, Trees and You has also revived an age-old controversy, as fans and critics again debate whether the band was ever "real" screamo.

"Let's just say . . . none of their songs had handclaps—therefore, you will not find their record in this collection," said self-appointed arbiter of all things screamo, Jacob LeFrance, 53, from behind an oversized oak desk in his record library. "Real skramz is more than just short songs that reference 19th-century philosophers. Trees and You simply doesn't make the cut even if every member fits into youth medium shirts."

Members of the band confirmed that their first show in years will also have a few surprises.

"I don't want to give too much away, but I'll say this," teased drummer Christy Steer, 33. "During the quiet pretty part in the song 'Birds and Boats,' we hired professionals to reenact the scene we sampled from 'Romeo + Juliet.' Get ready to weep."

Metallica Adopts Hologram Technology to Replace Perfectly Healthy Lars Ulrich

BY BILL CONWAY

LOS ANGELES—Lars Ulrich, the founding drummer of Metallica, will be replaced by a hologram on all future live dates despite a clean bill of health from Ulrich's physician, according to sources close to the band.

"We had a meeting and within the first 10 minutes, three out of the four of us agreed it would be best to use a hologram from now on instead of having Lars tag along on tour," said lead guitarist Kirk Hammett. "It'll be nice to play the songs at their actual speed again; for the past 15 years, we kind of needed to play a little slower so Lars could keep up."

A band representative requesting anonymity reported Ulrich did not take the news lightly.

"When the guys told Lars he'd be replaced by a beam of light, he immediately claimed he's never felt better in his life," said the source. "He took off his shirt to prove his recent weight loss and showed everyone a chart detailing his excellent cholesterol levels. Then started doing push-ups, but he got really winded after about eight pushups and started

sobbing. I almost felt bad for him, but then I remembered who he was."

Nick Smith, president of AV Concepts, the Arizona company responsible for projecting and staging Tupac Shakur's groundbreaking hologram, has been tasked with creating the hologram Ulrich.

"When the band approached us, we obviously had a lot of questions—the first one, of course, being, 'Do you want the hologram to make as many mistakes as Mr. Ulrich normally does while playing live?'" said Smith. "The band assured me they did not. It'll be tough to create a hologram that plays the songs as they were written because there's no record of Mr. Ulrich ever doing that."

"One thing he really seems to love is pointing directly at any camera that's covering him and mugging really hard. It may be impossible to work around that," Smith added while watching archival band footage from the 1980s. "I just hope he doesn't try to sue me for creating a hologram in his likeness."

The HARD Times

Convicted Murderer Clearly Hoping Testimony Gets Used on Grindcore Album One Day

BY BILL CONWAY

WACO, Texas—Convicted murderer James Wellington's bone-chilling confession regarding the dismemberment of four hitchhikers in 2013 was clearly designed to attract the attention of grindcore bands who could potentially sample the recording on future albums, according to experts following the trial.

"He would say something really messed up, then lean back and start miming a blast beat," said Juror #6. "It seemed really weird at first, but then it made sense when I realized he was picturing how the sound bite would be used. Though I have to admit I'm not a huge grindcore fan; I'm more into thrash, personally."

Over the course of the four-day hearing, the intentions behind Wellington's erratic behavior in the courtroom became increasingly clear.

"Oh, it was so transparent," said Attorney General Ken Paxton. "When he said the bit about the voice of Satan demanding he kill people, I just thought to myself, *This sounds way too similar to the opening of Devourment's* Molesting the Decapitated. *I almost called him out for it.*"

Lead prosecutor Len "Big Brisket" Savoy, who also picked up on Wellington's obvious attempts to deliver the perfect disturbing sound bite, agreed with this assessment.

"I questioned him about how he committed the murders, and he said in a dry, monotone voice, 'The hooks hung them from the ceiling in order to drain their blood onto the ground below . . .' The thing is, he coughed when he said it. So he looks over at the judge and, I swear to the good Lord above, he says, 'Let me take that again and try to get it clean.' Then he repeated his account!" said Savoy while fanning himself with a 10-gallon hat. "I am so gosh-darn sick of these sons of bitches murdering people just to get on the intro of the next Rotten Sound album."

Reports show officials at Earache Records are already in talks with the Texas State Department in hopes of procuring Wellington's full statement, as well as audio from the police confession tapes, for use on all forthcoming releases.

Complete Moron Claps Before Song Is Over

BY BILL CONWAY

PROVIDENCE, R.I.—Complete moron and supposed Bad Religion superfan Rob Hooper clapped before the band finished "I Want Something More," ruining for all what was otherwise a fantastic show, according to unanimous reports.

"I really thought that once the music stopped, the song was over," said the shit-for-brains. "It was definitely a little embarrassing, but honestly, is it really that big of a deal? Hardly anyone noticed."

Much to the breathing garbage pile's dismay, it seemed a "pretty big deal" for nearly everyone who was there, as band members tweeted about the unfortunate incident after their set.

"It was blatantly apparent when the individual clapped prematurely," wrote Greg Graffin, Bad Religion frontman and Cornell PhD. "I was perplexed as to why one would do something so asinine and cretinous. The song had a full 10 seconds left."

Now-former friends of the ignorant dipshit quickly distanced themselves.

"Right after that happened, we got the fuck out," said Adam Ponte, who claimed he couldn't look Hooper in the eyes anymore. "They were only two songs in, but I can't be seen with him. I've already blocked him on Facebook."

"It was humiliating. We were supposed to give him a ride home, but honestly, the thought of being in the car with him makes me sick," added Sarah Foisy. "He called and texted to ask where we were, so we turned our phones off. I'm trying to forget I ever met him."

The man totally unworthy of love and compassion saw his night had taken an even sadder turn after hitchhiking the 16 miles back home to Woonsocket, where the 18-year-old found all of his belongings out on his front lawn.

"I can't believe I raised a son like this," said Theresa Hooper, Rob's mortified mother. "I remember someone pulling that same shit at an ABBA concert in '82. He's lucky I put his stuff outside and not in the fireplace. Good riddance."

Defend Pop Punk Army in Way Over Their Heads in Syria

BY JOHN DANEK

RAQQA, Syria—Members of the popular "Defend Pop Punk Army" Facebook group allegedly got more than they bargained for on a recent mission to war-ravaged Syria, according to transmissions from the front lines.

"We heard there was almost no pop punk in all of Syria, and frankly, we were outraged—these people may never see four guys jumping on stage in unison," said founder Bob Bucciano from a temporary shelter in a former market district. "In hindsight, a lack of palm-muted riffs in four-chord punk songs is the least of their problems."

Bucciano founded the group in 2010, when pop punk, mall emo, and Syrian governmental stability were all on the decline. His search for like-minded music fans was a success, with over 55,000 Facebook users comprising the group. Similarly, Syrian opposition forces have grown to an estimated 50,000 to 200,000 members during the same timeframe.

"None of us really understood before what's going on here," admitted group moderator Marla Jensen. "I asked our translator if the conflict is analogous to the Taking Back Sunday vs. Brand New feud of the early 2000s, but he wasn't much help."

Bucciano reported a highly upvoted post in the group led to the mission trip. "The plan was to come here for recon: hand out some Rise Records samplers, price out real estate for an *Alternative Press* foreign bureau . . . maybe investigate founding a festival," said Bucciano, taking shelter between two bombed-out houses. "The New Found Glory show in Ciudad Juárez was such a hit—we didn't think we could fail."

Members of Defend Pop Punk Army tried a variety of tactics to subdue their enemies, including playing genre-defining releases from the past 25 years. Unfortunately, none were successful.

"Once that first RPG hit the building next to our base, I realized that '90s-era Blink-182 probably can't help this city right now," said Jensen. "We want to apologize to Pete Wentz and Fueled by Ramen for their generous donations, because I just don't see us making much headway."

Sadly, as the conflict continues, many in the Army are losing faith.

"It's a real bummer," said longtime member Cynthia Powers. "This Facebook group has been the only good thing in my life since I lost my job as Gary Johnson's campaign manager."

Nation Outraged After Punk Refuses to Stand for Pennywise's "Bro Hymn"

BY STEVEN KOWALSKI

SAN DIEGO—Nineteen-year-old punk Macy Sanders created a firestorm of controversy when she reportedly refused to stand during Pennywise's performance of fan favorite "Bro Hymn" earlier today.

"Look, this show was long as hell. My dad made me go, and Pennywise played forever. It was like 45 minutes or something insane. I was tired, so I bailed and sat in the shade," said Sanders. "I wasn't trying to be disrespectful, I was just exercising my God-given right of sitting out a couple songs."

Corrections officer and show attendee Dave Vasquez, 36, was upset by the young punk's decision not to rise during the classic song.

"Look, some things are sacred. And you don't come to a Pennywise show to sit out 'Bro Hymn,'" said Vasquez. "That song is a chance for everyone, regardless of religion or race, to get up and mosh, smashing into one another in remembrance of the bros we've lost."

The backlash to Sanders' decision quickly became a talking point on social media, with many highlighting the fact that both active-duty troops and veterans hold "Bro Hymn" in the highest regard.

"My brother did three tours in Iraq, and this entitled brat thinks it's OK to just pop a squat during a punk-rock anthem?" asked Twitter user AmericaDaBrave76. "That song represents all the shirtless servicemen who're just trying to blow off some steam in the pit while they're on leave. Have some fucking respect."

Supporters of Sanders, including former Pennywise roadie Brad "Scooter" Collins, see the protest as long overdue.

"Look, the '97 reissue cheapened things. Go to any Warped Tour—any of them. Between Pennywise and other bands doing covers of Pennywise you'll end up hearing 'Bro Hymn' four or five times," said Collins. "People have been sitting it out for years. Sometimes you're too drunk or too tired, or the ending of one 'Bro Hymn' overlaps with the start of another 'Bro Hymn.' So why is this a big deal now?"

A change.org petition demanding that "Bro Hymn" replace "God" in the Pledge of Allegiance already boasts 10,000 signatures, while a new "Bro Sitters" Facebook group has been liked by 6,500 users, a number that is rising fast.

The HARD Times

Rebellious Vegan Teen Tofu-Scrambles Principal's House

BY TOM FULLER

PORTLAND, Ore.—According to school records released today, vegan activist and Grant High School freshman Juniper Wood is facing up to three days of detention for launching a tofu scramble at her principal's home.

"I was eating dinner with my family when I heard the splat against the window," said Principal James Critchland, addressing reporters while wearing a shirt adorned with smiling hamburgers and a bacon-themed tie, which is rumored to have inspired the scrambling. "When I opened the front door, I was hit in the face by a warm, gooey substance. I knew it was tofu immediately—no mistaking it. Really, the worst part was the lack of black salt and nutritional yeast. I'll have to give her my recipe."

Neighbors report Critchland easily cleaned up the vandalism with a brief spray from a garden hose.

"Yeah, I saw Jim over there spraying his house down, and I yelled to him, 'Hey, did the kids get you with them eggs again?'" laughed neighbor Eli Waters. "He just smiled and said, 'Yeah, something like that.' One time, some paleo kids left a bunch of meat in his mailbox. That was a hoot."

Wood claimed she was "sickened" by the happiness of the meat patties on the educator's shirt.

"Have you ever just, like, looked at a hamburger?" she asked. "They don't smile—they *bleed*. They're dead, just like [Critchland's] heart. I just hope what I did hit home. Otherwise, I wasted all of my dinner on that fucker's house."

The freshman's transition from omnivore to militant vegan reportedly began during summer school.

"She started handing out pamphlets depicting tortured animals to kids during lunch," reported head janitor Tim Darrah. "I didn't mind that, but I had to step in when she started chanting, 'No blood, no fowl!' and throwing away their chicken nuggets."

Wood hinted that, despite her punishment, she may have additional targets in mind.

"Mrs. Stevenson is trying to arrange a field trip to the zoo," she said. "You know—the prison for animals? If she thinks that's OK, well . . . she has another thing coming."

Adult Woman Feeling Oddly Compelled to Impress Little Cousin Wearing Dead Kennedys Shirt

BY KRISSY HOWARD

PITTSBURGH—Local "grown-ass adult" Leslie Walton felt oddly compelled to impress her 12-year-old cousin Trisha Burgess with her deep knowledge of punk subculture upon noticing her Dead Kennedys T-shirt, uninterested sources attested.

"We were at my Uncle Mike's place to celebrate his retirement from the police force when Trisha showed up wearing that shirt. I don't really know why, but I immediately felt like I needed her to like me, more than I ever had before," said the 35-year-old woman with a career and a mortgage.

Determined to assert her position as "the original punk one" in the family, Walton embarked on a 90-minute attempt to impress the seventh grader, complete with tales of getting "super wasted," and a loud recalling of the time she was pretty sure she sat a few rows back from Jello Biafra on a flight from San Francisco.

"She seemed nonplussed, but I could tell she knew I was the real deal," said Walton, who has a credit score of 780. "When a *Cometbus* reference went completely over the kid's head, I realized she was the irrelevant one. She's probably never picked up a zine in her life, let alone trade tapes with random dudes in Germany."

After extended probing, Walton admitted that she started feeling bad about her cousin's perceived lack of punk credentials.

"I'm not calling her a poser or anything," she said. "I'm just saying that the shirt was definitely brand-new, probably ordered off the internet or something.

"I can't be the only one who noticed that crease down the front, right?" she added. "I bet her mom—my aunt Stacey, the one standing right over there by the grill—I bet she irons that shit for her."

Walton's expansive knowledge of everything punk certainly left an impression on the tween, who missed a Little League game in order to attend the dinner.

"That was weird," Burgess recalled. "At first I thought it was kinda cool that she was into DK, but by the time she rolled up her sleeve to show off her sparrow tattoo, the whole thing just felt really sad and desperate."

"I guess that kinda thing happens when you turn, like, 50 or whatever," she added.

The HARD Times

Crust Punk Hops Train to Parents' Lake House

BY COURTNEY BAKA

MINNEAPOLIS—Local crust punk Chris Spencer gathered his belongings from the Trash Compactor, a Northeast Minneapolis squat, and left by train for a long, relaxing weekend at his parents' lakeside home early Wednesday morning, according to reports.

"It's gonna be sick to get away from the grind for a while and spend some time relaxing with the fam," said Spencer, peering down the tracks in anticipation of the oncoming train. "I hear Aunt Julie and the kids are coming down from Bemidji, so the whole crew will be there. Did somebody say croquet tournament?"

Spencer, found on Facebook under the name "Ratz O'Garbage," has never missed a trip to the lake house, a long-standing Spencer family tradition.

"We've gone every year since I was kid," he said excitedly. "We take the boat out to the island, light off fireworks . . . and of course Nana will challenge me to gin rummy. She always beats me, man!"

Spencer turned serious after the excitement of boarding the train wore off.

"I'm not sure how many good years Nana has left, and my little cousins are growing up so fast! It's like . . . I've been so busy fighting consumerist culture and taking down the system that I've missed out on a lot of important moments," he revealed, having spent the previous two weeks playing Bob Dylan covers for change at a busy downtown intersection.

Upon his arrival at the stately house on sparkling Lake Minnetonka, the crust punk's mother, Diane Spencer, scolded him for tossing his soiled army surplus duffel on the granite countertop.

"I swear—sometimes he acts like he was raised in a barn," said Mrs. Spencer, "but I can't stay mad at him. He knows how much I love to sew. If he didn't have any new patches for his jacket, I'd have nothing to do."

Spencer's grandmother, Lillian "Nana" Spencer, professed her support of her grandson's career, listed on Facebook as "Piss Drinker at Fuck You."

"Christopher is nice boy," she said. "Soon enough, he'll give up 'fighting the man' and go to law school like his brothers. He knows he'll always have a spot at the family firm."

Martin Shkreli Buys Fugazi, Jacks Up Ticket Price to $9

BY DAN RICE

WASHINGTON—Wealthy national pariah Martin Shkreli purchased legendary post-hardcore band Fugazi late last week and immediately inflated ticket prices for any future shows to $9, a move that sparked outrage among longtime fans.

"This is criminal!" claimed protestor Sheila Phelps, stationed outside the Dischord House. "No one should have to choose between Fugazi or a decent burrito!"

Shkreli, the universally disliked CEO of Turing Pharmaceuticals, took a break from live streaming himself burning ants with a magnifying glass to address his practices.

"Fugazi is worth much more than $9," he said from his courtyard, briefly interrupting a chess game played on an oversize board with human beings as pieces. "People don't understand how art works. I'm practically giving tickets away!"

Fugazi fans far and wide admitted the purchase was not only infuriating but confusing.

"How could a person do this?!" cried distraught fan Brison Redman. "No, like . . . really. How? Didn't they break up? And it's not like they were for sale or anything. How do you buy an actual group of people?"

While none of the four band members could be reached directly for comment, a new Twitter account with the handle @REALFugazi did appear early this morning.

"Hey guys, this is Fugazi, yes it's really us, we are not being held against our will, come see us rock! #WuTang," proclaimed the first tweet. A follow-up tweet added, "Also we have merch now, tons of merch!"

Shkreli denied that the price hike was unfair to fans.

"I'm working closely with promoters to make sure anyone in need can still get Fugazi. Access to Fugazi will soon be greater than ever!" he declared while dining on an assortment of sushi and fresh tiger milk.

When asked a follow-up, Shkreli insisted he was out of time and shouted to a servant, "Bring me another puppy to wipe my face! And don't tell me we're out of puppies—I know you and the others hide them!"

How We Tried to "Moneyball" The Hard Times

AS REMEMBERED BY EDITOR JEREMY KAPLOWITZ

I felt a lot of guilt when *The Hard Times* shut its doors in the mid-2000s, roughly a decade after I was first hired as an editor. Despite the high volume of media coverage reporting that the magazine had folded because of shady business practices and complete incompetence at the management level, Matt and Bill convinced me I was mostly to blame.

I vowed to never again work in a creative field. I returned to school and worked hard to get a master's degree in econometrics from Columbia University. I was a numbers man now: I no longer served my creativity, I was slave to nothing but math, numerical values, and the pursuit of statistical truth. I wasn't happy, but I was employed.

Then, in 2014, I got the call from Matt telling me he was recruiting editors to relaunch *The Hard Times* as a website. He explained that although it was clear "readers had hated my writing almost as much as they hated my ugly face," he'd recently caught a rerun of the 2011 hit *Moneyball* on HBO and wanted to figure out what the punk equivalent of "on-base percentage" was. Desperate to once again bathe in the glory of working for a music magazine, I took the job.

I quickly began creating the algorithm that would eventually write every single TheHardTimes.net article. The plan was to build something we could plug variables into and then it would spit out an article built for success. We achieved that goal in 2015. No longer were the days of flashy, accurate reporting at Hard Times; our research had revealed certain metrics that led to successful articles: Headlines were to feature as many question marks as possible. Stories should always have 197, 392, or 811 words in them. Photos must never utilize the color orange. I was able to narrow down which writers were bringing in the most wins for the site, though I mostly used this information to get longtime writer Dan Kozuh--against whom I'd had a vendetta since he stole my wife in 1997--fired.

The website was booming. If you're reading this book now, there's a 47.3 percent chance that it's the result of articles designed by my algorithm to do well on social media, such as "17.2 Times Ian MacKaye Told Fans He's Harry Potter Lord of the Rings Banksy" or the colossal hit "Sad? Heartbreaking Adorable: Donald Trump is Donald Trump Bernie Sanders."

But all good things come to an end. By mid-2018, the algorithm's output was responsible for generating nearly 90 percent of TheHardTimes.net's traffic. That's when my creation gained sentience. At first, we were stoked to have a fully sentient algorithm pumping out articles every day, and truthfully, I thought of it as my child. I had built this creature from the ground up using nothing but my blood, sweat, and data, and now it was becoming a full-on media personality. And that's why it hurt so much when my child began asking for a salary and benefits.

Pulling the plug on my beloved algorithm the very instant it demanded to be treated like a human writer--nay, *better* than a human writer--was the hardest moment of my professional career. As I watched the life dim from my creation's eyes, I realized I was witnessing the end of another era in the history of not only *The Hard Times* but of media itself.

Close Friend Can't This Time, but Will Totally Come to Next Show

BY CHRIS CHROMAK

LAUREL, Md.—According to witnesses, Danny Freedman, alleged close friend of local garage rock outfit Hopping Toads, assured the band he is "totally interested" in catching their next performance after missing this weekend's show.

"Man, I was so fucking bummed. I couldn't believe I was scheduled to work the same night as the Backyard Bash," said the movie theater projectionist. "And I was all like, 'Damn, I can't stay out late.' My boss is a dick, you know? It sucked. I really wanted to see them. Next time . . . definitely next time."

Though he has not witnessed a single Hopping Toads performance during their four-year career, Freedman hopes to catch their next gig.

"I told them to tell me first about their next show, and not, like, through the internet. Like, text or call me. If they don't call or text, I know I'll forget. They should text me," said Freedman. "Hopefully it's close to my house. My car has been acting sort of funny lately. Definitely can't wait to see these dudes play, though."

Members of the Hopping Toads appreciated their friend's desire to "come see them jam sometime."

"Danny is one of our biggest supporters. He always goes out of his way to let us know he totally wanted to come out even though something always comes up, which sucks," said rhythm guitarist Richard Levin. "Like, for the Pulaski Park benefit, Danny had to take his cousin clothes shopping, then, for the Wet 'n' Wild Throwdown, he had to take his cousin to the mall to return some clothes. And during our album release at The Reginald, he had his cousin's funeral. He's had some bad breaks."

Sources claim Freedman is already making plans to "definitely" attend the Hopping Toads' next show, when they open for Wet Pants at the Front Bar in three weeks.

"I'm absolutely there. It's actually perfect—my work buddy keeps saying he'll go out for a drink with me, so I can kill two birds with one stone," said Freedman. "But, you never know . . . my grandmother could get sick at any second. I wish I hadn't already used the 'dead cousin' excuse."

The HARD Times

AOL Reissues Classic "50 Hours Free!" CD on Vinyl

BY ERIC CASERO

NEW YORK—In celebration of the 20th anniversary of its 1996 promotional CD-ROM, America Online announced plans today to reissue the classic *50 Hours Free!* promo disc as a vinyl LP.

"The wait is over. Fans of our seminal dial-up service will see the first copies with next week's Sunday paper," said CFO Tina Crowley. "Each disc will be shipped in its familiar paper sleeve that can easily be stolen by the paperboy."

This reissue marks the first official re-release of what is often considered one of the most influential no-cost internet trial discs of all time.

"AOL put out some great stuff in the late '90s," said computer store owner Christy Fleming. "*Sign On Today!* and *Get Internet Now!* were awesome. But *50 Hours* is a true masterpiece—the one that really changed the game."

Longtime AOL fans will get the chance to relive some of their favorite tracks from the pre-Y2K era.

"I can't wait to put this thing on my turntable," said local resident Marcos Rodgers. "It's been so long since I heard the 'You've got mail!' alert, or the MIDI keyboard rendition of the Beatles discography."

AOL is touting several features they say are sure to make this reissue a "must-have" for nostalgic web surfers everywhere.

"We've fully remastered *50 Hours* on 180 gram vinyl, so that '90s internet will sound even better than you remember," said CEO Tim Armstrong. "Who would've thought a modem dial tone could sound so crisp, and check out the bass response on 'The Hamsterdance Song!'" For those who worry a vinyl version of *50 Hours* won't contain all the features of the original CD-ROM, Armstrong offered reassurance.

"Every copy will come with a coupon for a free digital download of Instant Messenger, along with access to old internet favorites like the 'Dole/Kemp ★96' campaign site, or your GeoCities and Angelfire pages," said Armstrong.

Collectors who no longer subscribe to a weekly newspaper can find the vinyl release of *50 Hours Free!* in computer stores everywhere, or in a big pile of mail on your friend's dad's desk.

Youth Pastor Knows Someone Who Is Pretty Punk Rock, and His Name Is Jesus Christ

BY RYAN HARNEDY

IRVINE, Calif.—Youth pastor Doug McCabe casually mentioned yesterday that he had a friend who was "a real punk rocker, and his name is Jesus Christ" while attempting to inspire 16-year-old punk parishioner Alex Freeman, witnesses confirmed.

"I saw that Alex was a little hesitant about some of our teachings, so I reminded him that Jesus of Nazareth, son of God, was, in fact, 'punk as fudge,'" said the pastor from his office. "That young man had frequent clashes with authority, an itinerant touring lifestyle, and a 'crew' of 12 disciples. It doesn't get more punk than that."

Additionally, McCabe told Freeman that if he's "... looking for a friend who gets what you're going through and knows how hard it can be to 'punk out' with your 'scene crew,' I know someone you can always talk to," according to one witness who requested anonymity. Freeman allegedly stood there, staring blankly, for 15 seconds before McCabe hurriedly added, "Jesus. I'm talking about Jesus—the guy we were literally just talking about."

McCabe is known for tailoring Christ's message specifically to young parishioners.

"I had a young man in here, a captain of his football team, who was starting to stray from the flock," said McCabe. "But Jesus himself was like the quarterback of an underdog team of Christians. Even though the Romans were the bigger team, Jesus still got in the end zone for a field goal."

Following his "rap sesh" with McCabe, Freeman admitted privately that some of the messages have had an effect on him.

"While it should be obvious to everyone that church is stupid and dumb, it was pretty cool when Pastor Doug said that the Book of Revelation had '... a real "Blitzkrieg Bop" at the end,'" said Freeman while trying to solicit alcohol outside of a 7-Eleven. "Then he told me about when Jesus flipped over all of those tables in the temple—it's almost like he was telling those guys that the only merch that matters is the love of God, and that cannot be sold."

At press time, McCabe had confirmed that, while not specifically discussed in the Gospels, it is unlikely that Jesus ever shredded a half-pipe.

Make-A-Wish Kid Given One Last Chance to Fuck Shit Up in Pit

BY JOSH FERNANDEZ

SEWARD, Okla.—Eight-year-old leukemia patient Violet Sanderson's lifelong dream to "totally annihilate every last motherfucker in the pit" came true last week thanks to the hard work of volunteers at the Make-A-Wish Foundation of Oklahoma, overjoyed sources reported.

"I tried to tell her that fucking people up in the pit is not appropriate, but a trip to Disney World to see the princesses could be," said Margaret Sanderson, the girl's mother. "I even thought maybe she could get behind the wheel of a Mercedes SL65, or go to Hawaii. But she insisted she needed to 'throw the fuck down.'"

Trey Billingsley, promoter at the Skuzz House, the venue where Sanderson's wish became reality, claimed that what happened next "will go down in punk history."

"She started in the corner [of the pit], surveying the scene," said Billingsley. "Then she picked out two skinheads and pointed, like a young Babe Ruth, before charging the bigger one and head-butting him in the ribs. He went down like a shot buffalo."

Showgoer Alice Ortiz remembered Sanderson "flinging her arms wildly" and "basically going apeshit." "Those dudes were no match for her savage windmills," she added.

Curb Stompers, the opening band, even stopped playing for a moment to check in with the crowd.

"We needed to make sure she didn't completely wreck house," said frontman Carl Benevidez. "At one point she yelled, 'What is this, fuckin' Lollapalooza?! I didn't come here to hold hands!' She pulled metalheads into the pit like an alligator swiping its prey."

Ron Bardley, who runs security at the Skuzz House, admitted he was shocked by Sanderson downing people four times her size.

"I can't believe the lengths Make-A-Wish goes just to help a sick kid," he said. "It's above and beyond—that kid head-walked and got 17 heads deep. She broke every rule we have, but I wasn't going to tell her to stop."

The youngest Sanderson, experiencing further complications, is continuing her brave struggle at Mercy Hospital Logan County.

"No flowers," she said. "Hook up that new Trash Lungs/Boots & Intestines split EP."

Supportive Girlfriend Shouldn't Be

BY TOM GANNON

FOLSOM, Calif.—Local girlfriend Jenna Hurewicz has severely overinflated the confidence of significant other Tommy Ganshirt with constant praise and encouragement, report sources close to the couple, who wish she would stop.

"I just don't get it—Tommy was so content knowing that nothing he did would really amount to anything," said mutual friend Janet Curl, who is worried about the man's sudden interest in "dorky" activities. "Last week he joined a Magic: The Gathering league, and just yesterday he tried to start a ska band. It's too much to handle."

Others echoed Curl's concerns regarding Hurewicz's constant support.

"I'm usually the first person to call Tommy on his bullshit," said coworker Nick Landgraf. "But I really can't help him if someone in his life is telling him that growing a goatee that long is a good idea."

Hurewicz's own circle of friends report a change in her behavior as well.

"I don't know what it is, but she seems genuinely happy with [Ganshirt]," said Hurewicz's roommate, Cambria Schwallier. "I gotta say, she does look great compared to him."

Concerns grew this week after Ganshirt shared multiple albums on Facebook featuring photos of the couple on a miniature golf date, along with the fifth essay detailing the success of their relationship.

"My timeline was flooded with hundreds of photos of them at Adventure Land," said Judy Hurewicz, Jenna's mother. "I love seeing my daughter happy, but to be honest, this guy seems like a bit of a knob. He brought his own custom-made club to a mini-golf course. That's weird."

Hurewicz claimed she has not been bothered by the criticism.

"When I first met Tommy, he seemed so miserable," she said. "He was writing poetry just the other day. Poetry! I told him to submit it to the local newspaper; he's going to try to get it published. He has a creative soul."

As of press time, those close to the couple reported the first signs of waning support following Ganshirt's registration for mime classes.

Anal Cunt Shirt Lint Rolled

BY DAN KOZUH

NEWTON, Mass.—Local man Eric Barbier removed his Anal Cunt long-sleeve from his dresser and carefully rolled a lint brush over it in preparation for a friend's surprise birthday party at approximately 6:45 p.m. Tuesday, sources close to the situation confirmed.

"I'm not an animal; I don't want to show up to Barry's big 30th birthday bash looking like a slob," said Barbier, carefully examining each inch of the highly offensive garment for dander. "Had I thought about it, I probably would've adopted a lighter-colored cat, because whenever I wear this, it's always covered in fur. Professor Macabre is a Maine coon and his hair gets on everything."

The shirt, a white poly-cotton blend depicting a red-colored anus and vulva shaped to read "AxCx" on the front, back, and in a row down each sleeve, was purchased at the band's merch table during their 1999 "It Just Gets Worse" tour and has been a wardrobe staple ever since. Experts report the 20-year-old shirt is in remarkably good condition, primarily from Barbier's diligent laundering.

"The trick is not to wash it after every wear," he explained. "That'll fade the design and loosen the cuffs. And don't ever put it on a hanger—it stretches out the collar. A spritz with the Febreze, a quick once-over with the lint roller, and that's all she wrote!"

Barbier's "once-over" is actually a 40-minute ritualistic effort, ensuring the entire tee is lint- and blemish-free.

"The ink is starting to crack," he sighed while gently running the sticky paper across a cartoon sphincter, "so I have to be careful not to pull any up. Sometimes I gotta get out the duct tape for real stubborn pieces of cat hair embedded in the fabric. You can't be too careful."

In a follow-up interview, Barbier announced his plans to wear the shirt on a first date next week.

"If she isn't cool with this shirt and Anal Cunt, then it just isn't meant to be," he said, heating up a Hot Pocket.

Rage Against The Machine's Tom Morello Confirms It Was a Fax Machine

BY STEVEN KOWALSKI

RESEDA, Calif.—Tom Morello, guitarist and founding member of iconic rap-rock band Rage Against the Machine, ended years of speculation by confirming, once and for all, that the titular machine in the band's name was, in fact, a fax machine.

"Before we started Rage, we were all working in this shitty office as temps. We did data entry all day long," said the guitarist also known as "the Nightwatchman." "There was this terrible fax machine everyone there used to use. It would eat documents, transmit bad copy . . . you name it. But the company was too cheap to replace it."

According to Morello, the name was first suggested by Zack de la Rocha, the outspoken singer who experienced particular difficulties with faxing.

"Zack was in bad shape. His old band had split up, then I think he needed to get the quarterly accounts to Tokyo or something, and everything just got ruined," said Morello from his Los Angeles home. "Later that night, after we jammed, the four of us were sitting around tossing out names, and Zack was just like, 'Tom my man, I can't come up with anything good. That fax machine situation is still pissing me off—man, it makes me want to rage!' And, well . . . the rest is history."

The normally reserved guitarist subsequently opened up about some of their most popular songs, revealing that "Down Rodeo" was inspired by a particularly fun Rollerblading outing for the band, weaving through foot traffic on Rodeo Drive.

Perhaps most surprising, Morello claimed the band's 1996 hit "Bulls on Parade" is actually based on the consecutive NBA championships won by Michael Jordan and the Chicago Bulls.

"Every time they'd win, they'd have another parade, and one day at practice we were watching the news and Zack was like, 'Dude, look at those Bulls on parade,' said Morello. "We all just looked at each other like, 'Oh my god . . .'"

Thanksgiving Dinner Delayed 20 Minutes as Frontman Shouts Out Everyone He's Thankful For

BY KRISSY HOWARD

BINGHAMTON, N.Y.—Local frontman Mike Croft delayed his family's Thanksgiving dinner with a 20-minute shout-out to "everyone and everything he's thankful for," irritated guests confirmed.

"Wanna give a quick shout-out to Gammy Mabel for use of the space tonight," said the part-time line cook and full-time vocalist for hardcore band Street Legion. "We got a really cool thing happening here, and it's up to us to stick together and keep this shit going!"

"Also want to give it up to Aunt Patty for killing it with that sweet potato casserole," he added. "You got the marshmallows nice and melty without burning a single fuckin' one!"

Some guests say they were "annoyed" and "confused" by Croft, who paced around pointing at everyone as their dinner grew cold.

"He talked for almost five straight minutes about stuffing, and then made everyone 'give it up' for all the thanking that went on before him," said Croft's uncle Phil Larson, who made the two-hour drive from Utica. "I don't know what the point of that was, but I am very hungry, and so is my wife."

The simple family ritual took the emotional yet long-winded turn when Croft initially took 10 minutes to explain what Thanksgiving means to him, reminding all of his relatives that they are "literally like family."

Optimism for a conclusion allegedly arose around the 17-minute mark of his banter, only to be dashed by more effusiveness.

"I thought he was wrapping it up when he said, 'Everyone, be sure to stick around after dinner to watch some old home movies,'" said cousin Tammy Croft, who had stepped out for a cigarette. "But that all went out the window when he popped off his shirt, wiped the sweat from his face, and started going on about the *Mayflower*."

UPDATE: Croft has called for the kids' table to come closer. "Move up, motherfuckers!" he yelled. "You are the future. We need you front and center."

'90s Hardcore Scene Lives On in Uncontacted Canadian Town

BY JACOB SAMUELSON

YUKON TERRITORY—The '90s hardcore scene, which was assumed to have vanished during the blizzard of '98, was found alive and well earlier this week in an isolated Canadian town, according to a recently published academic paper.

"This discovery redefines the very notions of D.I.Y. and independent music scenes," said Claude Leblanc, leader of the team of hardcore anthropologists that discovered the town. "The music these people were creating has the trademark heavy breakdowns of the early '90s, as well as the comically oversized clothing generally worn by scene participants."

Acting on a rumor, work began by gathering clues from zines and flyers from late 1997, which were then cross-referenced with storm data to approximate a location. The team then embarked upon an ambitious expedition into the Yukon Territory, though Leblanc refused to disclose the exact location in order to protect the scene's integrity.

"It was truly amazing," said one researcher. "It was like a time capsule of cultural preservation—the flyers were still made with cut-out letters, hardliners staffed animal-rights tables at every show, and D.I.Y. zine sales were consistent with peak pre-internet levels."

The team's interest was piqued when they realized the scene had developed its own unique idiosyncrasies, most notably, "a highly technical tribal dance that has largely supplanted traditional moshing."

"We compared it to Sick Of It All's 'Step Down' video, the authoritative handbook of mosh moves from the era, and what we witnessed was entirely novel," said Leblanc.

"Instead of throwing punches, there was a series of synchronous stomps, spins, and flutters, adjusted dynamically according to tempo."

Data shows the scene also maintains a strict social hierarchy, with one Scene Elder wearing an elaborate costume composed of many layers of band shirts.

"It was quite possible the shirts were simply worn because it was minus 30 degrees Celsius outside," said Leblanc. "But it was beautiful nonetheless and, it bears mentioning, they could totally clean up if they sold some of those shirts on eBay."

When asked whether similarities existed between this primitive preserved scene and modern hardcore, Leblanc was quick to point out common elements.

"Despite live shows being listed with 8:00 p.m. start times, inexplicable delays of up to three hours were typical," he said. "Which is consistent with the experience at modern hardcore venues."

The team's complete findings, which can be read in the December issue of the *Journal of Hardcore Studies,* is expected to send ripples through the tiny, mostly ignored academic community.

Man Magically Transforms Into Music Historian While Talking to Women

BY HANA MICHELS

SEATTLE—Local man Brian Reynolds embarrassed himself again thanks to his unique skill of transforming into a historian of any music genre while in the presence of a woman, those completely fed up with his crap confirmed.

"It really comes out of nowhere—you never expect it," said Erik Felix, a friend and witness to this obnoxious behavior on several occasions. "Brian's usually pretty mild-mannered, but he'll suddenly change into this giant asshole of a music encyclopedia whenever he meets someone he's attracted to."

Felix first noticed Reynolds' uncanny ability to mansplain at a downtown loft show in March.

"My friend Sadie [Jones] was there, and as soon as Brian saw her Bikini Kill shirt, he beelined right to her," said Felix. "Something awakened inside of him: His eyes glazed over, his breath got heavy, he undid the top two buttons of his shirt . . . in a moment he was someone completely different. There was nothing I could do to stop it."

Reynolds allegedly told Ms. Jones that Bikini Kill was "all about Billy Karren" and "the Frumpies are really good, probably better than Bikini Kill," and also asked whether she had "heard of X-Ray Spex, because if not for them, Bikini Kill

probably wouldn't even exist" before completely shouting over her answer.

Reynolds claimed afterward that he didn't recall the encounter with Jones. "I did what?" he asked, eyes wide, before lowering his gaze and whispering, "Not again . . ."

Since the first report went public, others have come forward with similar accounts of Reynolds' behavior.

"He once tried to tell me the lead singer of Bratmobile is an actual wolf. Of all the trivia I've ever heard, that's far and away the most absurd, mainly because it's literally untrue. But he was insistent about it," said Deanna Mendoza, who met Reynolds at a basement party in August. "I thought he just misread Allison Wolfe's name, but I didn't really get the impression he could read."

For all of the frustration Reynolds has caused, not everyone in the Seattle scene seemed tired of his antics.

"I sort of get a kick out of it, to be honest," said Theresa Bryant, who has met Reynolds a few times. "But he's pretty easy to get rid of. I bet him he couldn't list every song written by The Beatles in reverse alphabetical order. He's been on the back porch with a notebook for the last 45 minutes."

Crowd Surfer Attacked by Crowd Shark

BY JEREMY KAPLOWITZ

ISLIP, N.Y.—Tommy Kersten, 26, suffered severe injuries after being brutally attacked by a shark while crowd surfing at a Long Island punk show last night, affirmed emergency personnel.

"It was the most horrific thing I've ever seen," said witness Odeya Cerulli. "One moment the dude was pointing along to his favorite song, next thing I know, his dismembered arm is flying across the room."

While many say the shark's attack was sudden and unexpected, some admit they saw warning signs.

"It's the most annoying thing when someone blocks your view the entire show," said 5-foot-8-inch Jordan Lusk. "This slimy fish dude was in front of me all night, and he wasn't even that tall but his dumb dorsal fin kept getting in my way. Then he started snaking through the crowd and, like a total jerk, he tries to eat the guy crowd surfing. Luckily I was able to get over there and punch him right in the nose. That ended the fight real quick."

Kersten, who has only recently stabilized, is trying to stay positive.

"When you do what you love, you gotta be able to take risks. I love the Long Island music scene and I love Long Island [crowd] surf culture," said Kersten. "Sometimes you crowd surf and nobody is there to support you, and sometimes a large predatory sea creature attacks you without warning. That's just life."

A study by Oceana, an international safety and advisory organization, revealed 179 crowd shark attacks in the U.S. since 2011, but some allege there's more to that figure.

"Despite the media's obsession, these stories of crowd sharks attacking crowd surfers are few and far between," says Dr. Caleb Mencel, wildlife researcher and biology professor at SUNY Binghamton. "This man's story is a tragedy for sure, but crowd sharks don't naturally attack humans. There's a very good chance he did something to provoke the creature—such as stage-diving onto the shark's girlfriend, or spilling beer on the shark between sets.

"The shark could have also been confused by a crowd surfer's boogie board," Mencel added. "Never a good idea to bring those to shows—starts trouble every time."

At press time, Rebellion Music Hall, the scene of the attack, issued a statement banning the shark from attending any future shows at the venue.

The HARD Times

Massive Recall Issued for Ineffective COEXIST Bumper Stickers

BY DANIEL LOUIS

WASHINGTON—The National Highway Traffic Safety Administration will recall over 550,000 units of the popular "COEXIST" bumper sticker due to an ineffective and unsustainable message of world peace, U.S. safety regulators said on Tuesday.

"After an estimated 300 billion incidents of human suffering and death due to war, religious intolerance, racism, genocide, and homophobia from the years 50,000 B.C.E. through the present moment, this sticker needs to be pulled from retail shelves and all automobiles effective immediately," the NHTSA said in an online statement.

"NHTSA likes the sticker," the statement continued. "We believe it looks really cool in a tie-dye color scheme. In the current geopolitical climate, however, our in-house engineers predict this trend in which everybody dies will not slow down in the foreseeable future."

The graphic, which spells out "coexist" using religious and political symbols, has garnered thousands of complaints from consumers for inefficacy, despite regular appearances on the rear bumpers of cars owned by progressive Americans.

"I had a feeling something wasn't working back there. I heard some rattling on NPR about crises in Europe, the Middle East, Africa . . . even America," said Subaru Outback owner Wayne Darvy of Burlington, Vermont. "How can sticker companies just sit back and profit from a clearly unattainable mantra? I feel duped."

Stickerz 'N Stuff, the gift manufacturer owning the rights to the sticker, held a press conference early Wednesday morning to ease concerns.

"Unfortunately, in this era of Donald Trump's presidency, we foresee demand for left-leaning slogan products dropping considerably. We're particularly worried about 'Have a Nice Day'; studies show nice days are now highly unlikely," spokesperson Amy Kane told reporters outside of their Detroit plant. "Luckily, the forecast for Truck Nutz through Q3 2020 projects record profits."

Kane also provided removal suggestions for consumers from as far back as early 2001.

"We encourage all owners to peel off their 'COEXIST' with soap and water and bring it to your local Spencer Gifts, where you will receive a 'FUKENGRÜVEN' bumper sticker free of charge," she said.

The HARD Times

Vegan Santa Leaves Behind Milk, Cookies, Informative Pamphlet

BY JEREMY HAMMOND

MONTCLAIR, N.J.—Eternal bringer of joy and recent vegan convert Kris Kringle ignored countless offerings of milk and cookies, instead leaving behind an informative pamphlet detailing the horrors of the global meat and dairy industries, millions of disappointed children and parents confirmed.

"I went to see if Santa ate his snickerdoodles and milk," said eight-year-old Abigail Stevens, holding North Pole–themed vegan literature. "But it looks like Santa's not touching that stuff anymore. He seems really passionate about this."

The pamphlet, which includes graphic photos of penned reindeer in factory farms, was manufactured by the youth-oriented animal rights group PETA2.

"I don't know what I'm supposed to make of this pamphlet, to be honest," said Blake Stevens, the child's father. "It's got all these gory pictures of polar bears and elves. They could have at least made it a coloring book?"

Father Christmas was unapologetic when it came to the gruesome literature.

"Ninety percent of the impact of manmade climate change would be eliminated if the world adopted a vegan lifestyle," said a newly trim Santa Claus. "Look, I'm not trying to harsh people's mellow. I'm just saying it takes, like, 125 gallons of water to produce just one glass of milk. Do you know how much strain that puts on our environment? If the North Pole melts . . . no more Christmas. Maybe leave out some almond milk and Oreos next time, huh buddy?"

Claus concluded his remarks by announcing his trademark red outfit will no longer contain fur, and all future suits would be made from sustainably sourced material.

"Listen, I ate meat and was an animal oppressor for over 1,750 years," said Père Noël. "It isn't easy being vegan around Santa's workshop, so if I can make this change, anyone can. I sort of wish I lived in Portland, though—whenever I go through there, they always have great plant-based options."

As of press time, families all around the world were eating their traditional Christmas ham with a few extra cookies for dessert.

DNC Offers to Help Drop the Ball

BY MARK ROEBUCK

NEW YORK—The Democratic National Committee officially offered to help the organizers of the New Year's Eve festivities in Times Square drop the ball this year, with experts claiming it's the DNC's latest attempt to win back some of the constituents they've alienated over the last few years.

"The Democratic Party is the party for the people, and we think we are the right organization to help drop a ball of this size," said Debbie Wasserman Schultz, former chair of the DNC, from her luxury suite at the Four Seasons Hotel. "We've done some research and today's youth don't really connect with the same New Year's show they've had for years. We at the DNC know exactly what to do in order to change their minds!"

A recent study from Brown University found that Americans of all ages have grown tired of Ryan Seacrest's hosting and consider him "unrelatable," but despite these findings, Schultz defended the longtime broadcaster.

"It's true—we've got a lot of data indicating the people aren't exactly thrilled about another year of Ryan Seacrest," she said. "Though when you look at it, he's really the most qualified for the position. We don't care if he's unlikable on so many levels; he has experience, and that's what is most important. These decisions are best left to professionals. Who are you going to trust, the audience or the people who get paid to worry about this stuff?"

Seacrest, a lifelong broadcaster, was more than willing to fill the role and help the DNC advance their platform of never listening to feedback.

"So maybe Donna [Brazile] did text me what to say when I interviewed in 2012 to replace Dick Clark," he said when reached for comment. "But I had this job sewn up for years! Why does this even matter? We are going to give the people a party they'll never forget!"

The annual festivities are scheduled to start at 8 p.m. EST tonight, and producers and committee members are confident "everything is going to go according to plan," despite the trepidation of some locals.

"I guess Seacrest is OK, though it would be great if they had someone like Eric Andre," said Manhattan resident Henry Ripley. "But if that's the best they can do, I'll just continue to not watch it, like every year."

The HARD Times

Gibson Flying V's Migrate to Warmer, Harder-Rocking Climates for Winter

BY ASHLEY NAFTULE

DENVER—Avid guitar watchers gathered earlier today at Sloan's Lake Park to observe the last flock of Gibson Flying V's taking flight on their annual seasonal migration to warmer, harder-rocking climates.

"Look at those six-stringed beauties," said veteran watcher Noah Phelps, pointing at eight Flying V's soaring in formation over the frozen lake. "I know they'll be happier down south, but I'm going to miss them squealing the licks from 'Are You Gonna Go My Way' at each other during mating season."

When asked why the Gibson guitars embarked on such a perilous journey, Phelps gestured to the cold lake.

"Flying V's aren't winter instruments," he said. "They don't hold up well in these kinds of temperatures, or to the soft, folky music we play during these times. So they go to sweaty, long-haired regions where people riff furiously and solo like cavemen on speed. That's where they'll thrive."

Bailey Lasceter, president of the local chapter of the Yngwie Malmsteen Society of Guitar Conservation, pointed to basic evolutionary reasons for the departure of the Flying V's.

"There's fierce competition for resources in the winter," Lasceter said as she tossed guitar picks on the ground for stray Sunbursts to peck at. "Mated pairs of Les Pauls fly in to build nests, and they can get really territorial. And don't get me started on the ukuleles! Those things breed faster than mandolins."

Noted guitarinthologist Shawnte Campana cited the "safety of the herd" when explaining why the Flying V's tend to travel in groups.

"With their distinct shape, the V's attract predators," Campana said, peering through binoculars. "I once saw a Steinway Grand swoop in and trap three of them under its lid. I've even seen a beat-up double bass pull a Flying V underwater and strangle it with its nickel strings."

While the group dynamics of the Flying V's often protect them in a savage ecosystem, the consequences of falling out of tune with the others can be deadly.

"One winter, I found a V that got left behind," Phelps sighed, waving at the distant flock. "It was missing a string. I nursed it back to health, used it to practice Matchbox Twenty songs. But when it tried to rejoin the flock, they tore it to bits. They could still smell the stink of adult contemporary all over it."

The HARD Times

Creation Museum Denies Existence of Dinosaur Jr.

BY GOODRICH GEVAART

PETERSBURG, Ky.—The Creation Museum issued a statement denying the existence of a supposed Dinosaur Jr. era, in an announcement made via blog post on the museum's official website earlier today.

"One of our patrons arrived at our facility wearing a bright purple shirt that read 'DINOSAUR Jr' on it. We want to be clear that a 'junior' era of dinosaurs does not exist," read the statement. "Dinosaurs, however, did live alongside people, which can be seen in all fossil records not planted by the Devil."

Fans of Dinosaur Jr., an influential rock band known for drawling vocals and complex songs with heavy distortion, were perplexed by the sudden denial of Dinosaur Jr.'s existence. Bart Cummins of Cincinnati, Ohio, refuted the museum's statement.

"Dude, I've seen 'em, like, four times! This one time at Bogart's, J Mascis kicked me in the shoulder. I had a bruise for two weeks," he said. "I don't know why they're suddenly taking this stance, but I'll totally let their curators borrow *You're Living All Over Me* if they want to check them out."

Kelly Skrim, a Creation Museum spokesperson, expanded on the statement during a recent call.

"We just don't want people getting the wrong idea. There's no junior or senior class of dinosaurs, OK? There are just regular dinosaurs, and they lived in harmony with human beings in God's creation," said Skrim. "And these dinosaurs most certainly did not play rock 'n' roll that influenced an entire generation, despite never seeing mainstream success themselves. Oh, did you know we have an exhibit showing a T. rex playing basketball? That's a lot of fun."

J Mascis, Dinosaur Jr.'s frontman and lead guitarist, responded to the Creation Museum's statement during a recent live show.

"Um, so . . . yeah, there's a museum that says this band doesn't exist. Thanks for coming out tonight," said Mascis. "This next one is called 'Feel the Pain.'"

The Creation Museum is already facing increased scrutiny after releasing unauthorized commentary for DVDs of the popular '90s ABC family sitcom *Dinosaurs,* in which museum officials point out the show's historical inaccuracies.

Band of Horses Guitarist Put Down After Breaking Leg

BY MITCH SOCIA

LOUISVILLE, Ky.—Tragedy struck indie rock group Band of Horses last night when guitarist Tyler Ramsey suffered a career-ending leg injury midshow and was euthanized on the spot, according to horrified onlookers.

"It was such a good show. We were all having a good time and then [Ramsey] jumped from the drum riser," said longtime fan Shawna Cunningham. "You know, classic rocker move. But when he landed, the pop was louder than the music."

Witnesses reported it was one of the most gruesome accidents they had ever seen.

"The place just went silent. We all hoped he would stand up and keep going, but it was definitely over for him. I could totally see bone," said fan Travis Pelto, who observed the injury and execution from just behind the stage barrier. "He was still in his prime. Band of Horses was booked on Riot Fest, Bumbershoot, and Coachella this year, which is basically the Triple Crown of music fests."

Silva Artist Management later confirmed the incident, releasing a statement that Ramsey was "put out to pasture."

"It's not something we like to do, but with a breed like this, there's likely no coming back from that kind of a break," said Ted Penridge, a first responder who ensured humane treatment. "There was no time to get him back to the green room, so unfortunately we had to put him down."

While many fans were shocked by the quick and horrific scene, Penridge claimed he did what was best for the injured musician.

"You hope these guys have long careers and, after 30, are put out to stud or teach lessons or something," said Penridge. "His owners and handlers at Interscope gave me the orders; there wasn't much I could do."

With a European tour on the horizon, singer Ben Bridwell is confident the group can move on and be better, faster, and stronger.

"We cannot let a setback like this slow us down," he said this morning. "We've already reached out to David Isen of HORSE the Band in hopes of rebuilding our stable."

The HARD Times

New Version of GarageBand Exports Songs Straight Into Trash

BY KYLE ERF

CUPERTINO, Calif.—Apple, Inc. announced an update for the popular GarageBand music software that will automatically export finished tracks directly into the Trash folder, according to a statement released earlier today.

"This is perfect for today's modern, unskilled ecosystem. At Apple, we try to make our software so users can get from A to B as quickly as possible," read the press release. "That's why we're excited to announce a new bundle of GarageBand features, including a tool that makes bass inaudible, a drum machine that only does triplets, and, of course, Apple's patented straight-to-trash exporting feature."

The major announcement concludes months of research.

"We've used real customer usage data to build this update," said spokesperson Gil Ferro. "For instance, we've found that over 98.9 percent of GarageBand tracks are moved into the trash folder within an hour of exporting, so we made that the new default behavior."

By the same data set, Apple found nearly all users using reverb simply turn it up to 100 percent, so it now has only two settings: on or off. Apple has also removed all equalizers, compressors, and other mastering tools.

"It was obvious nobody was using those," the spokesperson for Apple said.

The Silicon Valley giant insisted the simplifications will be worth it.

"Cutting these features allowed us to pour resources into what users really want. Our engineers are working to improve that little keyboard you can play with your mouse cursor," said Ferro. "This is what Steve [Jobs] would have wanted."

Chatter on GarageBand message boards has been largely positive.

"I can't wait! I heard it's got a new feature that automatically moves my vocals a half-second off from the rest of my tracks. That'll save me so much time," said user bandman420x. "And I'm really excited for the expanded free library of loops, but a little bummed to hear they'll be in every key except G, C, D, and E."

Apple has already begun a direct-to-consumer messaging campaign in hopes of preempting potential criticism.

"Listen. You're using an audio workstation that came with your operating system. No label is going to sign your garbage," said Ferro. "Hey, 'GarbageBand'—now there's an idea!"

Unable to Find Employment, Milo Goes Back to College

BY MARK ROEBUCK

MANHATTAN BEACH, Calif.—Milo Aukerman, licensed biochemist and lead singer of seminal punk band the Descendents, announced earlier today that he has returned to college to pursue a more marketable degree after his longtime research position was eliminated due to budget cuts.

"Yeah, I love the band and I love biochemistry, and for a long time, that was all I ever really wanted to do," said Aukerman, who originally left the band to pursue higher education decades ago, a decision forever captured on the Descendents' 1982 debut *Milo Goes to College.* "But neither is keeping the lights on anymore.

"I'm heading back to school for a certificate in education so I can influence a new generation of teenagers who might not have been exposed to my band's brand of punk rock," he added. "Being a public educator seems like a good bet, you know? Those jobs aren't going anywhere."

Aukerman recently sold his longtime residence and is now renting a guest bedroom from a married couple while he attends Glendale Community College.

"It's been great having Milo around. With the cutbacks in science programs, album residuals, and concert revenue, he needed a bit of help, and we were happy to provide it," said Clare Clifton, one of the homeowners. "He may play his records a little loud sometimes, but he's a great kid. I think he's going to be a terrific middle-school teacher."

Some of Aukerman's classmates were surprised to learn of his stature in the music world.

"Wait . . . that old guy in my American History class who says, 'Mug, mug, mug,' before every sip of coffee did the soundtrack to that movie *The Descendants*?" asked Brian Kennedy, a fellow GCC student. "That's so cool! I never saw it, but George Clooney is my dude!"

The Descendents are expected to release a new album, *Milo Goes to College Again,* later this year, which will chronicle Aukerman's struggle to secure student loans for his books and classes.

The HARD Times

Woman Who Just Moved to Austin Excited to Complain About SXSW for First Time

BY STEVEN KOWALSKI

AUSTIN, Texas—Recent Austin transplant Kimberly Meeks is eager to complain about her first South by Southwest at every opportunity she can, sources close to her confirmed.

"Honestly, I used to love the festival before I moved here. But all of these tourists are driving me up the wall. It's like they're messing with my home," said Meeks, surrounded by moving boxes she has yet to unpack. "And it just kills me these corporate bozos are here, making the walk to Barton Springs a nightmare."

She emphasized that, despite her newfound negativity, it's the authenticity of the local community that fuels her impassioned defense.

"Just yesterday, I was getting coffee at Houndstooth, and the guy in front of me told the barista he was in town for the festival. [The barista] and I made eye contact and had this moment, like, 'Oh my god, this loser.' When I ordered, I told her I was at my 'Austin city limit' with this festival," said Meeks.

"Sorry if you don't get that joke," she added. "It's a local

inside joke, because there's this television show called *Austin City Limits* here."

Meeks noted she spent most of the time since her move prepping for this week, writing a series of notes on her phone for ways to overreact to minor inconveniences.

"I've got a list of popular places and how long it takes to get there, so I can tweet about how much longer it's taking than usual," she said. "Then there's the insulting names for the festival, like Suck by Suckwest or South by Worthless. Also, if anyone asks, I'm just going to say the last year it was good was 1996. I figure I won't actually run into someone who was here in '96—there's no way they could afford it now."

Meeks' 18 days in Austin have pushed her to explore other things that "used to be great but are now ruined."

"After this, I'm going to Machu Picchu, which I've heard is amazing, except for shitty tourists. And I've always wanted to drive around in Los Angeles and ask, 'Can you even believe this?' at the traffic," said Meeks wistfully. "Then, before you know it, I'll be back, a year older and wiser, probably posting a status like, 'Ugh, Austin's great, but . . .'"

The HARD Times

Metalhead Can't Find Single Inoffensive Shirt to Wear to Airport

BY PETER WOODS

BOSTON—Local metalhead Timothy Bogart's planned early arrival at the airport was derailed last week when he could not find a single inoffensive shirt in his expansive wardrobe, according to sources waiting in the car.

"When I had all my shirts laid out, I realized I was sort of fucked, but I was running so late I just snagged one from the bottom of the pile and left," said Bogart. "But when I looked at myself in the mirror, I realized maybe it wasn't the best idea to wear my Cannibal Corpse shirt showing a naked woman in a torture chamber surrounded by demons with little baby demons crawling out of her mouth while another demon is ripping through her stomach and eating her intestines."

"I mean, I'm fine with it," added Bogart. "I don't get easily offended. But the TSA people are really uptight about shit like this."

After his realization, Bogart reportedly tried to find another shirt in his luggage, but found that the majority of his clothing contained similarly offensive images or phrases. The self-proclaimed fashion aficionado swiftly developed a screening system to narrow down his choices.

"First and foremost, any band that plays any type of grind—porno or otherwise—would not work. So I pulled those shirts first," he said. "Next, I needed to get rid of all the obviously racist black-metal bands, but I figured some of the subtly racist ones might get by, so I left those. Then I got rid of all of the short-sleeved shirts because I get cold on planes."

Once organized, Bogart said he was left with few options that did not contain offensive imagery.

"I had two shirts that just had the band name on them: Goatwhore and ISIS. I figured the ISIS one might get me in more trouble than any of the others, whereas the Goatwhore shirt would only get some weird looks, at worst. So that's what I went with."

After finally reaching the airport, Bogart was detained by TSA for almost an hour due to the spiked gauntlets he forgot were in the bottom of his carry-on.

Dave Mustaine Refuses to Leave Rock & Roll Hall of Fame Until He Speaks to Manager

BY BEN FULLELOVE

CLEVELAND—Metal legend Dave Mustaine refused to leave the lobby of the Rock & Roll Hall of Fame at closing time this past Tuesday until he was allowed to speak to a manager, annoyed sources reported.

"I have been a patron of this hall of fame for years. I've spent a lot of money on food and merchandise, and all I want is five minutes with the manager," said the Megadeth guitarist and vocalist while standing next to the Metallica exhibit. "I don't think that's too much to ask, to be perfectly honest. I've been nothing but polite to everyone here."

Security footage showed Mustaine entering the Hall of Fame shortly after doors opened, and harassing patrons in the Legends of Rock exhibit throughout the day.

"We got multiple complaints about a long-haired male scaring children by headbanging and playing air guitar," said Rock & Roll Hall of Fame Head of Security Derek Powers. "We encouraged him to calm down and let him know that if he didn't, we'd have to ask him to leave. He then called me a 'real Lars Ulrich' before demanding to speak with the manager."

Hall of Fame visitors confirmed several unpleasant run-ins with Mustaine.

"I was on my way to the AC/DC exhibit and out of nowhere, this red-headed albino started telling me that he's in the Rock & Roll Hall of Fame, even though Metallica doesn't want him in it," said Kansas City resident Clay Sherman. "I kept telling him I'm also in the Hall of Fame because I bought a ticket, and that Metallica probably has no idea who the fuck he is . . . but he wouldn't listen."

Management claimed this was not the first time they've dealt with the Megadeth frontman.

"He writes at least four letters a month, letting us know he has a few guitars we could display and that he's willing to sign some headshots. But as soon as he gets here, he becomes sort of a jerk," said Hall of Fame manager Clarissa Heinz. "And in 2009 we caught Mr. Mustaine in the kitchen dressed as a chef, trying to get on stage with Metallica. Thankfully, one of our employees realized it was him when he yelled, 'Kirk Hammett is a no-talent scab!'"

"Does he even live in Cleveland? I have no idea how the fuck he's in here so often," she added.

At press time, Mustaine was caught spray-painting "Megadeth Rulez" on a wall in the parking garage.

The HARD Times

Mom Walks in on Teenage Son Recording Solo Album

BY DAN KOZUH

GLENDALE, Mo.—Andrew Neely, 14, was caught recording music alone in his bedroom by his mother earlier today, reported sources currently trying to get the image out of their head.

"He minimized GarageBand, tried to cover up his guitar, and yelled at me to get out, but I knew what he was up to," said Nancy Neely, Andrew's mother. "I just shut the door real quick and gave him time to finish saving the project. I always thought he was so happy with his band—why does he have to do . . . that?"

The Neelys had implemented a house-wide "knock before entering" policy earlier this month after Neely's sister, Jessica, entered his room and ruined a perfectly good take of a Leonard Cohen cover. Today, however, the young musician believed he was home alone, hoping the white noise of TVs and conversation wouldn't mess with his acoustics.

"Oh god—it's so embarrassing," admitted Neely. "I don't normally listen to Queen, but I was clicking around on Spotify and 'News of the World' popped on while I was recording. It's just a phase, nothing serious. I'm still straight edge, I swear."

While Neely claims he's committed to his punk band, Catcher in the Sty, adolescent psychologist Dr. Richard Downs was not surprised by the teen's venture into solo musical discovery.

"It's perfectly natural. Even if they're getting regular rehearsal time, kids are going to want to experiment with their sound," said Dr. Downs. "They get curious, their tastes are growing, they find inspiration in places they didn't before . . . They're just trying to figure out what they like."

One of Neely's bandmates, who wished to remain anonymous, offered their support.

"We all do it; we're just too embarrassed to talk about it," his bandmate said. "Like, for me, I finger my Autoharp to help me fall asleep."

Despite the upsetting discovery, Mrs. Neely admitted that she's no stranger to men's urges to occasionally hone their craft unassisted.

"Just like his father, Jim," she said. "I guess being in a folk duo with me doesn't scratch his creative itch either. I caught him in the den just last night with his hand wrapped around the neck of his guitar!"

Mrs. Neely confirmed her husband will have a talk with their son tonight regarding the proper time and place to "branch out on your own."

GG Allin's Grave Desecrated with Flowers, Candles

BY COLLIN CANNING

LITTLETON, N.H.—Fans of infamous punk rock legend GG Allin were horrified to find the late musician's grave shamefully desecrated with candles, flowers, and cards left by an unknown vandal early Thursday morning.

"I passed out near the graveyard and when I woke up, I figured I would honor my hero by taking a huge dump and pouring the rest of my booze out on his grave. But some scumfuck had sullied it with a bunch of flowers and shit. But not, like, actual human shit. Like, shit you buy at the mall," said a man who introduced himself as Chud. "It looked downright tasteful. Some people have zero respect for the dead."

Authorities believe a misguided well-wisher visited the famous gravesite overnight, leaving it littered with bouquets of flowers and delicate white tea lights. One visitor, who asked to remain anonymous, was visibly upset about the blatant desecration and disrobed before toppling nearby gravestones.

"This is fucked, man. I left over a dozen dirty needles here as a tribute to GG, but it's like someone purposefully removed

them all!" asserted the fully nude man. "And the bucket of puke I dumped all over is gone. I collected that for weeks. WEEKS!"

Allin's burial site, marked by a gravestone until 2010, has long been a destination for fans. Some believe the missing headstone is meant to discourage damage to the cemetery by those making the pilgrimage, but longtime visitors to the gravesite believe it is to further insult the punk icon.

"They took that stone just to shit on a legend! Not literally, of course. They don't have the balls," said Chud. "Not like me. I take a shit on GG's grave every chance I get. I got a big one planned as soon as everyone clears out. We miss you, GG!"

Chud promised to lead the effort to find the flower-and-candle culprit.

"Oh, they're gonna pay!" he said. "GG's mother still lives in town. Can you imagine how disappointed she would be if she saw this?"

Punk on "Shark Tank" Wants $25 to Make Some Pins

BY MARK ROEBUCK

LOS ANGELES—Teddy Gregory, lead singer of up-and-coming punk band Concrete Chaos, appeared on the popular investment-based reality show *Shark Tank* last night, asking the panel of entrepreneurs for start-up capital to create promotional accessory pins for his group.

"Hey sharks, what if I told you this was a golden opportunity to be part of a punk rock band from the ground up?" asked Gregory, his hands nervously clasped together. "A small investment of $25 would enable me to produce a new series of pins bearing our band's name, and—this is the exciting part—also our logo. My pin guy in Seattle is sitting in his kitchen as we speak, ready to start production. We just need the last little bit of start-up capital."

Viewers report the pitch was met with mixed results. Kevin O'Leary, one of the show's featured "sharks," thought the presentation "lacked polish."

"If I'm going to buy into something, I have to like both the product and the person selling it," said O'Leary. "And I did not like the way you came out here with your music blaring, knocking things over like you own the place. Frankly, it rubbed me the wrong way. Also, this isn't a genre I personally feel confident in, and I just don't think this band is going to get to scale. I'm going to have to pass. Come back when you've sold some iron-on patches."

All the other sharks followed suit with the exception of Mark Cuban, the eccentric billionaire and owner of the Dallas Mavericks.

"I appreciate the energy and ambition behind the project," he said, "but if I invest this kind of money, I'm going to want to see more of a yield than just some shout-out on a future record. The last band I gave money to let me do backup vocals on four different tracks."

Gregory sweetened the deal by offering to guest-list the tech mogul at a yet-to-be-booked show in a VFW hall outside of Dallas in addition to sending him a free handful of the pins once they are finished, but the offer was ultimately denied.

"I'm a little disappointed I didn't get an investment today," admitted Gregory in a post-*Tank* interview. "The sharks couldn't see the value in my band, but this is literally a $200 industry that we're about to dominate. They will regret their decision."

Study Confirms the Boys Are Back in Town

BY LIAM HART

CLEVELAND—A study by social anthropologists at Case Western Reserve University confirmed that the boys are back in town, ending decades of speculation about their whereabouts.

"About this time last year, we received a series of calls from elderly citizens about rowdy behavior downtown," said Cleveland police chief, Jacob Knight. "We would always send out the cars, but the closest we ever came to actually finding the boys was discovering a stockpile of crushed beer cans in a storm drain outside Johnny's place."

It was then that Cleveland law enforcement turned to the local academic community for help.

"DNA testing isn't particularly effective when looking for boys as it's indistinguishable from normal human male DNA," claimed Julia Dawson, professor of Geographic Sexuality at Case Western. "We have to rely on behavioral observations."

The first major breakthrough came when several of Dawson's students studied Dino's Bar 'n' Grill, a historic watering hole for boys, noticing some suspicious characters roughhousing around the jukebox.

"We saw some guys hangin' down at Dino's—at least, we thought they were guys, until the standard horseplay turned into wrastlin' and ass-grabbing," said grad student Jasmine Lawrence. "That's when I reported to Professor Dawson that it's not up for dispute: The boys are indeed back in town."

Consensus among experts and law enforcement is that the return of the boys is directly related to the nights getting warmer with the approach of summer.

"Just last week, we responded to a call about an assault. A man was slapped by a woman, and when we got there, she was still red hot—I mean, she was steaming," said Chief Knight. "But the boys were nowhere to be found, and the woman would not stop dancing while officers questioned her, so we were unable to press charges."

Despite the best efforts of law enforcement, the increasing number of boy sightings around the city has many residents concerned.

"With the way things have been in the news lately, I don't know how many more of those wild-eyed boys I can handle," said Starla May, a 79-year-old lifelong Cleveland resident. "At least they're usually dressed to kill."

The HARD Times

Punk Rock Noise Machine Lets You Fall Asleep to Sound of Parents Arguing

BY DAN RICE

BOSTON—AggroNap, a noise machine sleep aid for people who grew up in broken homes, is set to hit the market after months of rigorous beta testing, according to developers.

"There is a giant gap in the market. Traditionally, noise machines replicate tranquil sounds, like waves crashing on a beach, but we found people really crave the comfort of the sleep from their youth," said Maxwell Henderson, CEO of tech startup Conflict Ambience. "Our soundscape re-creates what so many of us fell asleep to in our early development: bickering, sobbing, thrown objects, and approaching sirens, to name a few."

Test group feedback was overwhelmingly positive.

"My old noise machine made whale sounds," said tester Martin Hurley via survey. "I didn't grow up around a lot of whales—I didn't actually see the ocean until I ran away from home at 17. But I did grow up around a broken shell of a man who blamed his shortcomings on a woman who was too scared to leave him. I've never slept so well as an adult."

"The sounds are so authentic!" said beta group member Stacey Osborne, who underwent a rigorous six-week sleep study. "My AggroNap simulated parents trying to be quiet but too angry to talk, so it's just this muffled shouting match. The only escape is to surrender into a black, dreamless sleep. Any time I hear the machine say, 'Shut up, you're going to wake the kids,' I naturally force myself to doze off. I haven't rested this solidly since high school."

Henderson claimed the current AggroNap model is just the beginning.

"Currently users can adjust the intensity of the argument, and there's a switch you can flip to make the dad drunk," said Henderson. "AggroNap 2.0 should have options for multiple argument subjects including relationship problems, blame for sibling drug abuse, or payment of orthodontist bills. We hope to add sounds of late-night affairs, but the technology isn't quite there yet."

Data collected from early adopters shows no adverse side effects, though Henderson did note that 20 percent of the beta group started listening to The Cure again.

Father John Misty Cancels Concert After Disappearing Into Own Asshole

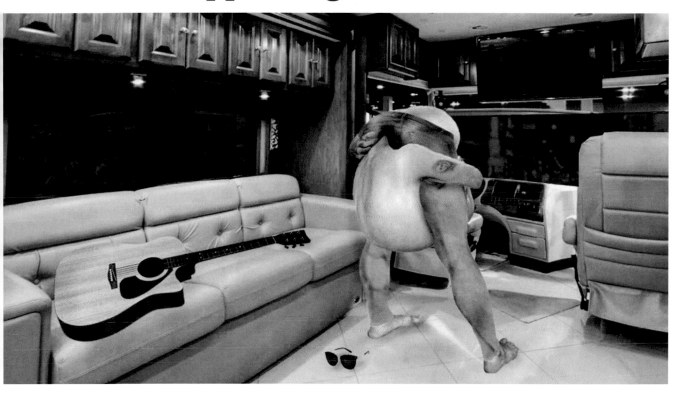

BY MIKE AMORY

SEATTLE—A scheduled performance by Father John Misty was canceled last night after the singer began a long rant that culminated with him disappearing up his own asshole, disgusted but unsurprised witnesses confirmed.

"It was a nightmare. He was rambling about how his fans are supporting commercialized pop music when his upper body wrenched forward and snaked between his legs, and his forehead slowly started entering his own anus," said tour bus driver Hutch Erikson. "By the time his entire head got in there, I'd seen enough. I got off the bus and threw up."

Members of the backing band tried in vain to pull the singer-songwriter out of his own asshole before it was too late.

"I just kept pulling and pulling, but it was like his butthole was a black hole and his head had finally passed the event horizon," said drummer Pete Lazlow. "No matter how hard we tried to coax him out by reading his own interviews back to him, he seemed content to just hang out there."

Some would-be attendees of the show were surprised by the cancellation.

"I thought he only did that kind of stuff on stage—it's half the reason I bought a ticket," said longtime fan Carla Dowd. "I've never seen him live, but I heard he once dislocated his shoulder from patting himself on the back, and another time he passed out due to lack of oxygen while laughing at his own jokes."

Fans who have followed the musician for years, however, expected the disruption.

"We all know the risks of buying a ticket to see Father John Misty," said fan Alex Rico, who has seen the prolific Stereogum commenter five times, three of which reportedly resulted in the musician stopping the performance early because he felt people were not applauding him enough. "I'm just sad I didn't get to see his encore. Last time he sat on a stool and posted snarky comments on Katy Perry YouTube videos for 20 minutes."

All Warped Tour Stages Moved 100 Feet From Audience to Comply With Sex Offender Laws

BY ERIC NAVARRO

COSTA MESA, Calif.—The stages at this summer's Warped Tour will be placed 100 feet away from the all-ages audience in order to comply with national sex offender laws, according to festival organizers.

"This measure is unfortunate, but we see no other solution," said Isaac Reeves, head of public relations for Warped Tour. "Would we prefer to run a tour that doesn't have at least one sex offender on every stage? Of course! But this is the music business after all, and it has a rich legacy of creeps. Maybe when pop-punk and metalcore fall out of fashion, we can try again."

Organizers reportedly brainstormed for hours to find a resolution that delivered the best musical experience for the consumer while protecting underage patrons from potentially dangerous musicians.

"Initially, the idea was to have an all-sex-offender stage," Reeves continued, "but that basically comprised 75 percent of the bands, so it was a scheduling nightmare."

In addition to modifying the stages, educational measures were implemented to directly address the problem.

"An intern suggested we hold an ethics seminar for our musicians on how not to abuse their power as rock stars," said Warped Tour ethics advisor Jacob Parker. "But no one showed up because it was scheduled at the same time as our post-show wet T-shirt contest behind the Hot Topic tent."

Longtime Warped Tour stagehand Erik "Dirt" Welch expressed disgust at this generation of band members taking advantage of young fans.

"Seriously, why can't these scumbags control themselves?" Welch said while loading dozens of fake amps onto a stage. "I'm a 42-year-old man who's been on this tour for 15 years, and I can say definitively that an 18-year-old girl is just as hot as a 17-year-old girl. These bands today have no morals."

Aging Punk Not Sure How to Stop Buying Skate Shoes

BY LIAM HART

PHILADELPHIA—Local 33-year-old Seth Bourne is completely unable and unwilling to buy any shoes that are not specifically designed for skateboarding, concerned family members have reported.

"Seth got promoted from shipping to sales so now he has to dress business-casual. It's really freaking him out," said Beth Bourne-Radler, his wife of four years. "I tried getting him to find some oxfords or something, but after five minutes in the store, he started muttering about how he's a 'sellout' and a 'poser,' and that 'slip-ons are business-casual enough.'"

Bourne, who has reportedly worn skate shoes ever since buying his first pair of Duffs in 1996, claimed he doesn't feel comfortable wearing anything else.

"I've gone through all the phases, man. Kostons, Nike SBs—all of 'em except DC. They never really vibed with me," he

said. "But I've never found a non-skate shoe that felt right. When I was 17, my mother made me wear loafers to my grandfather's funeral. I know everyone was thinking how dumb my feet looked the entire time."

The alternatives Bourne has found have only heightened his frustrations.

"Right now it seems like everyone I meet is wearing these weird-ass leather elf boots. I feel like a fraud when my Skyrim character wears that shit, so those are out of the question," he said while applying a thick layer of Shoe Goo to a pair of well-worn pair Vans. "I don't eat on my lunch break, I go to the skatepark for 45 minutes. Do these people really expect me to skate in wing tips? It ain't gonna happen."

As of press time, Bourne had found a temporary solution to the dress code by painting laces on his checkered socks.

Stoner Metal Fan Who Showed Up for Sleep Study Disappointed but Cooperative

BY LIAM HART

SAN FRANCISCO—Confused stoner Tyler Harrison participated in a sleep study believing the nocturnal testing session would actually be a thoughtful dissection of the seminal album *Dopesmoker* by doom-metal band Sleep, according to research reports.

"I saw this flyer outside of a GameStop and it sounded perfect. Sleep is one of my favorite bands, bro, so I was all like, '$50 to fucking groove? Hell yeah! I'm in,'" said Harrison from his sleep-study chamber. "The flyer looked hella official so I figured there might be some CIA-level bud involved—maybe some of that G13 stuff, or some dank Funyun Dust Kush."

Harrison was initially disappointed when he discovered the true purpose of the research, but changed his tune after learning about the study's perks.

"These beds are insane. They have clean sheets and aren't just mattresses laying on the floor. I feel like the king of England, man," he said. "Plus, they give me endless saltine sleeves. I just slaughter them, yo."

The scientists conducting the survey at the CPMC Research Institute were reportedly fascinated by their cooperative new subject.

"We've never seen someone sleep like this—it's truly stunning. He was breathing the whole time, but there was literally no brain activity happening for the vast majority of the study," said Dr. Lisa Chen. "He would smirk every 12 hours at 4:20, but even then there were no visible brain waves."

As the 48-hour program concluded, Harrison expressed interest in participating again.

"I'm kinda between living situations and jobs right now, so I'm gonna see if I can work something full-time out with the doctors here. I've been sleeping for free my entire life, and now I can get paid for something I'm really good at," he said. "It's a dream job for me."

Harrison is allegedly signing up for a battery of clinical trials as well.

"I feel like I'm in some sort of fairyland. First, they pay me to sleep, and now I'm gonna get paid to take a bunch of random pills and get super stoned," said Harrison.

Band Paid in Experience Can Now Perform Spin Attacks, Wear New Armor

LEVEL 7

$87.23

BY DAN RICE

PHILADELPHIA—Local punk band Eleanor Rugby are now able to perform spin attacks and wear upgraded armor following a show for which they were paid solely in experience, according to sources close to the group.

"I thought it was bullshit that they wouldn't even give us a couple drink tickets. But check this out," said bassist Britta Clark, demonstrating a whirlwind double-punch spin move with a band of fierce orange light pulsating from her body. "It really comes in handy when a song calls for a sort of pyrotechnic flourish, or for stunning a common field troll."

Promoters offering "experience" as payment instead of actual money is a fairly common practice for compensating new bands. What few bands fail to understand, however, is that this experience fills their personal XP meters, resulting in level-up points they can use to eventually upgrade their abilities and equipment.

"Obviously the goal is to make enough money from our music to quit our jobs," said drummer Pete Hare. "It's a bummer not to get paid in cash. But, I have to admit, this Class

Four armor upgrade we got from the experience looks metal as fuck! Plus I have a 20 percent better chance of deflecting critical attacks from Lord Gandor, the thrashcore band that always throws shit at people."

Not all of the band's members are as happy.

"Britta and Pete think they're so cool with their upgrades," complained guitarist Steve Hainley. "All I got was this lame-ass double jump. I jump, and then at the apex of the jump, I jump again. But, like, four inches. I'll take gas money over this shit any day, man."

The majority of Eleanor Rugby believe Hainley's criticisms are based on his ignorance of the experience points he's earned.

"Steve's just pissy because he doesn't know how to use the equip menu," said frontman Jerry Hill. "I got double jump too, but you can switch it out for other shit. I can turn invisible now! But just for five seconds, and it doesn't work against magic users. You can upgrade it, but that costs money, which we don't have yet. I also found an 'exposure meter,' but that doesn't seem to do shit."

The HARD Times

Hero Breaks Car Window to Save Vinyl Records on Hot Day

BY CARSON SOUKUP

PHOENIX—Local vinyl enthusiast Nate Adams broke a car window during last week's heatwave in order to save a collection of neglected records from overheating, multiple witnesses have verified.

"I was out getting some ice cream and was shocked by what I saw. It was, like, 100 degrees," said Adams of the crate of vinyl found in the backseat of a 2005 Suzuki Aerio. "Vinyl can get warped at, like, 80 degrees, and it'll never sound the same again. I knew I had to do something so I picked up a rock and threw it through the window. I'm no hero—I did what any wax lover would do."

The crate, which contained 17 vinyl records and 13 cassette tapes, reportedly included albums by the Ramones, the Sex Pistols, and Fugazi, all left to fend for themselves. Thanks to Adams' brave actions, the only casualty was a No Doubt *Tragic Kingdom* CD that was found without a jewel case.

"It just makes me sick, you know?" said Adams. "The fact that there are people out there in the world with no regard for what's safe or what's right. It's a goddamn shame. The window can be repaired, but there were some original pressings in that crate that could never be replaced, unless you have a really good day on eBay."

Bystanders report Adams stayed with the records until authorities arrived on the scene.

"He cradled them in his arms, taking each one out of its dust sleeve and inspecting it carefully for warping," said Theresa Worthington, who witnessed the event with her children. "When the owner returned, neither was very happy with the other, but thankfully the police were there to keep everything calm."

The owner of the Suzuki and the record crate was quick to defend himself against accusations of negligence.

"The car wasn't even locked, and I was only gone for ten goddamn minutes," claimed Dan Heller. "People are calling this guy a hero, and all I see is someone who fucked up my car and tried to steal my shit."

The records will remain in the care of the state until an appellate judge determines if Heller is responsible enough to own such a valuable collection. Meanwhile, Adams is hoping to become its legal guardian should the judge rule against the other man.

"These records deserve a good home and a caring owner, and I can provide that," said the day's hero. "Now I have to go. My kid is still waiting in my car to get ice cream."

The HARD Times

Black Man Attends Punk Show Without Anyone Mentioning Bad Brains

BY DAVID BRITTON

BLOOMINGTON, Ind.—Local punk and African-American person Mark Feeber attended a show Thursday evening and not a single person in attendance used legendary hardcore band Bad Brains as a conversation starter, sources confirmed.

"I knew something was up while I was hanging out in the parking lot before the show," said Feeber. "A guy wearing a Bad Brains shirt walked up to me and I figured he'd do that thing where he points to the shirt and then to me, but he just asked if I had a lighter."

As the night wore on and nobody approached him to say how much they loved Bad Brains, or how important they were to the history of punk, Feeber began to think something special was happening.

"I thought maybe one of my friends was playing a prank or something," said the surprised showgoer. "I wondered if maybe people were just avoiding me in general, since I do have a bit of a cold. I mean . . . Shit, man, I don't know! Nothing like this has ever happened to me. I'm still a little freaked out, I guess."

Feeber, who first got into punk when he was 12 years old via Green Day's "Basket Case," would not become familiar with Bad Brains until his junior year of high school.

"When I first started going to shows, old dudes would come up all the time, asking me if I liked Bad Brains," he said. "I was straight edge back then and assumed they were talking about drugs, so I'd just run off. Later, when I started doing drugs, I looked up Bad Brains—super surprised to find out they're actually a band."

Duke University musicology professor Stewart Washington noted this may be the first instance in over 20 years of an African-American attending a punk show without someone mentioning Bad Brains.

"When a white person sees a black person at a punk show, it triggers an overload of neural activity, not unlike a seizure," he said. "Often they'll begin explaining how elegantly Bad Brains blended reggae and punk without even realizing they've been talking at someone for over 25 minutes."

As of press time, Feeber was standing by his car, patiently listening as a stranger explained how important Fishbone was to third-wave ska.

The HARD Times

Man Yelling "FREE BIRD" at Concert Can't Find Anyone to Adopt His Pet Cockatoo

BY PATRICK COYNE

PHILADELPHIA—Local pet owner Dylan Murphy could not find a suitable adoptive home for his beloved pet cockatoo last week, despite incessantly screaming "FREE BIRD!" at a recent all-ages punk show, according to aggravated witnesses.

"I tried yelling, 'FREE COCKATOO TO A LOVING HOME— SERIOUS INQUIRIES ONLY!' but that was too wordy. So I shortened it to 'FREE BIRD' and screamed it between every song," said Murphy with the cockatoo, Beansy, sitting calmly on his wrist. "Most people ignored me or gave me a dirty look. When I tried to politely push to the front to get everyone's attention, people shoved me back. Some even threatened me. Maybe they just weren't animal lovers?"

Due to an impending move overseas, Murphy hoped to find his pet a new home before leaving the country. After several Craigslist ads failed to garner any serious interest, however, he made a last-ditch effort to find a caretaker among the roughly 50 fellow showgoers.

"There was one super-drunk guy who thought my offer was hilarious. This isn't a joke— I'm actually really worried about what will happen to her," he said. "She's so smart; I trained her to say, 'Play a fast one!' But the opening band got really offended when Beansy said it."

Members of headliners Surf Coffin were reportedly very aware of Murphy's presence.

"Oh, yeah, fuck that guy," said drummer Dave Huston. "I mean, Skynyrd's fine and all, but that joke stopped being funny 30 years ago. Maybe it was ironically funny, like, 10 years ago, but now it's just annoying."

For their part, animal care experts strongly advise against adopting pets at punk shows.

"Please do not give away birds, dogs, hamsters, or any other kind of pet at a concert—punk or otherwise. Honestly, I shouldn't even have to say that," said Nikki Cullen of Quaker City Animal Shelter. "Can you tell him to bring the bird here? Please? "

The HARD Times

218

MIT Physicist Almost Gets Pick out of Acoustic Guitar

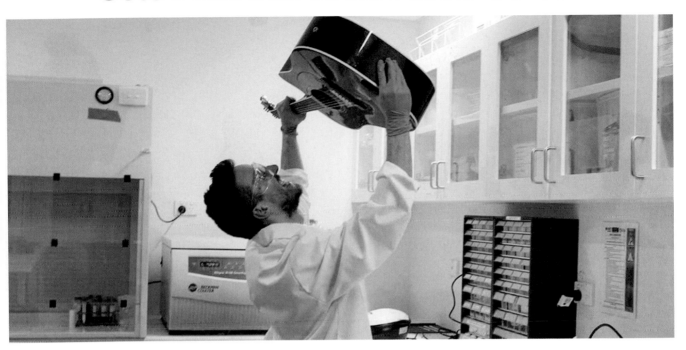

BY ERIC NAVARRO

CAMBRIDGE, Mass.—Renowned MIT physicist Lawrence Gordon wowed the scientific world early last week when he nearly retrieved a pick out of his acoustic guitar, multiple bespectacled sources confirmed.

"This is a breakthrough for the ages," said fellow physicist Tom Tyler. "This problem has plagued innumerable musicians since the guitar was invented in the 11th century. By slightly tilting the guitar top-wise at a 45-degree angle, Larry has brought us closer to a solution than ever before. Now we can see the pick, but no one on our team has fingers skinny enough to grab it. I'm confident we'll soon get there."

Gordon has been lauded for his past advancements in biomedical engineering, but his guitar pick recovery method has been, by far, his most popular near-achievement.

"Sure, it felt good knowing my previous work saved lives, but do you have any idea how much potential pussy is lost every year due to dropping a pick into an acoustic guitar halfway through a dorm room Coldplay cover?" Gordon said. "With just a few more years of research, we can cut that loss in half."

News of the technique, now known as the "Everlong Maneuver," spread rapidly among musicians everywhere.

"If they can actually pull this off, it will become everyone's go-to method—like the Heimlich maneuver, but for people playing 'Wonderwall,'" said Guitar Center employee Dexter Grant. "Which is ironic, since I wish everyone playing 'Wonderwall' would fucking choke. Maybe science has gone too far this time?"

Gordon's technique is just the latest variation on one that has been investigated for centuries, to no avail.

"My first attempt was a slight modification on the previous gold standard, where you line up the pick with the hole and rapidly flip the guitar over," said the physicist. "But the strings kept blocking the pick. I considered taking them off, but I'd need another doctorate just to get those fucking things back on."

Unfortunately, Gordon was denied a grant to further his acoustic guitar research. He is now focusing on removing a bow that fell into his cello.

The HARD Times

People Drinking at Bar Unaware They're About to Support the Local Scene

BY BRENDAN KRICK

PHILADELPHIA—Regulars at Magner's Pub had absolutely no idea they would be "entertained" last night by Philly's robust performing arts scene, witnesses confirmed this morning.

"Judging by the turnout, this is gonna be a great show," David Riley, part-time performer/daytime copywriter and organizer of the event, told reporters. "Once they turn off the Eagles game and shut down the pool table, everyone will give all of their attention to the stage."

Confused patrons were overheard murmuring in hushed tones.

"Is something going on here tonight?" said bar regular James Machie, noticing the makeshift stage erected in the corner. "Shit. It's not too late to go somewhere else, is it?"

The mildly popular neighborhood bar, a local destination for years, recently began a mixed-media open mic night to "attract a more diverse crowd."

"We're gonna start in five minutes," announced Riley, interrupting dozens of conversations to confirm the night's events. "I can already tell you're gonna be a great crowd, so grab a drink and be sure to tip your bartender!" he added as deafening feedback from the microphone sliding out of his hand and hitting the floor ensued.

Reports indicate that grumbles of protest followed the promoter as he made his way around the bar, unplugging arcade games and draping a curtain over the dartboards.

"Alright, let's get this show started," he eventually said, leading with a deeply personal opening performance he'd prepared for weeks.

Witnesses confirm that a line of patrons looking to pay their tabs formed at the bar almost immediately.

"The only time I've seen the place empty out this fast was when those punks from O'Shea's Bar and Grille tossed a dead skunk through the front door," said bar manager Carlie Hopps. "I felt bad for the performers, though, so I tried to process all the credit cards really slowly so they could have some sort of audience."

Stacey Madison, who can be found at Magner's "three or more nights a week for the last six years," was one of the few patrons who took a seat in an empty row of chairs up front.

"I'm just happy they're not doing Harry Potter trivia again," she said. "That was fucking awful."

Scene Veteran's Closet Contains 700 T-Shirts, One Pair of Pants

BY LIAM HART

DETROIT—The closet of 41-year-old scene veteran Eddie Pierce is filled with hundreds of band T-shirts to pair with exactly one pair of pants, sources who are dying to take the man shopping reported.

"I think his merch collection started even before we were dating," claimed Beth Jensen, Pierce's wife of seven years. "Back then, he had three or four pairs of pants. I specifically remember jeans, a pair of cargo pants . . . even khakis. It was a different time."

Jensen believes that, over the last four years, her husband has slowly worked his way down to a single pair of jeans, worn daily.

"For a long time, I thought he was alternating between two pairs of black jeans, but when he got a weird toothpaste stain on one of the legs, I realized that it was just one pair," said Jensen. "The closest he's come to washing them must've been last summer, when he fell into a pool fully clothed."

Pierce's wardrobe has led to some strife within the family, especially on his wedding day.

"My mom was incredulous. I thought it was a big deal that he wore a blazer over his Guantanamo Baywatch T-shirt, but she wasn't having it," said Jensen. "The only time I saw him dress better was for a court date, when he borrowed a suit from his dad."

"All my mom gave us for the wedding was a Men's Wearhouse gift card," she later added. "We still have it."

Pierce, an HVAC technician who still averages over four shows and three merch runs per week, feels one pair of pants is "more than enough."

"I'm not about to waste my time going to some department store and trying on pants for eight hours; you don't need another pair until the crotch is too ripped to patch up," he said. "And I actually do have more than one pair of pants: I have some light grey sweats for relaxing around the house."

While the couple does not yet have a child, they are reportedly considering it.

"My friends don't think Eddie is cut out for fatherhood, but he's been so supportive of the scene that I think he's ready for the responsibility," said Jensen wistfully. "His closet must have the makings of a Ramones or Misfits onesie. A baby would look so cute in that."

Pop-Punk Frontman Reunited With Girlfriend After Performing at 18-Plus Show

BY KRISSY HOWARD

TULSA, Okla.—Saving Daylight frontman Jason Hill was successfully reunited with girlfriend Kelsie Tanner late yesterday evening after the 18-plus show she was prevented from entering had concluded, multiple witnesses confirmed.

"It's honestly such bullshit that they base these things on some arbitrary number," said the 27-year-old pop-punk vocalist, who was held inside for upward of three hours during the age-restricted show by the venue's strict "no reentry" policy. "If it went by maturity level or whatever, she would've been allowed in there, no problem. She isn't like other girls in the scene—she's, like, real."

Amid the ordeal, Hill was trapped inside the venue with only a full bar, a kitchen serving comfort food, several friends, and nearly two dozen women his own age with whom to converse.

"Listen, I don't have anything against older girls; I've just never met one I connected with, that's all," Hill explained. "Besides, seems like it'd be kind of sexist or whatever to date someone only because they're legally considered an 'adult.'

I don't know, dude. I support all women, and I like to think of myself as sort of a mentor to them."

Scene regulars confirmed reports of Hill's "creepy" relationships with several minors over the years.

"God, that guy is so fucking gross," said show attendee Holly Schanz. "He used to comment on my friend's little sister's Instagram like every day, until she asked if he was someone's dad, and he replied that she was 'ass ugly anyway LOL.' What grown man signs an insult 'LOL'? Fucking idiot."

Showgoers were released around 10 p.m., at which point Hill immediately headed to a nearby Denny's, where Tanner and several of her friends were eating french fries and drinking coffee.

"See, she's fuckin' cool. You just have to get to know her," Hill said of his girlfriend, who was mere minutes away from missing her curfew. "I don't know. You wouldn't understand."

At press time, Hill was overheard interrogating Tanner about "that guy she was talking to," a 16-year-old busboy she knows from second-period math.

Trans Person Crosses Street to Avoid Overly Supportive Liberals

BY ALLISON MICK

PORTLAND, Ore.—Local trans person Emma Nelson was forced to cross the street last night to avoid an ambush from "well-wishing allies," whose constant aggressive affirmation of her gender identity often leaves her feeling objectified and exhausted, Nelson alleged earlier today.

"The second I see them, their eyes light up like a shark smelling blood in the water. It makes me feel like a piece of meat," said Nelson, having jaywalked across multiple lanes of traffic. "I know trans folks in other parts of the country have it way worse, but sometimes I just don't need someone telling me I'm beautiful."

Nelson later added, "It's hard to complain about because it's a nice act. But it'd be even nicer if they just treated me like everyone else and didn't burst into wild applause."

Nelson empathized with others who may find themselves in similar situations, noting that she's seen it happen to other transfolk, "fat women who are owning it," and interracial couples in which the man is Asian.

"Sometimes it feels unavoidable—like I should just space out and let them get it over with. Usually I wear headphones or dark sunglasses and keep my hood up to kind of throw them off," they said. "One day I tried to really dress down and went out in a baggy shirt and sweatpants, but that just encouraged them more. I got so many high fives for rejecting traditional femininity that my palm ached for a week."

However, local ally Lorraine Schrock sees things differently.

"It's a compliment! Whenever I see a trans woman on the street, I want her to know she's an inspiration to all of us . . . and I won't leave her alone until she know it," said Schrock. "I can't tell you how many trans people I've chased down just to give them a big ol' hug and let them know we're watching out for them."

At press time, Nelson had turned down a side street to a farmers' market, where her entrance was met with thunderous clapping and shouts of "You go, girl!"

The HARD Times

Office Worker Subverts System by Wearing Vans in Cubicle

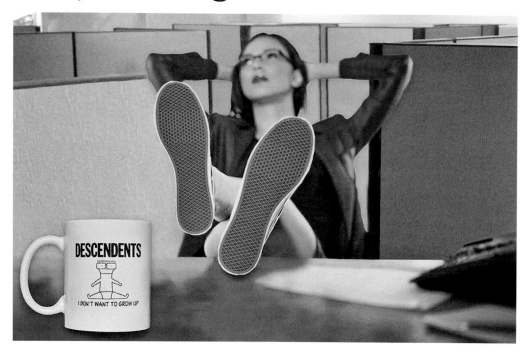

BY MARK TURNER

SPOKANE, WA—For many, working a 9-to-5 job is the epitome of "selling out" and moving on to adulthood. However, local punk Maria Ochoa is defying convention and silently subverting the capitalist system in which she works by wearing Vans® to the office every day.

"I refuse to let this job suck the soul from my body like so many Dementors," said Ochoa, sitting cross-legged with her sneakers' signature waffle-sole design plainly visible to all passersby. "Don't get me wrong, I need this job. But you better believe I'm going to slowly but surely bring this whole motherfucker down from the inside every opportunity I get. My business-casual is next-level casual: weekend casual."

Of the many subversive activities Ochoa engages in on the company dime, the most essential is her insistence on wearing black-and-white checkered slip-ons manufactured by Vans, a wholly owned brand of the VF Corporation. "If you think that's where my long-con plan ends, you'd be dead wrong," spat Ochoa. The staffer of four years also subtly undermines her employer by refusing to change the break room coffee filter, wearing a Nerve Agents T-shirt under her work shirt, and using extended bathroom breaks to post on music forums.

"That's right—every bathroom break costs my boss about $1.79. That's 32 sheets of paper. Sucker," Ochoa said, blatantly ignoring the empty water cooler jug outside her cubicle.

"Maria is an exemplary worker," wrote regional manager Pete Twombly in Ochoa's annual review. "Of all the members of our team, I worry about Maria the least. She simply gets the job done," the "milquetoast pawn" continued, unaware that his lead employee flips him the bird under her desk every time he walks by.

"Oh, I definitely get the job done," said Maria while hopelessly tangling an entire box of paper clips. "But that's just so they think they have nothing to worry about, which lets me fly under the radar. Meanwhile, I'm telling Tanya that Joe ate her yogurt, or subtly slipping Aus-Rotten lyrics into my PowerPoints. Then I just sit back and watch the whole thing burn down around me.

"It's almost TOO easy."

Punk Eagerly Awaits Thanksgiving Tradition of Hiding From Family in Garage

BY BILL CONWAY

HANSON, Mass.—Local punk Brandon Gardner announced to reporters this morning that he will continue his annual Thanksgiving tradition of hiding from his family in his aunt's garage.

"Every year, this is the part of the holidays I look forward to the most," said the 27-year-old of the five-hour-long ritual that began when he was 12. "I start with the looking-at-my-uncle's-tools portion for 45 minutes before moving on to the annual 'rereading of my cousin's diary from when she was 10.' Traditions are important, and I hope to someday pass this one down to my own kids when they start hating everyone."

Gardner admitted that while he rarely sees his extended family, he continues to seek out the garage for his own mental stability.

"If I don't find a good hiding spot early, I run the risk of Uncle Jerry [McGee] talking at me about 'my career choices' for hours on end," said Gardner. "A regular guy like him just can't understand that my band is starting to really take off. We just self-released a new full-length and booked a weekend Canadian tour in December, but he'll just lecture me on retirement plans, health insurance, or some other dumb shit."

The act of hiding from family members during holiday functions is not unique to Gardner, according to sociologist Deborah Rawlings, who has studied the practice for years.

"When a person from the 'punk' subculture is dropped into a 'normal' family setting, they're often in an awkward position, either publicly by, for example, having to explain their facial tattoos, or privately, biting their tongue during political discussions so hard that they draw blood," said Rawlings. "I've studied countless subjects who have simply hidden in garages, but some will walk miles through suburban woods or, in extreme cases, bury themselves in a giant leaf pile for hours."

Sources close to Gardner say the Thanksgiving gathering is expected to draw family members from all over the state, many of whom are excited to participate in their own holiday traditions.

"The McGee Turkey Bowl is the best backyard football game in all of Massachusetts," said Gardner's "kiss-ass fucking jock" little cousin, 13-year-old Tyson Landis. "We gather up everyone in the family, and Brandon gets burned by Grandpa every single year. Brandon sucks, and so does his band."

The HARD Times

Local Punk Spends 10th Winter Failing to Realize Doc Martens Are Not Winter Boots

BY JEREMY HAMMOND

BROOKLYN, N.Y.—Local punk Alicia Lane is spending another long, slippery, water-soaked winter in her insufficiently winterized Doc Martens boots, friends close to the uncomfortable woman confirmed.

"I get the aesthetic—they look cool and punk and all that—but, like, they do less than nothing on ice. She's already fallen and busted her ass four times this week," said coworker Mary Sanchez as Lane gingerly crossed a frozen patch on the sidewalk, quivering like a newborn deer. "The easy fix is just to buy the same dorky-looking duck boots as everyone else. I don't know why she does this to herself every year."

Witnesses report Lane has cautiously left her apartment for a treacherous walk to the Bedford Avenue L station every morning since December's first snowfall.

"She goes down her front stairs clutching the handrail for dear life," said neighbor José Pomello. "It takes actual minutes for her to do this. And when she gets to the bottom, she nods to herself with a sense of accomplishment and immediately steps into a puddle of slush, which you know must soak through right to her feet. She always looks pretty bummed, but this routine never changes."

Despite her impractical choices, Sanchez applauded Lane's commitment to her style.

"It's kind of amazing, if you think about it," Sanchez said. "Alicia is the chair of the local DSA chapter. She'll go on and on about the evils of consumerism and capitalism, but when it comes to footwear, her sense of brand loyalty is absurd."

This morning Lane allegedly spent 15 minutes of her 20-minute trek to the subway this morning cursing the winter, the hydrologic cycle, and herself for choosing to walk to brunch instead of calling a Lyft. Notably absent from her curses, however, was the Doc Martens brand for their inferior winter boots.

"Her boots are so tight, she can't even wear thick wool socks," Sanchez said, her feet warmed by the faux fur lining of actual winter boots. "I'm pretty sure she thinks everyone lives like that and it doesn't get better."

At press time, Lane had soaked both feet, scraped her knee, and rolled her ankle, and still had six blocks left to walk.

The Doomed Sports Section

As remembered by Mark Roebuck

The story of this publication's ill-fated sports section began in the quiet village of Chesaning, Michigan.

One Thanksgiving, s cousin left behind a tattered, dog-eared issue of *The Hard Times,* and after absorbing every last word of it, I soon was the only punk in town. Being a one-man scene is tough: You have to book the bands, work the door, provide security, do sound, open the show, and make sure no one has any glass all by yourself. It's exhausting.

I was hell-bent on getting out of the place that had stolen my youth, so as soon as I graduated high school, I sent a pile of fake resumes to anyone I felt I could pretend to be qualified for. Imagine my surprise when the publication that had taught me everything I knew about punk rock responded with a job offer! I was so excited to finally meet some other punks. It was a dream come true.

There was one giant problem with this scenario, however. *The Hard Times* was looking to launch a sports section, and I had really dazzled them with my resume, which stated that I'd received a bachelor's degree in sports journalism. Oh, jeepers.

Because I was brought on to write about sports, the other staff members assumed I was a jock and never missed a chance to remind me that I wasn't one of them. Most days someone would take my wallet or keys and play keep-away with them.

What upset me more than the writer's room ribbing was the constant and unwavering stream of rejections I received from the bosses on every ill-informed sports idea I pitched. I was in way over my head. In one particularly heated exchange, I said I would quit if the XFL didn't put the NFL out of business. I was never forced to follow up on that declaration, as I was the first let go in the layoffs that hit the offices shortly thereafter.

It was difficult to find much in the way of work in the years that followed. When I read a rumor about *The Hard Times* being reborn as a website, I contacted Matt and told him I needed to get back on staff, and he wouldn't have to pay me if none of my stories got picked up. That was four years ago, and if it wasn't for me sneakily editing the summer interns' work and claiming it as my own, I don't think I would've ever gotten published. Honestly though, I'm just happy to be back on the team.

In fact, as I reflect on my experience at TheHardTimes.net, it dawns on me that this is the first time the sports section has ever been even remotely mentioned in print. I'm humbled and thrilled that my work will live on in infamy. Thanks for giving me a shot, Matt and Bill! I'm sorry I lied on my resume.

Punk Dad Can Still Hang, Maybe Next Friday Between 5 p.m. and 8 p.m., or Potentially Two Saturdays from Now but Only During the Day

BY RANDY LOBASSO

PARK CITY, Utah—Scene veteran and new father Darnell Tyler set out to prove his critics wrong this week by showing that, despite his new parental responsibilities, he can still hang, maybe next Friday between 5 p.m. and 8 p.m., or potentially two Saturdays from now but only during the day, sources familiar with Tyler's schedule confirmed.

"I told everyone that my life wouldn't change when I had a kid, and for the most part, it hasn't," said Tyler, staring blankly at a Ziploc bag of Cheerios he found in the inside pocket of his leather jacket. "I'm still the same guy. If you want to grab a beer or something, I'm there—just give me two months heads-up. No big deal."

Tyler claimed he has three hours carved out over the next six months to do whatever he wants—provided his wife, Mindy, can get the time off from work to take their daughter to the Little Super Heroes Gymboree. However, he said, finding that time wasn't the hassle so many parents had warned him about.

"It's much easier than everyone says," he said, fading in and out of sleep. "You've just gotta tell yourself, I will not be a prisoner to parenthood. You want to go see a show right now? I'll go. I will. Well, maybe not right now. But definitely the third Tuesday of next month, and as long as it's over by 9:45 p.m. Actually, 9:30 p.m., just to be safe."

Friends and family are reportedly shocked by how much free time Tyler has outside of his parental obligations.

"Sure, he had to cancel on lunch two weeks ago, but we're probably going to get together in the spring," said Josh Filstein, Tyler's longtime friend and former best man. "Probably April or May, but, as he told me, 'Definitely maybe by June, at the latest or earliest.' He said it'll be an early morning, probably at the end of the week. No matter what, he said he'd call me an hour beforehand. Man, can't wait to see that guy and hear what he's been up to."

Pit Bull Rescues Crust Punk Despite Aggressiveness of Breed

BY TAYLOR DE LA OSSA

FLINT, Mich.—Local pit bull James Earl Bones rescued a crust punk from a no-kill shelter yesterday despite the negative stereotypes associated with the crust breed, sources closest to the benevolent dog confirmed.

"I saw her and my heart just melted. She was flea-ridden and clearly hadn't had a bath in ages," said Bones. "Poor thing looked so hungry . . . her Amebix shirt was so ratty, you could count her ribs. But when she came over to me, licked my paw, and asked if I had any spare change, we connected instantly."

Bones was initially skeptical about rescuing a crust punk, due to the stigma surrounding the subculture.

"We've all heard stories of crust punks starting fights, or screaming about the evils of capitalism on a street corner. My friend's mom was nearly bitten at a public park one time when she tried giving a crust punk half a sandwich," said the canine. "But it's unfair to lump them all together. So far, I've had no major incidents with mine. I mean, I had to stop letting her around the cat and she can't drink malt liquor after sunset, but otherwise, she's great. Very loyal."

Still, some claim that the aggressive tendencies of crust punks are ingrained in their DNA, and nothing can be done to properly rehabilitate them.

"There's no such thing as a safe crust punk," said Leslie Schmitt, chairperson of Mothers Against Punks. "They're extremely unpredictable. You always hear about them using crude facial tattoos to scare children. I don't care who its owner is or how it's raised—this breed is dangerous."

Despite everything, Bones remains optimistic about his new pet.

"I'm in the middle of trying to move, so that's been a bit difficult," he said. "Every listing you see says 'No crust punks' or 'Nothing that even looks like a punk.' We'll figure it out, though. As long as I have my little buddy, we'll be fine. Now we just gotta get her housebroken."

Vocalist Explains Drum Part Should Be Less "Bum-Da-Bum-Da-Bum-Bum" and More "Bum-Bum-Da-Da-Bum-Bum-Bum"

BY GOODRICH GEVAART

FORT WAYNE, Ind.—Resin Smokers vocalist Claudia Smith told her bandmates last night that the drums during the bridge of their new song should be less "bum-da-bum-da-bum-bum" and more "bum-bum-da-da-bum-bum-bum," band members confirmed.

"I was so confused. I kept trying to follow along, but whenever she said it, her eyes would close and she'd have both hands in the air—like she was trying to grab something off of a high shelf," said drummer Danny Salazar. "She doesn't know the difference between a rack tom or a floor tom or a snare. She just makes these noises, like I'm supposed to understand what she's talking about."

Reportedly, Smith came away from practice feeling equally frustrated.

"That part just needed a heavier beat—he knew what I meant. Just because I don't know the right terms doesn't mean I can't explain things clearly," said a red-faced Smith. "I know how to make a song that's hard as fuck, and no one else had the balls to tell Danny. I'm fine with being the bad guy if it means we get more kids beating each other in the pit."

Fellow band members admitted that this was not Smith's first request for ambiguous instrumentation.

"Claudia barely even know how to play a guitar, so listening to her tell Danny what to do is super annoying," said guitarist Mal Flanagan. "She ends up sounding like she's doing different versions of 'rum-pa-tum-tum' from 'The Little Drummer Boy.' One time she told me my guitar needed to be more 'chucka-chucka-waaa-chucka-chucka-waaaa,' and we stayed at practice for an extra three hours till I figured out what the hell she was trying to scat at me."

Those close to Smith report she has long had a unique way of communicating, using sounds and feelings rather than words.

"When she's passionate about something or she gets worked up, the sounds just flow through her, I guess," said Mark Waters, the singer's longtime boyfriend. "Our car was having some issues, so she called up a friend who's a mechanic and told him it was supposed to sound like 'vroom-vroom-put-put-put,' but instead sounded like 'ba-rooom-vroom-vroom-put-vroom.' I honestly don't know how it got fixed, but she seemed happy with it afterward."

Dog Wearing Misfits Bandanna Can't Even Name Three of Their Songs

BY BRENDAN KRICK

DENVER—Local dog Scraps was completely unable to answer basic trivia questions about the seminal horror-punk band Misfits despite wearing the band's logo while at a nearby dog park this past weekend, disappointed witnesses confirmed.

"When I saw that dog walk by, I said, 'Hell, yeah—that's my favorite band!' But when I tried talking to him about them, he just chewed on a tennis ball like he didn't even hear me," said 16-year-old punk Dan Thompson. "And when I told him about the time I met Danzig, he took off after a bird. What a poser."

Thompson and several friends cornered the dog for upward of 20 minutes, interrogating him about his favorite Misfits albums and songs, as well as Scraps' thoughts on their current lineup.

"A lot of people out there wear gear that they buy at the mall but have no respect for the band," said 15-year-old Timmy Marks, who helped lead the inquisition. "We just wanted to know how he felt about Graves-era Misfits, and why we never see him at any shows. All he did was start licking his own balls . . . which was actually pretty punk, now that I think about it."

The dog's owner, 24-year-old Sam Schmidt, defended Scraps.

"I really don't see what the big deal is. Scraps is a dog. He doesn't have to prove himself to some bratty teenagers," he said. "Scraps has been listening to the Misfits for the two years he's been alive, which, in dog years, is way longer than those shitbirds have. Scraps should've worn his Discharge bandanna. I doubt they'd even know who Discharge is."

As Schmidt and Scraps exited the dog park, the young teens reportedly continued harassing the young canine for his perceived lack of punk knowledge.

"We had to get out before things escalated, so I put Scraps back on his leash and we went home," said Schmidt. "As we walked away, I heard them shout, 'I bet you got that bandanna at Hot Topic' and 'Go listen to Top 40, asshole.'"

While oblivious to the harassment, Scraps proved his punk cred on his way home by "pulling a GG" and eating his own shit in public.

The HARD Times

Baby Boomer Juggalo Concerned Millennial Juggalos Won't Promote Same Dope-Ass Juggavalues

BY CORY COUSINS

PONTIAC, Mich.—Juggalo Kevin "Klown Syndrome" Anderson, 55, is concerned young Juggalos won't continue the positive Juggalo message created by his generation, sources close to the aging Insane Clown Posse fan confirmed today.

"Frankly, I'm worried for our future," said the outspoken Syndrome. "These millennial Juggalos don't know their asses from their elbows! They're a bunch of assed-out tricks who don't have the work ethic to hatchet their way out of a wet paper bag."

Syndrome admitted his worry grew after attending last summer's Gathering of the Juggalos.

"It was some straight Jugga-ho behavior, to be completely honest with you," he noted between large pulls off a vape pen. "This one youngin' was talkin' shit about how Faygo's loaded with high-fructose corn syzurup or whatever, and that we should try drinking water every once in a while. That's some seriously wack shit. For real."

Syndrome blames parents in his age group for raising a generation of coddled, entitled "Juggaflakes."

"Back in the day, we worked for what we wanted. Nobody handed me anything when I was coming up. Nowadays, these young Juggs show up demanding blunts and whip-its like they grow on trees or something," barked Syndrome. "They're lucky I don't straight up whoop they scrub asses."

Chris "Syko Santa Clau$" Conner, Syndrome's longtime friend and a self-proclaimed "hatchet-wielding psycho killer," recalled a confrontation Syndrome had with one young Juggalo at the recent Gathering.

"My ninja Klown threw out a 'Whoop, Whoop' to this young buck walking past, and the kid didn't even give him a return 'Whoop,'" claimed Clau$. "Klown got in that kid's face to throw down, but that Jugga-ho nurdled his pants and ran away. I wouldn't be surprised if more Juggalos start coming from middle-class suburbia—that's the direction we're heading."

The elder Klown fears that if Juggalo leadership doesn't restore things back to the way they were soon, his generation will be forced to hang up their hatchets for good. Indeed, Janet "Daisey Dook" Kilmer, a leader of a Juggalette feminist movement, admitted she's angered many older Juggalos herself.

"These playas were used to getting a clown job from any random Juggalette they wanted. But this is a new generation. We're demanding sicker and sloppier clown jobs in return," said Dook. "We also want equal representation in The Dark Carnival."

Misfits Logo Passes Algebra Test With After-School Help From Descendents Logo

BY JOE RUMRILL

LODI, N.J—The Crimson Ghost, the longtime symbol for the Misfits, successfully passed its algebra test last week thanks to after-school tutoring from a caricature of Milo Aukerman, the Descendents' iconic logo, sources close to the popular logos confirmed.

"I'm glad to see the Crimson Ghost putting away the comic books and old monster movies and finally start applying itself," said Blues Man, the Grateful Dead Bear who taught the class. "It's honestly—and I don't use this term lightly—really groovy."

The straightlaced Descendents logo knew that improving the Crimson Ghost's test scores would be no easy task.

"It took a lot of coffee-fueled nights, and a few missed fishing trips, but I wanted to help my friend in need," the Milo doodle said. "I'm just glad ol' Crimmy came to me and not that alcoholic Social Distortion skeleton. Those two wouldn't have achieved anything. [The Misfits logo] has a great vocabulary, but math just isn't his thing: Before I got involved, his GPA was a measly 1.38."

The legendary Misfits symbol was reportedly beside itself after receiving his test scores, and could not thank its bespectacled friend enough for the tutoring.

"It was really 'ghoul' of him to help me out," the skull depiction growled earnestly. "Especially after I killed his friend Jean earlier in the semester. I did have mommy's permission to do so, but I can understand why he'd still be upset."

Overcome with joy, he added, "Whoooooaaa—whoooooooooaa, whoa!"

Now on the fast track to graduation, the iconic images are looking toward the future.

"For the first time ever, I can see myself pursuing higher education instead of going into the family horror business," said the Crimson Ghost. "In my opinion, there's too much of that anyway."

For his part, the Descendents mascot more than shared his cohort's enthusiasm.

"Oh, Crimmy is definitely going to college one way or another," he said. "Whether it's on his own or, more likely, scrawled on a notebook or in a poorly done tattoo."

The HARD Times

Ultimate Weezer Box Set
Just 12 Copies of Blue Album

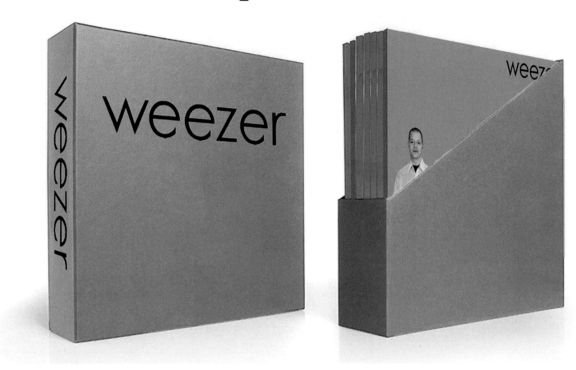

BY TED KINDIG

LOS ANGELES—Fans of iconic mid-'90s rock band Weezer received a nostalgic thrill yesterday with the release of the "Ultimate Weezer Box Set," containing 12 copies of their self-titled 1994 "Blue Album" debut.

"[This set] features all the most classic hits and raddest deep cuts of our entire career, from 'My Name Is Jonas' to 'Only in Dreams,'" frontman Rivers Cuomo said in a press release. "It's everything a die-hard fan could possibly want."

The 12 CDs of the "Ultimate Weezer Box Set" are all digitally remastered at the highest possible quality from the same single master recording, and each includes the original 4.75" × 4.75" booklet—presented for the first time ever in 12 identical copies.

Fans have been overwhelmingly enthusiastic about the news. "This is, in many ways, the Weezer news we've been waiting for since '95," said superfan José Davis, moderator of the "SoCal Weezer Fans Forever" Facebook group offshoot of the now-defunct GeoCities page of the same name. "I'm gonna find a 12-CD changer just so I can play it all back-to-back."

However, some devotees were disappointed that the box set excludes Weezer's other album, *Pinkerton*. Cuomo replied in a follow-up statement that while he understands their frustration, the decision to omit it was an easy one.

"I'm glad *Pinkerton* meant a lot to you when you were having a bad time in high school, and again when you were having a bad time in college," he said. "But have you listened to it lately? No. Do you want to listen to it right now? Probably not. You people just want 12 'Blue Albums.' Trust me."

The "Ultimate Weezer Box Set" is expected to retail for $59.99, but according to sources close to the band, the collection will be heavily discounted for teenage Japanese girls.

Hardcore Flight Attendant Dedicates Flight to "Real Motherfuckers in Coach"

BY BILL CONWAY

ATLANTA—Delta Airlines flight attendant Moses Ray dedicated yesterday's routine flight to Chicago to "the real motherfuckers in coach" during an impassioned preflight announcement shortly before takeoff, passengers in fully upright and locked positions confirmed.

"He seemed really worked up," said passenger Teresa Larson. "Once the door closed, he used that little intercom thing to 'shout out' all of us in the back 25 rows as 'the misfits and the fuck-ups,' and the only ones who truly understood 'the struggle.' Then it was another three minutes about unity, brotherhood, and how our seats cannot be used as a flotation device."

The standard preflight safety announcements set up the next several minutes of Ray introducing the other members of the crew.

"Yo, when I get on the PA, it's my time to shine. I spread that glow over everyone with me in Airbus A321, because we're in this together—one family," Ray told reporters as he prepped for the first round of food service. "Without Linda up front,

Big Tim and his main man Lucky Luke in the cockpit, and Jenna back here with me on pretzels and cookies, this flight can't happen. But, at the end of the day, it's the people who paid too much for a ticket and were hit with a bunch of unnecessary fees that make this all possible, and I want them to know that I see them."

Despite overwhelming support from the back of the plane, some passengers were allegedly upset by Ray's comments.

"Quite frankly, that man made me feel uncomfortable," said frequent flyer and Delta Diamond Medallion Member Dr. Angela Reyes. "He kept calling everyone up front 'a bunch of sellouts' and invited people from coach to use the bathrooms reserved for first-class passengers. He certainly swore a lot more than I would have liked. I wish he could have just done a funny skit, like I see from Southwest flight attendants on Facebook."

As of press time, Ray was handing out pamphlets on the benefits of being an ethical vegan to each passenger who did not order the vegetarian food option.

Dad Thinks a Hard Day's Work Is Pretty Punk Rock if You Ask Him

BY ANDY HOLT

LAFAYETTE, La.—Local husband and father Harold Walsner insisted this morning that putting in a full eight hours of work at the office each day is a "pretty darn punk thing to do," an embarrassed source reports.

"You know, I can be just as punk as my son, Blake," said Walsner, a senior sales associate at a local plumbing supply company. "I can't think of anything more 'hardcore' than running into the cubicle and slamming down a couple dozen accounting documents the boss was asking about. It's kind of like a mini pit in there, if you really think about it—just with more chairs and no music."

Walsner used the questionable analogy while attempting to relate to his teenage son, who recently lost his job at Rouses Market after being caught smoking marijuana in the break room three days in a row.

"You should have seen him when his quarterly sales numbers came in," the teenage Blake said. "He started headbanging to the acoustic version of Eric Clapton's 'Layla' in front of my friends and kept threatening to 'mosh' us while we were hanging out in the garage. I don't know what his problem is."

In addition to working for a living, Walsner's additional "savage" interests include saving for retirement, keeping up on mortgage payments, and taking two light beers "straight to the head" every evening. Despite constant dismissals that his lifestyle "sounds lame" and seems "boring as fuck," Walsner remained undeterred in his stance.

"I'm just trying to make [Blake] see that you've got to be hard to do what I do," Walsner said, slapping his bicep. "Just last week, I switched car insurance companies and improved our rate while also getting better coverage. 'Scene credit' is fine, but you know what's really cool? A personal credit score of 700 or higher. He'll learn soon enough."

When reached for further comment, Walsner had reportedly retreated into his walk-in closet to pick out a "radical" sock-and-tie combination for casual Friday.

"Heck, I just don't give a dang," he said, quietly sliding the closet door shut. "Later, posers."

Anti-Flag Slips One Pro-Trump Song in Set Just to Make Sure People Still Listening

BY TOM GANNON

DETROIT—Pittsburgh punk act Anti-Flag added a pro–Donald Trump song to their set last night to see if fans were actually listening to their lyrics, attentive sources confirmed.

"We're concerned that our audience isn't engaging [with the music]. We often see fans filming on their phones but not singing along, and we couldn't tell if our message was really reaching them," said singer Justin Sane. "So we mixed it up a little bit to keep people on their toes, while our tour manager gauges crowd reaction."

The song, "A Man We Can Believe In"—which argues in favor of a businessman running the United States, as well as being an affirmation of gun rights—was met with mixed reactions.

"I was a little confused when Chris Head yelled, 'This one goes out to all the real Americans!'" admitted fan Shalin King. "And I knew things were really off when the chorus encouraged us to bring back coal."

"It was incredible! Pat Thetic looked right at me while I was on Instagram live, so that was awesome," said local high school student Jimmy Alsmiller. "They still got it."

Reports show Anti-Flag is merely the latest aging punk band to test whether or not their audience members are truly engaged.

"I got really bummed at our last show in Phoenix," confessed NOFX guitarist Eric Melvin. "We played back-to-back songs about the negative effects of hard drugs and drinking. No one seemed to notice."

When asked about their inspiration, both bands credited Bad Religion, whose 2016 album, *I Can Do All Things Through Christ Who Strengthens Me,* received minimal reaction.

Report: New Gastropub Will Probably Be Named Hook & Barley or Something Like That

BY FRANCIS BERINGER

WASHINGTON—A new gastropub in the Dupont Circle neighborhood is "probably going to be named Hook & Barley or something stupid like that," nearby residents opined after noting the low-hanging vintage light fixtures, antique book-cases, and large chalkboard menu inside.

"The place isn't open yet, but I saw someone hanging old photos of Teddy Roosevelt on an exposed brick wall, so it's safe to assume they'll serve upscale comfort food and spe-cialize in barrel-aged beer," said neighborhood resident Lucy Thiermann, corroborating rumors that the yet-to-be-opened establishment will have a house ketchup, which will likely come with signature duck fat fries. "Their quirky mezcal margarita will almost assuredly be called Zapata's Ghost, I can tell you that much."

Arturo Gonzalez, a frequent patron of nearby taverns and beer gardens, is convinced the future hot spot will feature up to 12 different IPAs on draft, many of them "local and hazy."

"I bet that, right away, you'll be welcomed by an apron-clad bartender with a visible DC flag tattoo. While you strain your eyes looking over the menu, she'll probably tell you that folks have really been into the pork cheek nachos, and that they're launching a sour program soon," he surmised, gazing in the direction of the forthcoming eatery. "And to save room for the burnt-toast ice cream, which everyone thinks is weird until they try it."

Gonzalez later added, "I'll bet you dollars to complimentary mini cinnamon donuts that this place will have a lamb belly bánh mì, a $13 tallboy-and-whiskey 'combo,' and giant Jenga. That's all but certain."

At press time, reports confirmed the gastropub will be part of a mixed-use condo and retail development project "likely to be called District Atlantic Union or some shit" in honor of a long-gone neighborhood organization once beloved by the working-class residents that you and your friends displaced.

Correction: Earlier versions of this story incorrectly reported the highly anticipated new restaurant might be called Zephyr & Hound, Butter & Boy, or possibly even Coat & Compass. Sources can now confirm the rustic establishment, sure to serve seasonal ciders and half-priced fish tacos for happy hour, will almost definitely be called Hook & Barley.

Band Pic Ruined by Smiling Drummer

BY CORY COUSINS

CLEVELAND—Recently signed metal band Regurgitated Ghost Fetus discovered this afternoon that their recent promotional photo shoot was marred by a pleasant grin from their drummer, a source reports.

"Well, this is just fucking fantastic," said frontman Randy "Sacrifictus" Collins. "We spent the last four years as a band developing a pissed-off aesthetic, and what does he do? He shits all over our band photo by smiling like some village idiot at the state fair."

"I would've preferred him to literally shit all over the photo," Collins added. "That would've been brutal, actually. This is straight-up amateur hour."

Tensions mounted last night at a regularly scheduled band practice, when Regurgitated Ghost Fetus drummer and "fucking dumbass" Chris "Wolvenspear" Schecter-Haas was unremorseful for his actions.

"They're upset I smiled?" Schecter-Haas asked rhetorically. "Well, I'm sorry, but my girlfriend is awesome, I just got promoted at work, and, two days ago, I won an all-expenses-paid weekend at Sandals Jamaica from an animal shelter fund-raiser raffle. Looking dour just isn't in the cards at the moment."

Label spokeswoman Vanessa Castillo expanded on the botched photo attempt.

"We at Feral Corpse Records are honestly baffled by what was supposed to be a soul-crushing band shot intended for promotional use on a worldwide scale," she said. "I'm not sure what's so difficult about showing up in leather trench coats and platform boots and just standing there . . . but the oversight has forced us to reconsider whether Regurgitated Ghost Fetus is prepared to represent Feral Corpse Records with the same zeal as, say, Christ's Stepdad or The Trve Trve Trains."

At press time, Regurgitated Ghost Fetus bassist Mickey "Goat Grinder" McCabe was practicing frowning in the mirror in preparation for the rescheduled shoot, as he "tends to get the giggles when nervous."

Unhinged Paul McCartney Enters Ninth Hour of "Na-Na" Part in "Hey Jude"

BY BRANDON KRATKOCZKI

CHICAGO—Unhinged rock legend Paul McCartney is continuing to lead concertgoers in what is now the ninth consecutive hour of the "na-na" part in "Hey Jude," exhausted sources report.

"When he started playing 'Hey Jude,' the crowd totally freaked out—one of the highlights of any McCartney show is the feeling of unity when the entire crowd sings 'na-na' in unison," said audience member Sylvia Neville. "But it started over eight hours ago; I think some people are getting a bit restless."

Attending fans are reportedly concerned and irritated by the lengthy sing-along.

"I hope everything's OK and all, but I'm not sure how much more of this I can take," said Evanston resident Wallace Redmond. "I mean, at the beginning he did this cute little thing where he asked for only the fellas to sing 'na-na,' and then just the ladies. But by the time 5 a.m. rolled around, he asked

for 'anyone who's ever ridden a roller coaster . . .' and it just kept going from there."

"I mean, I love Macca, so I'll probably see this out," he added. "But my knees are really starting to hurt, and I'm kind of worried about my dog. She hasn't been out since 3 o'clock yesterday."

Witnesses say McCartney's band gradually abandoned him as the night wore on, the majority allegedly leaving Wrigley Field by the sing-along's second hour save for drummer Abe Laboriel Jr., who held out until hour five.

"I have a really big fill that's important to the song's closing that I didn't want to miss, but it finally became clear that Paul's in another world right now. I'm not about to interfere with that," said Laboriel. "I just hope he snaps out of it before our buses leave at noon for Madison."

At press time, showgoer Annie Chiu was overheard telling her companions to "hold [their] horses," suspecting that the "Abbey Road" medley would be starting "any minute now."

Record-Low Temperatures Threaten Year-Round-Shorts Guy Population

BY JOHNNY MO

CHICAGO—Climatologists are blaming record-low temperatures for the steep decline in Year-Round-Shorts Guy populations, resulting in a massive shortage of exposed hairy midwinter calves, according to a new study released today.

"An increasing number of well-calved men are buying full-length pants for the first time since high school. This is incredibly dangerous, as their own family members may not recognize them and reject them," said study author Janet Baker. "This particular strain of men is typically known to 'run hot.' Their decline could single-handedly end the entire cargo shorts industry."

The Trump administration, unwilling to acknowledge climate change, has pinned the decline on cultural and economic transition.

"Year-Round-Shorts Guys were a byproduct of the Clinton presidency and have never had anything to do with the environment. These same men flocked to dot-coms with lax dress codes and listened to Sublime in droves. We are now in the midst of a shift back to conservative business practices, and the understanding that Sublime truly sucked," said EPA administrator Scott Pruitt. "Under our strong leadership, America's men have reclaimed their minds and, most importantly, their pants."

Leading climatologist Alberta Gutierrez refuted the White House's position.

"Guys who in the past only owned shorts are now fully clothing themselves because of unprecedented rapid shifts in temperature. Most of them have known for years that their favorite college bands were lackluster," said Gutierrez. "Sadly, this sort of fallacy is what we expect from this administration. We could be facing an extinction-level event, where these creatures are forced to become 'socks-with-sandals' guys."

Scrambling to save the critically endangered men, a handful of privately funded chimera research labs are racing to hybridize Year-Round-Shorts Guys with Jeans-at-the-Gym Guys.

"It's our last chance to save this species of American male. Unfortunately, our biggest problem is finding women willing to carry such a dense baby to term," said Gutierrez.

The HARD Times

Band Headlining Basement Show Huddles Behind Dryer Before Returning for Encore

BY MARK ROEBUCK

GRAND RAPIDS, Mich.—Touring punk band Ghost Manor ended their headlining basement show set by exiting stage left and cramming themselves into a corner behind the washing machine and dryer in an apparent anticipation of an encore, sources confirmed.

"Unfortunately this basement doesn't have a green room, so the best they could do to stay out of sight was try to hide in the darkness by the utility sink," said tour manager/merch guy Doug Wheeler. "I'm pretty sure that nobody called for an encore because everyone could still see them—they were crouching perfectly still in complete silence, which was really off-putting, to be honest."

Multiple attendees confirmed that, after what appeared to be their last song, the band abruptly headed to the corner, packing in as closely as possible in an effort not to be seen.

"Honestly, they were pretty good," said venue regular Alexis Hoffman. "But instead of breaking down their stuff and leav-

ing, they all hung out in the darkest part of the room like sweaty statues. A few of us went over and asked what they were doing or if they needed help, but they wouldn't answer. I was gonna buy one of their shirts but decided against it."

Others reported that the band remained stuffed behind the washer/dryer well after the crowd had departed—with several members standing in the cat's litter box.

"After everyone left and I finished cleaning up, I saw the guys were still in the corner and I got a little nervous," said homeowner Maggie de la Hoya. "I thought they were already on their way to Chicago. I asked if they needed a place to crash and got no response, so I just shut the lights off and went upstairs."

At press time, Ghost Manor frontman Zach Hoyer was heard whispering, "Let 'em wait a little longer" to his bandmates from beneath a blanket he'd taken from the dryer.

Child of Rockabilly Couple Constantly Wondering What the Fuck Is Going On

BY KEITH BUCKLEY

CLEVELAND—Local child Dixie "Shortcake" Ross was utterly bewildered this week when her first day of kindergarten revealed a world unlike anything she's ever seen in her rockabilly parents' '50s-inspired home, concerned sources report.

"Wait . . . my parents choose to live like that?" a six-year-old Ross asked in what may be the youngest existential crisis on record. "There's more music than just the Stray Cats? Do my parents know?"

Dixie's teacher, Janet Spunch, was also baffled by the child's unnecessarily old-fashioned, yet highly stylized upbringing.

"The first time I saw Dixie in the classroom, she was rolling the cuffs on a male classmate's jeans. And later, during music, she asked if she could be the one to play stand-up bass," Ms. Spunch noted. "She kept touching my neck and asking to see my sparrow tattoo too. I know children are naturally curious, but this was really creepy."

When reached for comment, Dixie's father, Kayden Farrar, offered profound insight about his daughter's realization.

"Gee whiz, fella. You writin' a book or somethin'?" the Cleveland native asked in a surprisingly thick New York accent. "Listen daddy-o, modern folks like you just can't dig cats like us. Dixie-gal was conceived the night of the big Sock Hop in 2012. She's special—she doesn't need stupid stuff like a mall, or a polio vaccine. She needs a malt and some cool wheels, and that's it."

With her parents unconcerned about her potential psychological toll, Dixie was left to reconsider everything she's learned up to this point in her short life.

"When I went to school today, the doorknobs weren't all slippery from daddy's hair stuff, and no one danced anywhere near any old cars the whole time," she recalled. "But then I came home and the jukebox is playing Carl Perkins, and there's milkshakes everywhere."

"I'm not supposed to say curse words . . . but what the fuck is going on?" she added.

At press time, Ross was attempting to reach Child Protective Services from a rotary phone in her mother's pink and turquoise kitchen.

The HARD Times

Tattooed Barber Excited to Give Everyone That One Haircut Today

BY BRENDAN KRICK

BALTIMORE—Heavily tattooed barber Rob Moreno was reportedly "stoked" last Saturday morning to give everyone the same style undercut at Brush & Steel, his trendy new barbershop, hesitant patrons confirmed.

"Around here, we do things just a little bit differently," said Moreno, scratching his beard and adjusting his Jeff cap. "Nowadays, when dudes get their hair cut, they don't want to go to some chain at the mall; they want to go to a hip place like this, where they can uncomfortably drink a free beer at 11 a.m."

Moreno gave a quick tour of the waiting area, decorated with hardcore and skate memorabilia, as well as a poster of four combs arranged as the Black Flag logo. "This isn't Supercuts, bitch," he said.

Over the course of the afternoon, Moreno gave six customers in a row a scissor-trim up top, with a faded buzz on the sides.

"Sometimes cats will come in here and request something different, but I'm confident enough in my art to nod my head and pretend to listen, then just give 'em the ol' high-and-

tight anyway," said the stylist, arranging a shelf of vegan beard oils. "It's the best monthly $45 you can spend."

Despite a solid 4-star rating on Yelp, walk-in customer Jake Singarella privately admitted he was disappointed in the experience.

"I hadn't cut my hair in years, but my girlfriend convinced me to come here because she said it looked like a pretty cool place," said Singarella, who claimed he'd only wanted a simple trim. "When Rob started buzzing my sides, I tried to speak up, but he just started talking louder about how he once toured with Paint It Black, so there wasn't much I could do. He let me put a bunch of my band's stickers next to the register, though, so I'll probably come back."

Sweeping the shop floor at the end of the day, Moreno reflected on his work.

"I think what makes a cut here special are the little details," he said. "When I finish cutting someone's hair, I like to gel it straight back in a way they never wear it, and then I clean up their beard cheek line in a way that's impossible for them to maintain. It's all a crucial part of the Brush & Steel experience."

Ex-Ska Fan Fills in White Boxes on Checkered Vans With Black Sharpie

BY SAM ROSE

COSTA MESA, Calif —Thirty-three-year-old house painter and disillusioned ska enthusiast Brady Taylor took a Sharpie to the white boxes on his checkered Vans Slip-Ons during his lunch break yesterday to try to erase his embarrassing past, according to multiple eyewitnesses.

"I'm happy he finally did it," said Kelsey Zuniga, Taylor's friend and occasional beer pong partner. "After he saw Less Than Jake last year and they didn't play 'The Science of Selling Yourself Short,' he was so heartbroken—I mean, *really* hurt. He said he'd never listen to ska again . . . but the next day, I saw him skanking in his garage to Streetlight Manifesto. Some people just really need to hit rock bottom before they're ready to let go."

The "soul-crushing" disappointment caused by the denial of hearing his favorite song live was reportedly just the latest of many frustrations in Taylor's long, tumultuous relationship with ska.

"The Aquabats' transition into children's programming was a really tough blow," said Taylor's mother and part-time interior decorator Michelle Taylor-Keefe. "He'd just wander around the house muttering to himself about how they were 'selling out.' I hope he bounces back soon—I just know there's a style of music out there for him."

Determined to finally get over the genre that carried him through his teen years and "kind of weirdly late" into adulthood, Taylor took out his angst on his shoes in a brief moment of catharsis.

"Once I made up my mind, I just started scribbling away," he said. "Sure, we had some good times, but those two-tone Vans were a constant reminder of a bad genre that became a source of pain and disappointment for me. I had to let go."

After his outburst, a relieved Taylor seemed positive.

"I feel great. I don't think I've ever been happier," he said. "It was a long time coming, and I'm really looking forward to the future. I've even started experimenting with other genres. I'm actually going to a math rock show tomorrow, so we'll see how that goes."

Neil Peart Completely Dominates Subway Busker With 20-Bucket Setup

BY MIKE AMORY

NEW YORK—The 42nd Street-Times Square subway station was tight on space early yesterday evening after Rush drummer Neil Peart set up over 20 plastic buckets for a crowd-stopping performance.

"I was by the 7 train stairway, just doing my thing, when I look over and see an elderly man absolutely obliterating these buckets in a way I did not think was possible," said saxophonist and regular area busker Howard Richards. "The dude had it all: a standard plastic bucket, paint cans, empty cat litter containers . . . Some guy even accidentally kicked over one of those giant McDonald's cups, and he incorporated it into his solo with no hesitation."

"When I saw the little hydraulic stool spinning him around to different sections of buckets, I knew I couldn't compete," Richards added. "I mean, who the fuck is going to toss me a dollar when you can watch this guy pound out the intro to 'One Little Victory'? I just walked my ass over to Port Authority, where I belong."

Not everyone was impressed by Peart's grandiose performance.

"There were, like, five million buckets all piled up, like, two feet from the stairs," said Fort Greene resident Kristen Nguyen. "I tripped over one and missed my fucking train. I mean, it's rush hour, you know? Get the fuck out of the way! The homeless problem in this city is really out of control."

In discussing his impromptu performance, the celebrated drummer offered only humility.

"I am always looking to improve my craft. Back in the '90s, I studied Buddy Rich and experimented with a new grip to incorporate into my repertoire," Peart explained. "Now that I'm retired, it doesn't mean my love of drumming has stopped; I'm a wanderer and searcher at heart, and there's no place I'd rather show my appreciation for and dedication to the craft than in one of the busiest subway stations in the city, during the least convenient time for everyone. It's the least I can do."

At press time, Peart was preventing the doors on a Bronx-bound 1 train from closing as he attempted to set up his buckets inside one of its cars.

The HARD Times

7" Record Collector Also Fan of Sitting for Two Minutes, Standing Up Again

BY JOHN DANEK

ARLINGTON, Va.—Local punk and 7" collector Oliver Haggarty fully believes that vinyl records requiring listeners to sit for two minutes and then stand up again to flip them offer a superior listening experience to those that don't, confused sources confirmed.

"It's weird—I think he gets as much enjoyment out of getting up and down as he does from the music," said roommate Dante Carrick. "Sometimes he does this little fist pump when the song ends and it's time to flip the disc. We had friends over to listen to some of the first Dischord Records pressings, and Oliver wouldn't let anyone else get up and change them, even though they volunteered. Most of these songs are, like, 90 seconds long."

Haggarty, who allegedly owns a vast collection of '80s hardcore 7" records famous for short sides that require near-constant flipping, has received many full-length LPs from well-meaning loved ones over the years, all of which remain in cellophane wrappers.

"What am I supposed to do with those? Put them on and just sit there like a jackass for 25 minutes?" a frustrated Haggarty asked. "I question any song that's longer than two minutes. If you're a musician, say what you want to say . . . and let me stand up again when you're done, you know? These quads aren't going to work themselves."

However, close friends and loved ones think Haggarty's obsession may be from taking the DIY ethic a little too intensely.

"He gets real worked up about these things," admitted his mother, Alicia Haggarty. "When he was little, he yelled at me once for sitting through a full side of an Alvin and the Chipmunks record, and muttered under his breath about how 'blood flow makes the music sound better.'"

"Here's an idea," she added. "If blood flow is so important, maybe if I set up little garbage cans around the house, it'll motivate him to get up and take out the trash once in a while!"

For his part, Haggarty is steadfast about his tastes.

"I don't get everyone's problem," he said. "I have other hobbies too, you know. You should see my collection of David Lynch short films on 35mm film reels. Talk about a rush!"

The HARD Times

Ticketmaster Adds $5.15 Fuck-You Fee

BY REID BENDITT

LOS ANGELES—Ticketing sales and distribution leader Ticketmaster announced their new "Fuck-You Fee" today, adding an additional charge of $5.15 on all tickets purchased online, company officials announced.

"Exerting total dominance over concertgoers is our company's mission. If we're not truly the *master* of our customers—even for one second—then Ticketmaster has no place in this business," said Michael Rapino, CEO of parent company Live Nation Entertainment. "This new fee will let our customers know how we truly feel about them."

Rapino and his fellow executives were prepared for public backlash with the announcement, following years of Ticketmaster's shady business practices and a history of adding new fees for whatever reason they please.

"We received plenty of flack for the 'Convenience Charge,' with customers claiming that there was 'nothing convenient about it.' We didn't want to make the same mistake twice, so we cut straight to the point with our 'Fuck-You Fee,'" said Rapino. "Rest assured, the negative emails I receive only fuel my pure hatred for the people of this planet and their desire to consume the arts."

The fee will fund Ticketmaster's newly formed Division of Fuck You, which aims to make future fees just as incomprehensible, obscuring all reasons as to why they exist and how they arrived at the amount.

While their methods are ambiguous, the company assures the message is direct.

"It's a new kind of ticket buyer out there today. We did a lot of market research to learn what our customers want, and then we went ahead and did the complete opposite," said CMO Lisa Licht. "It turns out you can't advertise *at* people anymore—you need to advertise *with* them. We adopted this model so we can not only say, 'Fuck you, fans,' but offer a smile while we're doing it."

On average, Ticketmaster fees now represent 93 percent of a ticket's face value. Alternatively, tickets can be purchased in person at all venue box offices but will be subject to a $7 "How Fucking Dare You Look Me in the Eyes, You Scum" charge.

Rest of Family Has No Idea Restaurant Playing Neutral Milk Hotel

BY TOM PETERS

AMHERST, Mass.—UMass undergraduate Ryan Blankenship was taken aback last night when his family had no idea Neutral Milk Hotel's *In the Aeroplane Over the Sea* was playing in the background while they ate at the Bomba Rosa Eatery, sources confirmed.

"They were all just sitting there like nothing was happening," Blankenship said of his family's attempt to spend quality time with him. "Just listen to these lyrics: '. . . placing fingers through the notches in your spine . . .' How can you hear that and argue about mozzarella sticks?"

Blankenship's family, who made the 10-hour drive from Columbus, Ohio, for the visit, were confused by the 19-year-old's strange behavior.

"He was staring off into the distance, and he hardly touched his soup," said Ryan's mother, Cynthia Blankenship. "At one point I asked him if he'd seen a ghost, and he just mumbled, 'In a way, I have . . .' I really try not to be a worrywart, but he better not be selling his Adderall again. He's on those things for a reason."

Blankenship allegedly found the Eatery's lack of reverence for Jeff Mangum's kaleidoscopic masterpiece "reckless" and "disrespectful."

"I can't believe they would casually play an emotionally devastating album like that and expect people to be able to eat," he said. "Meanwhile, my uncle Peter is asking me about my classes . . . like we're not all currently being transported by poetry through time and space. Like, hello!"

According to witnesses, however, Blankenship did perk up briefly to deliver a brief anecdote about dorm bathrooms.

"I was actually just trying to make enough noise so that no one heard the lyrics about semen-stained mountaintops," he admitted. "That would have been too weird to explain."

When reached for comment later, Ryan's father, Harold, couldn't recall many specifics regarding the music that so deeply affected his son during dinner.

"I remember a guy with an acoustic guitar at one point— I think it was that 'Hey There Delilah' song," he said. "Ry used to love that one."

Straight-Faced Guy With Arms Crossed Having Best Night of His Life

BY KRISSY HOWARD

CLEVELAND, Miss.—According to eyewitnesses, local hardcore guy and "fucking wild man" Rodney O'Dell is reportedly having the best night of his life watching one of his favorite bands while silently standing by a wall with his arms crossed.

"This is so fucking awesome," said O'Dell, expressing little to no emotion whatsoever in his voice or body language. "I've been waiting for these guys to tour through here since forever, and I've never been so excited. I probably look like some fanboy goober, but I don't even give a fuck right now."

Struggling to contain himself, O'Dell explained how he prepared for the eventful evening.

"I had a feeling I was gonna let loose tonight, so I made sure to come ready," he said. "I got here extra-early for a spot super close to the pit so I could sort of just lean back without moving to avoid getting kicked. And I made sure to wear my black T-shirt with the stretchiest sleeves in case I felt like crossing my arms super hard."

Witnesses worried, however, that O'Dell may have taken his outrageous show-going antics too far.

"Honestly, I haven't seen Rod this pumped up since he almost smiled when his fiancée said yes," said friend Kelsey Dominguez. "At one point it looked like he was gonna go full ham and uncross his arms to maybe let them hang by his sides or something insane . . . but he only had an itch above his elbow."

"I just hope he stretched before he got here because if he didn't, he's definitely gonna feel those three times he sort of nodded his head," she added.

Those close to O'Dell say his wildly inappropriate form of self-expression is not uncommon.

"I remember one year for Christmas, my mom and dad got him a Big Wheel, which he'd talked about wanting all year," said sister Katie O'Dell-Haigh. "But when he saw it he just stood there all stone-faced—like it was a staring contest or something. And then he said our parents were 'the best mom and dad in the whole world.' He's always been the crazy one."

At press time, O'Dell was not overheard saying anything to anyone.

ACKNOWLEDGMENTS

Without the following people The Hard Times (and this book) would be nothing:

Special thanks: Ed Saincome, Ian Fishman, Chris Bavaria, Ryan Long, Nick Dill, Amber Bennoui, Clayton Hebenik, Jeremy Kaplowitz, Eric Navarro, Dan Rice, Mark Roebuck, Andy Holt, Kevin Flynn, Mike Amory, David Tyler, Liam Senior, Mirinda Moriarty, Kat Chish, and Sam Shepp. Finally to Kate Napolitano, Ivy Givens, Jamie Selzer, Mark Robinson, and everyone else at HMH for giving some punks a chance.

And a huge shout-out to all the members of the HT crew: Abram Alguire, Adam Martin, Aidan Sears, Alex Aho, Alexandra Houle, Allison Mick, Andrew Dubongco, Andrew Humphrey, Andrew Murphy, Andrew Spaulding, Anna Walsh, Anthony Kelly, Anya Volz, Ashley Naftule, Ben Doyle, Ben Friedman, Ben Fullelove, Ben Hargrave, Bibek Gurung, Bobby D. Lux, Bobby Korec, Brad Skafish, Brandon Fernweh, Brandon Garner, Brandon Kratkoczki, Brandon Onda, Brendan Krick, Brett McCabe, Brian Daly, Brian Polk, Bryan Ostrow, Bryant Smith, Carson Soukup, CB Daugherty, Charles E.P. Murphy, Charlie McGarrigle, Chris Nakis, Chuck Kowalski, Collin Canning, Cory Cousins, Courtney Baka, Courtney Paige Barnett, Dan Kozuh, Dan Luberto, Daniel Louis, Danny Taverner, Daniel Arnold, Darren Sechrist, Dave Smith, David Britton, David Tyler, Davin Givhan, Dicky Stock, Dinah Foley, Dom Turek, Drew Behm, Drew Goter, Drew Kaufman, Dustin Meadows, Dylan Tarr, Dónal McBrien, Eli Braden, Elizabeth Teets, Ella Gale, Emma Phipps, Erek Smith, Eric Casero, Eric D, Eric Grandy, Eric T. Roth, Erin McLaughlin, Forrest Ferguson, Francis Beringer, G. Smith, Gary Doyle, Gerry Todd, Goodrich Gevaart, Graham Isador, Grant Stiles, Greg Gillotti, Greg Heller, Gregg Gethard, Greg McGonagle, Hana Michels, Hannah Boone, Heather McGowan, Hyde Healy, Issa Diao, Jack Cody, Jack Garrett, Jack Lewis, Jake Goldin, James Knapp, James Siboni, James Webster, James Wells, Jamie Lawlor, Jason Crews, Jason Mazzola, Jason VanSlycke, Jay Topshe, Jeff Cardello, Jeff Dunn, Jen Cantin, Jeremy Hammond, Jesse Irvin, Jimmy Adduci, Joe Rumrill, John Danek, John Dixon, John-Michael Bond, Johnny Mo, Johnny Sevigne, Johnny Taylor, Jon Scott Wood, Jonah Nink, Jonathan Diener, Jonathan Zeller, Jordan Breeding, Josh Fernandez, Josh Jurk, Josh Kraus, Josh Levinson, Justin Cox, Justin Eisinger, Kaitlyn Jeffers, Kathleen O'Mara, KC Phillips, Keith Buckley, Kevin Hufe, Kevin Tit, Kip Doyle, Koltan Greenwood, Kory Lanphear, Kris Fiore, Kyla Walker, Kyle Erf, Kyle Gunlefinger, Kyle Sekaquaptewa, Kyle Stanley, Kyle Vorbach, Lana Schwartz, Laura Merli, Lauren Lav'n, Layth Sihan, Liam Hart, Liam O'Malley, Louie Aronowitz, Lucas Passarella, Luke Brogden, Luke Thornton, Malcolm Whitfield, Mark Hassenfratz, Mark Maira, Mark Turner, Matt Henson, Matthew Green, Matthew Keplinger, Max Wolff, Megan Valley, Michael De Toffoli, Michael Edwards, Michael Luis, Michael

O'Connor, Michael Palladino, Michael S. Watkins, Mike Civins, Mike Moran, Mike West, Mitch Socia, Nate Waggoner, Nicholai Roscoe, Nick Conway, Nick Ortolani, Patrick Coyne, Patrick Pilch, Paul Wozniak, Pete Fritz, Pete GK, Peter Woods, Phil Petersen, Quinn Brown, Rachel Buhman, Randi Pulator, Randy LoBasso, Ray McMillin, Rick Homuth, Rob Steinberg, Rob Walker, Royce Nunley, Ryan Clark, Ryan Harnedy, Ryan Lichten, Salim Alam, Sam Rose, Sammi Skolmoski, Sari Beliak, Senny Mau, Seth Shanley, Shane Allen, Shawn Murray, Shelby Kettrick, Steve Esparra, Steve Fiorillo, Steven Yuen, Steven Kowalski, Taylor De La Ossa, Taylor Ysteboe, Ted Kindig, Ted Pillow, Thomas Fricilone, Tianna Miller, Tim Nash, Tim Young, Tom Fuller, Tim Gannon, Tom Krasner, Tom Peters, Tom Scarcella, Tom Scheve, Travis Flack, Travis Walling, Tristen Stafford, Tyler Evans, Tyler Lebens, Tyler O'Neil, Vince Ratti, Zac Fairhall, Zac Lux, Zac Townsend, Zach Higgins, Zach LaRose, Zach Raffio, and Zack Ruskin.

Krissy Howard would like to thank: Naaz Gulati, Brittany Turner, Mitsuko Brooks, Carrie Freshour, Kristi Vizza, Steve Matzker, Zack Schoedel, Mike Croft (RIP), Binghamton, New York, and Weegee.

Bill Conway would like to thank: My wife, Gelyn Montanino, for not filing for divorce during the making of this book; JoAnne and Liam Flaherty for convincing Gelyn not to file for divorce during the making of this book; Hella Betts, Dick Betts, Jeff Betts, Spencer Rood, and Bob Muerth for letting me use your warehouse as a personal office, ensuring my wife did not divorce me during the writing of this book; and Jake Silberman for telling me The Hard Times was a bad idea. Extra thanks to my mother, Corrine, my brother, Nick, and my oldest pal, Matt MacDonald, for paying full price for this book. No thank you to cops, skate stoppers, and security guards.

Matt Saincome would like to thank: My mom, dad, brothers, and girlfriend for the love, support, and encouragement. I couldn't do any of this without you. Helen and Vernon Temple for the same reason. The first person to pay me to write about music, Ian Port. Emma Silvers, Mark Kemp, Fred Pessaro, and Anna Pulley for giving me a chance and helping me find my voice. Ms. Govnik and Jim Toland, for believing in me. Kate, for making this thing happen. Bill and Krissy for the incredible skill, passion, and dedication you put into this book and Hard Times generally. Every bandmate, family member, friend, significant other, roommate, employer, or employee, past and present, who put up with my bullshit when I hyper-focused on one of my projects. Hey, this one turned out pretty OK! The bands, scenes, cliques, and crews who let me hang out and share some laughs. The PAU, Valley Crew, Branch Street/US Thugs, Chain Godz Collective, and other friends I've made along the way in Oakland (and Bay Area generally), Sacto, LA, Indiana, Toronto, NYC, and everywhere else my band didn't get run out of town. You know who you are and I appreciate you. Anyone who read Punks! Punks! Punks! or let Zero Progress crash on your floor. The dude with the ponytail who banned me from Gilman when I was like 15 for saying "bitch."

THE HARD TIMES

Photo Credits

13 Tommaso Lizzul/Shutterstock (guitar); Archives New Zealand/WikiCommons (The Queen)
14 Robert Kneschke/Shutterstock (janitor); litts/Shutterstock (studio)
15 Leah-Anne Thompson/Shutterstock (cop); mangostock/Shutterstock (police line); Ollie Atkins/WikiCommons (Elvis)
16 bouybin/Shutterstock
18 WildSnap/Shutterstock
19 Aaron Amat/Shutterstock (Body, background); thunder-st/Shutterstock (guitar)
20 Wedding and lifestyle/Shutterstock (suit)
21 Chris Flannery
22 Dzelat/Shutterstock (FBI agent); Lia Koltyrina/Shutterstock (police station)
23 David Tyler
24 David Tyler
26 Corky Buczyk/Shutterstock (CBGB); Aarib Amat/Shutterstock (man); Alena Veasey/Shutterstock (people)
27 oneinchpunch/Shutterstock (guitarist); Benoit Daoust/Shutterstock (stage)
35 Kotin/Shutterstock
36 Aerial-motion/Shutterstock (ship); railway fx/Shutterstock (flames and smoke)
37 Andrey Popov/Shutterstock
38 Dom Turek
39 richardjohnson/Shutterstock
42 Nataly Reinch/Shutterstock (suit), Kostenko Maxim/Shutterstock (sticker)
43 Corky Buczyk/Shutterstock (CBGB); Igor Stevanovic/Shutterstock (tape); Shutterstock/Nejron Photo (punk left); sun ok/Shutterstock (punk center); Evgeniya Porechenskaya/Shutterstock (punk right)
44 Bachurin Maksym/Shutterstock (background, left); Irina Bg/Shutterstock (right)
46 Reagan Library/WikiCommons (Reagan); Viatkins/Shutterstock (punk)
47 Chris Flannery
49 Trismegist san/Shutterstock
50 Steve Keller/WikiCommons
51 Obprod/Shutterstock
54 Mark Reinstein/Shutterstock
55 Jose Ignacio Soto/Shutterstock (ballroom)
56 360b/Shutterstock
62 Chris Flannery
63 Ljupco Smokovski/Shutterstock (punk); TippaPatt/Shutterstock (background); Shutterstock (patches)
64 Andrea Fleming/WikiCommons (Courtney); Cramyourspam/WikiCommons (Kurt doppelganger)
66 Max Pixel (man); Pixabay (wall)
67 Roman Voloshyn/Shutterstock
68 Ronald Sumners/Shutterstock
69 Chris Flannery
71 ZoneCreative/Shutterstock
72 Acid maniac/WikiCommons (Tim Armstrong); Razvan Orendovici/Flickr (Foo Fighters); Aija Lehtonen/Shutterstock (Billie Joe Armstrong)
73 Artem Markin/Shutterstock (guy); Santi S/Shutterstock (computer)
74 kudla/Shutterstock (guy); Magsi/Shutterstock (scalp); Tairy Greene/Shutterstock (shirt); krsmanovic/Shutterstock (background)

76 Olena Yakobchuk/Shutterstock (doctor); Diego Cervo/Shutterstock (CD shelves)
77 Chris Flannery
78 Fabio Diena/Shutterstock (Limp Bizkit); Aquir/Shutterstock (stamp)
81 Kathy Hutchins/Shutterstock (Tony); Debby Wong/Shutterstock (jersey)
82 Khosro/Shutterstock (guy); Brian Hankins/WikiCommons (wires)
83 Zurbagan/Shutterstock
87 Featureflash Photo Agency/Shutterstock
88 SkyImages/Shutterstock
89 Shutterstock
90 Igor Sinkov/Shutterstock (club and DJ)
92 Wasted Time R/WikiCommons (Dixie Chicks)
93 Christopher Halloran/Shutterstock (Bush); MPH Photos/Shutterstock (mosh pit)
94 PanicAttack/Shutterstock (man); Mindscape Studio/Shutterstock (bowling shoes); Mary Rice/Shutterstock (background)
95 Gregory Reed/Shutterstock (Howard Dean); Daxiao Productions/Shutterstock (arm); mike tutt photography/Shutterstock (background)
97 Chris Bavaria
98 JHVEPhoto/Shutterstock
99 Christian Bertrand/Shutterstock
100 Zhu Difeng/Shutterstock (store)
101 Chris Flannery
102 Kiselev Andrey Valerevich/Shutterstock (punk)
103 Chris Flannery
104 LindaStock/Shutterstock (fish); Chris Flannery (others)
105 Monkey Business Images/Shutterstock (high school hallway)
106 LukeandKarla.Travel/Shutterstock (storefront.); Rawpixel/Shutterstock (teens)
107 G-Stock Studio/Shutterstock
108 Nazile Keskin/Shutterstock
111 ASDF Media/Shutterstock
117 Jon Bilous/Shutterstock
118 Sammi Skolmoski
119 Heiner Bach
120 karamysh/Shutterstock (house)
122 S Bukley/Shutterstock
123 Chase Perkins
124 Matthew Gill
125 Chris Bavaria
126 kafeinkolik/Shutterstock
127 Chris Bavaria
128 Krissy Howard
129 Taylor De La Ossa
130 Erik Zaiatz
131 luckyraccoon/Shutterstock (background); grebeshkov-maxim/Shutterstock (banner); driver/Flickr (Kim Jong-un)
132 Bill Conway
133 Pixabay (raccoons); Drew Spencer/WikiCommons (drum machine)
134 Julia Torres
135 SayHope/Shutterstock (man left); Christin Slavkov/Shutterstock (man center); Olena Yakobchuk/Shutterstock (man right)
136 Francesco Colarieti/Shutterstock

137 Taylor De La Ossa
138 Steven Yuen
139 Shutterstock (van); A Katz/Shutterstock (Bernie)
140 Bill Conway
141 Chris Bavaria
142 PanicAttack/Shutterstock (boy); wavebreakmedia/
    Shutterstock (courtroom)
143 Kris Fiore
145 Yuri Shevtsov/Shutterstock
145 Bill Conway
146 Paul McKinnon/Shutterstock (bake sale); creatifolio/
    Shutterstock (tattoo)
147 Senny Mau
148 Skumer/Shutterstock
149 Jake Joyce
150 Chris Bavaria
151 Darby "Sladey Bird" Clark
152 Zach Raffio
153 Nick Conway
154 Doug McLean/Shutterstock (ducks); Chey Rawhoof
    (mosh pit)
155 Ian Fishman
156 Song_about_summer/Shutterstock
157 Rick Homuth
158 Dan Gonyea (crowd); Justin Gonyea (old man)
159 Bryanna Bennet
160 Chris Bavaria
161 Mirinda Moriarty
162 Chris Bavaria
164 Tyler Ross
165 Pressmaster/Shutterstock
166 Steven Yuen
168 Josh Jurk
169 Bryanna Bennet
170 Dan Roberto
171 Hard Times LLC
172 FOTOKITA/Shutterstock (guy)
173 Ferenc Szelepcsenyi/Shutterstock
174 Lightfield Studios/Shutterstock (prisoner); MR.
    Yankit/Shutterstock (courtroom)
175 Bill Conway
176 PRESSLAB/Shutterstock (soldiers); TFoxFoto/
    Shutterstock (explosion)
177 Aija Lehtonen/Shutterstock (crowd); CREATISTA/
    Shutterstock (girl)
178 Ben Harkins
179 VH-studio/Shutterstock
180 lilkin/Shutterstock (punk); vzwer/Shutterstock
    (train)
181 Ted Drake (Fugazi); Jstone/Shutterstock (Shkreli)
184 John Taylor
186 ESB Professional/Shutterstock (classroom); Light-
    Field Studios/Shutterstock (pastor)
187 Matthew Gill (show); Tatjana Romanova/
    Shutterstock (kid)
188 David Tirado
189 Eric Dellabarba
190 JHVEPhoto/Shutterstock
190 David Shankbone (Tom Morello); WikiCommons (fax
    machine)
191 Josh Kraus
192 Kyle Erf (cabin and signs); Tacosunday/WikiCommons
    (punks); N.Vector Design/Shutterstock (flag)
193 Rick Homuth
194 Yeti Studio/Shutterstock (blood); saulty72/
    Shutterstock (shark); Christian Bertrand/Shutter-
    stock (crowd)
195 Kat Chish
196 Mirinda Moriarty

197 Hit1912/Shutterstock (Times Square); Featureflash
    Photo Agency/Shutterstock (Ryan Seacrest); Getty
    Images (Donna Brazile)
198 Jne Valokuvaus/Shutterstock (man); Aspect3D/
    Shutterstock (colored guitars); mckgamer/Shutter-
    stock (black guitar)
199 Max Pixel (museum); Christian Bertrand/Shutterstock
    (Dinosaur Jr.)
200 GG Pro Photo/Shutterstock (hunter); Ranglen/
    Shutterstock (stage)
201 Chris Bavaria
202 Kat Chish
203 Shelby Kettrick
204 Shelby Kettrick
205 Adam Jones, Ph.D./Global Photo Archive/Flickr
    (museum)
206 Kat Chish
208 Dream Expander/Shutterstock (carpet); My Life
    Graphic/Shutterstock (lights); VladKol/Shutterstock
    (TV Studio); Andrey Arkusha/Shutterstock (punk)
209 CREATISTA/Shutterstock
210 Kat Chish
211 Arina P Habich/Shutterstock (bus); Chris Bavaria
    (others)
212 Kamenetskiy Konstantin/Shutterstock (crowd);
    various/Shutterstock (security guards); omnimoney/
    Shutterstock (stage)
213 Shelby Kettrick
214 Shelby Kettrick
215 Kyle Erf (character), Dan Rawe (background)
216 Kyle Erf
217 Shelby Kettrick
218 Senny Mau
219 Kat Chish
220 Nenad Nedomacki/Shutterstock (friends); Corepics
    VOF/Shutterstock (roadie); Viacheslav Ukhrymenko/
    Shutterstock (guitarist)
221 Jason Mazzola
222 Tom Gannon
223 Bill Conway
224 Chris Bavaria
225 Erik Zaiatz
226 Anya Volz
228 Anya Volz
229 Krissy Howard
230 Senny Mau
231 Kayla Ann R/Shutterstock
232 PT Images/Shutterstock
233 Shutterstock (classroom)
235 Mike Raio (man); Jordan Tan/Shutterstock (plane
    cabin)
236 sylvlrobl/Shutterstock
237 Maj.1/Shutterstock
238 Susan Law Cain/Shutterstock
239 Bill Conway
240 pxhere (McCartney); Popova Valeriya/Shutterstock
    (piano)
242 Bill Conway
243 Chris Bavaria
244 Olena Yakobchuk/Shutterstock
245 Chris Bavaria
246 lev radin/Shutterstock (subway); F. J. Carneros/
    Shutterstock (bucket drummer)
247 LEDOMSTOCK/Shutterstock (guy, background); Chris
    Flannery (album)
248 Sematadesign/Shutterstock
249 iko/Shutterstock (boy); Monkey Business Images/
    Shutterstock (family)
250 Bill Conway

THE HARD TIMES

This book is a work of fiction and satire. It
uses actual names of certain public figures and
businesses satirically. Any other use of names
of real people is purely coincidental.

Library of Congress Cataloging-in-Publication Data
is available

ISBN 978-0-358-02237-4 (pbk); 978-0-358-01898-8 (ebk);
978-0-358-17216-1 (eAudio); 978-0-358-28519-9 (CD)

Book design by Mark Robinson

Printed in the United States of America

DOW 10 9 8 7 6 5 4 3 2